Form and Decision

Form and Decision

ESSAY ON THE EUROPEAN CULTURAL FORM

Emanuele Castrucci

Contents

We might all perish; I, however, want at least
to select the field of interest for which I am to perish,
namely the civilization of Old Europe.

Jacob Burckhardt 1846

To have gathered from the air a live tradition
or from a fine old eye the unconquered flame
This is not vanity.

Ezra Pound, Canto LXXXI

to Roman Schnur
in memoriam

Introduction

Form is an original concept. In philosophical usage it indicates the entity – not empirical but ontological (Aristotle) or transcendental (Kant) – that makes possible the relationship between orderer and ordered at the origin of all knowledge. But the meaning we give to this concept in these studies is extensive and metaphorical. Form, while not belonging to time, is profoundly linked to it, in ways that the sociology of knowledge has the task of clarifying. I therefore mean here by "era of form" the era in which mankind still had the option of achieving an overall synthesis, a true ethical understanding of reality, capable of "salvaging" phenomena (τὰ φαινόμενα σώζειν). This capability came to a radical crisis with the scientific-technological organization of existence.

But what then is the "classical" era of form?

If by this expression we wish to indicate a historical era, it's very difficult to answer the question. It's nevertheless true that classical Platonic-Aristotelian onto-theology has exercised a decisive "forming" intervention over a long stretch of human history. Thus we adopt it – careful not to make it the exclusive symbol of our Western experience – as a key example of the historicizing of an overall metaphysical form, as in effect a synthesis that has been "successful" for centuries.

In onto-theology *form preceded decision*: this is the aspect that, in ethical and political terms, is most relevant to our discussion. The "forming" intervention consisted in the discovery or recognition of the ontological structures of reality, substantially unchangeable by human beings. If ethical form was a subsection of general ontology, ethical decision was merely its mirror image. In this context, an *ex nihilo* decision was truly unthinkable.

But the emergence of the is-ought problem, i.e. the split of norm from the human nature, typical of modernity, undermined the basis of the ancient-classical concept of form. This split found its philosophical model in the Cartesian dualism of body and soul, *res extensa* and *res cogitans*. How could the one now be deduced from the other? The ridiculization of their point of contact, which was now reduced to the fable of the "pineal gland" is one of the bitter ironies of modernity.[1] But irony, merciless daughter of intellect, produces an ethically paralyzing attitude. Those who have intellect can't help but love her, without however forgetting that she brilliantly eludes inescapable core problems.

To the inner history of this complex issue the present studies seek to furnish a simple set of juxtapositions, "shortcuts" mapped out in the dense network of European culture. The starting point understandably lies in the seventeenth century break of modernity, which highlights the detachment of ethical-political decision from metaphysical form, no longer considered pre-existent. While it is true that onto-theology was inextricably linked, in the great Western-Christian era, to an eschatology, it is in the Baroque period that it fails for the first time. Profane life thus seems separate from transcendent *Veritas:* no harmonious line of continuity is any longer drawn between the two planes.[2]

Decisionism – namely, decision free of form and posited *ex nihilo* to come to terms with the world's events – is, as is clear, an obligatory outcome, once certain radical epistemological conditions are determined, which the all-encompassing order of the scientific-technological organization of existence by its very nature requires.[3] But the price to pay for decisionism is ethical irrationalism: rationalizing the realm of the means brought about the irrationalization of ends. Already in Kant's categorical imperative it can be interpreted as a mere "fact" of reason,[4] which rendered dangerously precarious the alleged universality of ethical discourse. In the early twentieth century the attempt undertaken by Scheler to reconnect to an ontological basis the predicament inherited from Kantianism constituted a serious approach to this problem.[5]

Actually, decisionism is a more important way of thinking for what it presupposes than for what it explicitly theorizes. In other words, more than on the obvious level of political and juridical doctrines, it develops its major interest on the metatheoretical and epistemological level. The fact is that decisionism can only reject any discourse on the foundational procedures of its method: on any analysis of the *sense*

(*Sinnfrage*) of practical systems. Any control over the truth of its contents is precluded. The criterion of ethical validity – which substitutes, according to the non-cognitivistic canons, that of truth – interprets the problem of form in terms of formalism. From Scheler to Kelsen, after Kant, this is the almost obligatory path of contemporary ethics.[6] But all this, you might say, is common knowledge. What has been said relates to decisionism's inability to question the foundational procedures of its own method, and is a rule generally accepted (at least in practice) by modern thought.[7] The problem, though, is perhaps another: is decision (decisionistically understood)[8] able to *create new form*? In other words, can decisionism avoid the risk of ending up to coincide with a mere, subjectively (un)founded, essentially fragile and uncertain ethical occasionalism? Further: is it really unthinkable and unproposable to pose the question of "bridge principles"[9] which somehow reconnect being and having to be, reducing occasionalistic arbitrariness? Certainly, it must be distinguished that the problem of a *new form* would in any case make the greater claim, and the "bridge-principles" the lesser claim in the matter. But the question that lies at the core is the same: how to get beyond the arbitrariness of ethical subjectivism?

The philosophic-historical inquiry into an universal force embodying the metaphysical unity of order in the medieval Christian *respublica* was, according to Carl Schmitt, an attempt to provide an answer to the problem we are dealing with here. Its operation today could only move on an overtly literary level – a level which however is not to say senseless for problems of ethics and political philosophy. Thomas Mann's Naphta, in *The Magic Mountain*, who possesses a formidable intellect for dealing with philosophical-political questions, has something to say on this point.[10] Because it is literature (much more than the longwinded debates between metatheoreticians) that is able to provide valuable pointers on issues of modern ethics in general, overcoming vacuous occasionalism in particular. I have in mind especially Wittgenstein's fundamental ethical issues as they are expressed in the second part of Robert Musil's great novel *The Man without Qualities,* in the theme of the ecstatic society, namely the discovery of the "silent world" that lies *beyond* decision – *utterable* decision.[11]

The studies contained in Part III of this volume hinge on these points. They intend to suggest that the way to overcome ethical occasionalism, the perennial risk of any decisionistic epistemology, can be sought not only in an overall historical-metaphysical form – as Carl Schmitt said about Saint Paul's mythical image of *katéchon* (*2 Thess.*)[12] – but by relating ethics with *mysticism*. In other words: if decision can only intervene *within* the margins of the utterable, of practical, mundane speech, it is clear then that language – and the language of ethics in particular – is able to embrace only *a part* of human experience, leaving out – such as mysticism – «what matters most».[13] Surely, with Wittgenstein, the awareness of having to relegate to a parenthesis that other part of experience which at its core is linguistically incommunicable – but that is the very source of ethics, without which ethics would make no sense! – means that «our vital problems aren't yet even touched upon». But is it really so certain that «there is no longer any question» and that «in fact this is the answer»? Isn't it instead that the task of the mystical experience may be, among other things, to provide fresh energy, new life blood to an *utterable* ethical reflection?[14] I'd like the studies of the third part of this book to be read bearing in mind the (at least) non-senselessness of this question.

As for the final two studies of this third part, they can even be considered independently of the rest, since its aim is to develop in a consciously unilateral way the problem of form already addressed from various points of view in the preceding chapters. The juxtaposition I offer is between form and *creative doing*: *constructive* or *"poietic" doing*, in the profoundly Platonic sense Paul Valéry attributed to this term, and – in other respects – between "poietic doing" and *conventionalist ethics*. Obviously, the indication the last two chapters suggest must needs, here, remain sketchy. However, I believe that it isn't out of the question to imagine it stimulating further philosophical development in the field of ethics, whose phenomenology would thus be enlightened by the problem of "formal constructing", or by a fundamental human activity that in its necessary laws eludes decisionistic arbitrariness, and clearly touches on what the Platonic Valéry would have defined as the "inhuman".

But while the *Ekstatische Sozietät*, which concludes *The Man without Qualities*, indicates, in mid-twentieth-century Europe, the possibility of a connection between ethical reflection on form and the mystical dimension, it is also true that the first decades of the twentieth century in Europe elaborated, through the thought of Heidegger and Schmitt, another possibility, which in my opinion is not in conflict with it, but integrates the path traced by Musil, "Musil's way". It is the possibility whose most significant features are described in the Epilogue, linked to the chthonic element that makes up the mythical basis of European identity, in its deep symbolic roots. This is the way that leads to formulating the problem of a theory of political myth in the age of full-fledged nihilism – a problem that contemporary philosophical reason has difficulty framing, or that in any case erroneously considers devoid of a solution.

Part I

Aesthetics and Politics.
Seventeenth-Century European Politics
and the End of the Classic Concept of Form

I. *Political Physicalism?*

1. *Metaphorization of Copernicus.*

The 'machine metaphor'– aiming to mean the elimination and outrunning of the "natural ends" of a given system – can be especially applied to the structure of the early modern State. The Copernican reconfiguration of the cosmos[1] acted as a metaphor (that is: not conceptually, or at least: not immediately at a conceptual level), transposing acquirements of the modern natural science to the ethical and political field. The State, as a 'neutral' machine, carried within itself intellectual and ideological characteristics that could not fail to undergo an atheistic reversal, within European civilization, of what still remained a Christian ethical construction.[2]

On the other hand, the machine of the Leviathan-State functionally guarantees and distorts the individualistic foundation of Blumenberg's idea of a *Selbstbehauptung* already perfectly legitimized in itself. It presupposes:

a) an acentric cosmos, in which the *Sinnproblem* can no longer be foregrounded as such by any philosophical-political reflection that claims to be generally valid;

b) the recognition of decisionism as the only form of thought adequate – by reason of its *ex nihilo* proceeding – to the so-called "Age of Technology";

c) the principle of the integral manipulation of being (or the legitimacy of an unlimited transformative intervention on human nature), decided and planned on a large scale within the framework of an absolute immanence.

Political physicalism in the early modern age is founded on the concept that being, reduced to matter, is indefinitely mouldable and tendentially reproducible; it constitutes simply a matter waiting for a form or an energy that awaits some exploitation; the forms assumed by nature in the course of cosmic evolution are contingent and non-normative; mankind can impose new ones at its pleasure; human nature itself is a casual and changeable product; mankind becomes the inventor, producer and author of itself, *causa sui*, tending to no longer owe its essence and existence to anything but itself. A modern conception of the philosophy of history sees libertine individualism as leading, in what will be the immediately post-Hobbesian political experience, to the idea of an unstoppable, self-justifying "progress-process"[3] and tending to consider every relationship from 'political' to classical natural law (and before that, from the 'political' to the 'theological'), on which the hermeneutic hypothesis of secularization is founded, as «a category of historical wrongdoing».[4] Schmitt observed about this position that

> constructing [for it] a fresh political theology is no longer possible, so to speak a political theology *ab ovo*; there is absolutely no *ovum* in an ancient or renewable meaning; there is still just a *novum*; what is lacking are all the de-theologizations, de-politicizations, dejuridifications, de-ideologizations, dehistoricizations, and the further set of expressions with 'de-' in the sense of a *tabula rasa*; even the *tabula rasa*, which collapses together with the *tabula*, is *de*-tabulated; the new science, purely human-earthly, is an incessant process-progress, and consists in a renewal and expansion of nothing other-than-earthly-human knowledge, sustained by an incessant human curiosity. [...] Thenew man who in this process produces himself is not a new Adam, not even a new pre-Adamite, and still less a new Christ-Adam, but rather the prestructured product of the process-progress posited and kept going by man himself.[5]

The subject of historical action, notwithstanding that its initial hypothesis was that of the libertine *Selbstbehauptung*, was therefore already lost in the background between the seventeenth and eighteenth centuries, up to being reabsorbed into the functional impersonality of the process. The idea of history tended to be linked to that of "plan",[6] while the libertine's original "privatistic" introversion started to socialize itself in public opinion. It was at this point that, in the eighteenth century, the philosophy of history would oppose with the moralistic force of an enlightened utopia the political monopoly of Leviathan, dismembering it from within.

This interpretation (Schmitt-Koselleck) has within it a great clarity: for it "free thought" (and especially, I would add, its eighteenth-century manifestation, which can be defined as a "left-handed Enlightenment")[7] was destined to sharpen the conflictual substance implicit in the 'political', appearing as an intellectual reflection of society's ultimate ungovernability.[8] However, subjectivity reduced to a function of the progress-process marked the transfer on the political context of the scientific physicalist model, and as such expressed its complete detachment from what in the history of Western metaphysics was defined *onto-theo-teleology*, i.e. the dominant epistemological model in ancient-classical thought. In connection with this, we should consider the fact that the self-legitimization of human action undermines at its basis the concept (of great significance in both the legal and aesthetic sectors) of *representation*, which appears in Baroque symbolism as a guarantee of the profound unity between sensible and supersensible dimensions (one thinks of metaphors such as those of 'projection' or 'reflection').[9]

The decline of the classical concept of representation was already implicit in Hobbes, when in his *De Cive* he highlights the ine-vitable tendency to mechanization not only of the 'body' of the State, but also its 'soul': sovereignty.[10] In fact, «there can be no representation in the case of automata or machines, and much less can they themselves represent or be represented; when the State becomes Leviathan, it disappears from the representative universe».[11]

The machine is also «devoid of tradition», and Eric Voegelin is right to see in it a means for affirming the human passions. Thus the «arrogance» with which Voegelin associates the origin of the machine[12] is intimately linked to the *curiositas* that Blumenberg speaks of, and both to the *amour propre* that unmistakably marks the psychology of the modern age.[13] But it is also true that authors such as Voegelin and Strauss tend to unilaterally emphasize the risks involved in the modern reversal of Aristotelianism, to the point that the tone of their discourse may sometimes appear to be determined by a substantial disorientation.

The two principles that, in Hobbes, mark the separation from Aristotle's theory of motion, conceiving of motion as «change of place» (*Decameron Physiologicum*, chapter II) and, reciprocally, in the assumption that «every change consists in movement» (*De Corpore*, I, VI, 5) have the effect of reducing the entire horizon of metaphysical know-ledge in a physical-mathematical key. In fact, movement, for Hobbes, is infinite, that is, it has no order, no structure, no limit, no end: it is a constant tension without end or purpose, without teleology. Movement has no cause, because it is itself the only cause of the universe. But if nature is nothing but movement, we evidently arrive at the conclusion that the concept of nature has a much greater importance in Hobbes' thought – which has also emptied it of any finality – than in Aristotle's thought. It is to this paradoxical conclusion that the analysis of Hobbes' moral theory inevitably leads: Hobbes deprived man of his nature, but at the same time he affirmed man's need for one. He then assigned to the political power and science the task of building an artificial nature. But this was at bottom a door left open to totalitarianism, that is, the possibility of realizing a radical transformation of the very foundations of human existence.

The paradox lies above all in the fact that this potentially totalitarian characterization of Hobbes can easily coexist with what – dominant in Schmitt's interpretation – according to which Hobbes avoids binding man in any way *in interiore sphaera*. An aporia that is entirely intrinsic to Hobbes' thought. On the one hand, Hobbes (subjectively) does not require the State to intervene in human nature and therefore boldly excludes political obligations of conscience;[14] but on the other hand it poses the necessary premises for human nature to be artificially transformed as soon as technical progress has come to provide adequate means for this type of intervention.[15]

2. *Political physicalism and the philosophical problem of means.*

To critically approach the problem of the modern separation of fact from value – which in sixteenth-century Europe was characterized by the affirmation of decision-making arbitrariness in the field of political and legal science and by physicalism in that of natural science – we must first reckon with the objections that Leo Strauss made against Weber's approach, the latter containing the highest theoretical awareness that a methodologically informed historicism has been able to achieve. Strauss observes:

Natural law in its classical form is connected to a teleological view of the universe. All natural beings have a natural end, a natural destiny, which determines what kind of operation is good for them. In the case of man, reason is required for discerning these operations: reason determines what is by nature right with ultimate regard to man's natural end. The teleological view of the universe, of which the teleological view of man forms a part, would seem to have been destroyed by modern natural science.[16]

But if modern science has now decided irrevocably in favor of a non-teleological conception of the universe, Strauss feels that it is still possible to maintain a «finalistic science of man», to wit a substantial rationality in the choice of the ultimate values of orientation for human behavior. His clash with Max Weber was, at this point, inevitable.[17] For the purposes of our discourse, it is interesting to point out that Weber completes that strand of thought – arbitraristic decision-making regarding the problem of ends and rational-instrumental with regard to that of means – which we saw inaugurated with a modern slant in the theoretical context provided by Hobbes and the French libertines. This framework is characterized by

> a variety of such comprehensive views, each as legitimate as any other: we have to choose one; neutrality or suspension of judgment is impossible. Our choice has no support but itself; it is not supported by any objective or theoretical certainty; it is separated from nothingness, the complete absence of meaning, by nothing but our choice of it.[18]

These views are determined and imposed by a *destiny*, a philosophy of secularized, circular history, to which the subject is compelled to adhere,[19] and which registers within it the most complete interchangeability of what is "right", fueled by the dissociation between opinion and action, inner conviction and external behavior,[20] but also between ends and means, if it is true that now, in the line of thought that goes from Hobbes to Weber (perfectly opposed to the one that relates Aristotle and Leo Strauss), «the dimension in which the moral problem is posed in philosophy is the dimension of the means, not the ends».[21]

The reversal point of the classic trend line is certainly given by Bacon, who posed for the first time the problem of the «selective function that means have toward ends».[22] This function is now dominant as «the only possible action to select that cannot be effectively exercised by any morality that tends to replace the emotional motives of man with non-existent rational motives».[23] It is in this sense that Hobbes «had to recognize that man has been assigned no privileged ends or purposes by nature, but that the selection of ends is a *problem* that can only be solved in special conditions».[24] Hobbes' effort was precisely to highlight these conditions.

But then, if these are really the defining terms, we may again legitimately question, with regard to Hobbes' position, the qualification of nihilism (though «noble nihilism») that Strauss attributes to Weber: he, from the assumption concerning the ultimate unknowability of ends, came to the view «that every preference, however evil, base, or insane, has to be judged before the tribunal of reason to be as legitimate as any other preference»: Weber saw this alternative in the possible future prospects of civilization: on the one hand a spiritual renewal («wholly new prophets or a powerful renaissance of old thoughts and ideals»); on the other, a «mechanized petrifaction, varnished by a kind of convulsive sense of self-importance»: that is, the end of every human possibility, except that of «specialists without spirit or vision and voluptuaries without heart».

However, the really significant point in this disenchanted and widely shareable diagnosis is that Weber, faced with such an alternative, «felt that deciding in favor of one or the other possibility would be a judgment of value and faith, and therefore beyond the competence of reason».[25] This amounts to declaring oneself completely impotent with regard to the problem of the choice of ends as elements unrelated to any evaluative rationality.

We conclude our *excursus* on the problem of means in Strauss's critique by noting that this twentieth-century development of relativism would be hard to analyze and situate within the methodology of European science if we neglected to relate it to Hobbes' seventeenth-century tendency, where the first steps in this direction were taken. Within this type of thought there was now a widespread awareness that only from the problem of means could we shed light on that of ends, which therefore depend almost exclusively on means 'technically' chosen in the meantime. The fact is that from the balanced relativism contained in this last statement to Weber's nihilism the derivation is in the last analysis obligatory: based on unstoppable logical steps.[26]

3. *Sorbière, Hobbes, Pascal.*

Samuel Sorbière, translator and popularizer of Hobbes' work in late seventeenth-century France, well exemplified the libertine cynicism that arose from the recognition of an equal intellectual legitimacy «toward every preference, no matter how base or insane it may be for its wickedness».[27]

The neutralization of ethics produced, among other things, on a scientific level the result of considering man as a pure and simple object of curiosity: in Sorbière there is no such "participatory" form of depth that lies in the serious dedication to one's aim of research. He – it has been said – «effleura beaucoup de genres de sciences»,[28] pushing the instrumental use of reason to the point of making the "fantasyless specialist" (that is, the pertinence of *technique*) coincide in Weber fashion with the hedonist curious about the world (the pertinence of *pleasure*).

The political option for absolutism was grafted onto the framework of this logic which was at the same time – and without intimate contrast, since pleasure also appears to be founded on artificial bases – the logic of technique and passions. Sorbière, who had already translated Thomas More's *Utopia*,[29] shared Hobbes' radical anthropological pessimism. But in his *Discours Sceptiques*[30] the real object of the controversy is not so much 'evil' man of the state of nature, as man inserted in the 'temperate' government of civil society: not subjected to the strict rules of the absolute State. Where in Hobbes there is a dyadic rhythm – from the universal war of the State of nature to the conventional peace of the political order – in Sorbière the movement is triadic: from an initial concept of a nature without conflict, through a *temperée* civil society in which the conflict emerges and breaks out, up to the absolute state (*Estat de l'Empire*), which resumes imposing artificial peace. Pintard's observations are very pinpointed:

> Different starting points, but intersecting paths: Sorbière soon found himself on the same road as Hobbes [...]. Thus for Hobbes, since natural man is evil, authority and fear become

the necessary elements of society; but, for his disciple, the naturally good man has become corrupted in the state of sociability, and so authority and fear are needed to prevent him from doing harm. In any case, coercion is necessary: an anticipation of Rousseau's ideas leads back to the erudite Hobbes, whose memory of Montaigne had removed from Hobbes.[31]

Sorbière thus focuses his criticism on the so-called "mixed" forms of government, which he deems inferior compared to "pure" forms, the only ones capable of ensuring, along with order, the happiness of peoples, and of surpassing the collective memory – already dangerous in itself – of civil wars: «The history of our civil wars is recent, and it is so penalizing for our nation that it would be desirable to suppress it».[32] For Sorbière – it has been said, unlike Hobbes – peoples who are at a still primitive stage in the development of civilization live happily in proximity to the law of nature:

> Each of them seeks what it needs, and divides the superfluous with those who have not been able to go in search of their necessities or were not as lucky in obtaining them. Hunger, thirst, bad weather are what they fear. [...] They help each other, regret the loss of friends, and proceed on a path of happiness that shows them a small ray of common sense more constantly than it does to us, since all our great enlighteners succeed in showing us the most diverse paths for the sole end of more easily losing our way.[33]

The real causes of conflict and separation develop instead in civil society, starting with the chaos of "indirect powers", and above all starting with public opinion, which in the eighteenth century will become the new worldly power, uncontrollable and full of imbalancing effects on the political order:

> I doubt that all our misery and wickedness depends on the fact that we do not live, in our European civil societies, either under a true state of dominion or in a state of nature. We find ourselves in a place, as in the intermediate layer of the air, where storms and tempests are formed. Our spirits are as though divided between these two states, and as the subjection to sovereign powers abases our courage, so thoughts of freedom heighten it,

with the result of making us recklessly insult the first persons we encounter.[34]

This last passage also makes it clear that in Sorbière the anti-humanistic choice of libertinism has been led to its actual fulfill-ment: the degradation of the individual to potential enemy also deri-ves from the fact that concepts such as *«pensée de liberté»* are always seen in a negative light, as a source of danger for society (*«nous font insulter temerairement contre les premiers qui nous rencontrons»*), crudely exaggerating Hobbes' discourse.

But it is above all in his third skeptical discourse, *«Où les raisons d'une fausse prudence luy sont proposées à refuter»*, that we witness the totalitarian degeneration of certain intimations, originally much more problematic, of Hobbes' moral philosophy. Faced with the now clas-sical problem of «whether a prudent and wise man who lives in a State in which all is in disorder, and in which the perversion of customs is so generalized that there is no way to see the principles of honor and virtue prosper, must adapt himself to the times, and so allow himself to drift on the current, sacrifice something of his usual rigor, behaving like others and trying to save himself by following the same path taken by everyone else», Sorbière responds by re-embracing the thought of Naudé, for whom it is indeed necessary «to sacrifice something of that rigorous virtue which the Stoics testify to us, and which is extremely difficult to imitate».[35]

And again:

> It is said that necessity has no law, and this is said not without reason. Necessity is a kind of force majeure that com-pels us to obey, while violence makes fun of justice. There is no need to labor to have proof of this, since every day we have experiences that confirm what we are saying. The salvation of the people is the supreme law to which sovereigns can sub-ordinate the interest of individuals when the public interest re-quires it. Whatever the occasion may be, the *raison d'état* must prevail.[36]

What interests us here is, first of all, that libertinism *à la Sorbière* constitutes the *trait d'union* between Hobbes and the European-conti-nental theme of reason of state, understood as a technique subordi-nated to glorifying political power as force, *kratos*.

Secondly, that attention to the problem of force, or insistence on this aspect as an element that actually characterizes the worldly political order, places in relation – as has repeatedly been noted[37] – Hobbes' anthropological pessimism with that, supported by a strong mystical-religious impulse, of the Jansenists. But even more, we should clarify, it relates the environment of the 'Hobbesian' French libertines, and therefore the Naudé-Sorbière theoretical-political line, with the realism of Pascal's *Pensées sur la justice.*[38]

Certainly, in Pascal similar concepts, similar political indications to those of the 'Hobbesian' libertines, are quite differently founded and motivated with respect to the ends of the so-called "State of security". This is so obvious that it can be taken for granted. In fact, Auerbach notes that Pascal

> emphasizes, as does Hobbes, the necessity and legitimacy of a powerful State, but makes it even more profound and penetrating, since that 'legitimacy' is evil. It is not so much a matter for him of a reciprocal service between the State and the individual, where the individual owes the state obedience and material sacrifice to the State and the State owes the individual peace and security, as it is much rather one of a subjugation of the Christian to the evil of this world, regardless of whether the evil offers or not some counter-service.[39]

And Spink adds:

> There is good reason to think that Pascal borrowed many of his observations from Hobbes, but he did not at all accept the basic scheme of Hobbes' political philosophy, and chose only those points that were useful to him for his bitter indictment against human nature [...]. For Pascal, only in a purely hypothetical state of grace would the self-love of all men be transformed into charity and would a truly civil society be established. In the present state, no matter how perfect the social organization is built on the principle of individual interest, it is a pure fiction that hides the essential corruption of human nature.[40]

It is therefore above all on the level of the philosophy of history that Pascal's unique combination of reason of state and of Augustinianism, as a lucid Christian representation of a *linear* path of worldly time, aimed solely at salvation in transcendence, is opposed to the *circular* time of the libertines, whose course is linked to Earthly life, the tragic-nihilistic conception of a destiny incumbent on politics, and determinant of its laws.

Recalling the thought of Karl Löwith, one is perhaps able to shed light, conclusively, on the philosophical weakness of some fundamen-tal nodes of the passage from libertine "historicism-processua-lism" to the philosophy of Enlightenment history, a passage that in the European sensibility began in the last decades of the seventeenth century. In the eighteenth century, in particular, the philosophy of Enlightenment history – which as a global ideology of bourgeois society had reached a very advanced level of its development (Koselleck) – ends up neglecting, on the one hand, to take seriously, on the theoretical level, the depth of the Christian view of the world (subordinating the value of politics to the problem of salvation), and, on the other, must also show itself inferior to the task of further problematizing the atheistic-nihilistic perspective itself (associating, as Nietzsche later does, the laws of human action with the ontological problem of the will to power).[41]

4. *Philosophy of history and political theory between Libertinism and Enlightenment.*

As Löwith clearly sees, the modern overemphasis on secular history – rather: the very interpretation of the world as history, or historical process – is the product of our alienation from the natural theology of the ancients (whose pagan experience seventeenth-century libertines continually hark back to), and from the supernatural theology of Christianity. The 'alienated' time of libertines can therefore be considered with Löwith as a dimension «foreign to wisdom and faith».[42] It is worth recalling here that wisdom and faith are the traditional elements of conscience, against which the Enlightenment's social ideology of process-progress (the first nucleus of what will then be contemporary technological scientism) decidedly struggles.

After 1660 (Pintard conventionally suggests this date)[43] it happened that – above all because of the powerful socializing effects of bourgeois ideology – the very psychological assumptions that throughout the century had supported the "libertine phase" of the bourgeoisie slowly began to change. The Enlightenment appeared then to be something quite different from the mere continuation of a libertarian inspiration in a geometric-rationalist key. In the first place, it rediscovered *teleology* beyond the well-enclosed space of mechanistic causalism: history as a process no longer admitted the quietism with which the libertine accepted being ousted from political life and the functioning of the «great wheels and cogs». In contrast to any political mechanism – determined by the metaphorical extension to the sphere of the historical-political values of the principle of natural causality, which the Leviathan had been a symbol of – history now claimed to have a *goal to be achieved*, which was added and claimed to give meaning to the instrumental element constituted by modern science.

Secondly, all of this paved the way to a serious review of the philosophical-anthropological corner-stones on which seventeenth-century pessimistic realism was based, and principally to rethink the question of the *immutability* (or non-perfectibility) *of human nature*, which was indisputably dominant in Charron as in Naudé, Hobbes and Pascal. The secularization of the Christian idea of "providence" allowed history – seen as an all-encompassing process and a gigantic self-propelled organism – to redeem the *natura lapsa hominum* and hope for a constant improvement of the human world.

The atheism implicit in the Enlightenment philosophy of history was also visibly dissociated here from libertine 'paganism' and the circular horizon, overarched by destiny, which was typical of the Baroque period, to be paradoxically relinked to eschatological assumptions of Christian derivation. Moreover, as has been maintained, it «is possible only within the Christian tradition: in fact the intuition that the world is completely without God and abandoned by God presupposes faith in a transcendent creator who takes care of his creatures».[44] Hence the modern historical thought that formed on Enlightenment roots remained substantially halfway between the Christian and the pagan mentality: «it eliminates from its progressive concept the Christian elements of creation and consummation, while it also absorbs from the classical intuition of the world the idea of an infinite, continuous movement, depriving it of its circular structure». This is why its view is finally «necessarily confused, as compared to Greek or biblical thought».[45]

This opinion, which the Enlightenment *Weltgeschehen* posed, despite all appearances, in clear correlation to Christian *Heilsgeschichte*, was embraced by Del Noce, who observed among other things that

> between the rationalism that terminates in libertinism and the other that begins in the Enlightenment there is a clear caesura, in the sense that the Enlightenment appropriates what is the Christian meaning of time, symbolized in the ascendant line. Moreover, modern rationalism begins when the spiritual type which libertinism has given rise to, the erudite who looks to the past, who does not fall for present-day impostures because he recognizes their substantial sameness with those of yesterday, is replaced by the enlightened philosopher who looks to the future, toward a humanity free from mythologies; when the thesis of the dual truth, for the learned and the ignorant, which was essential to the first type of rationalism, gives way to the idea of the construction of the future city, when the model of the political philosopher represents itself in a non-utopian form.[46]

The relationship between libertinism and Enlightenment is therefore not, all told, as simple and straightforward as it might appear from a now classic historiographic reconstruction.[47] There is especially implicit in the libertine view of the world an *atheistic negation of work*, understood as an activity – whether individual or collective – bolstered by fundamental transformational optimism. The libertine denial of work is abides, as has often been observed, in the tendency to exalt private wisdom as a heritage of small coteries, in clear opposition to the Renaissance-Enlightenment *homo faber*, who attempts to change the world by forcing it towards a mythical, albeit 'rational', collective liberation. (The heroic sensitivity of the sixteenth century is linked – so to speak – to encyclopedism and reflection on the technique of the eighteenth, overleaping the stagnant pond of the Mannerist and Baroque crisis).

On the contrary, there was a line that, in negating "constructive action", linked the still balanced libertine interiorization to the pure logic of Sade's pleasure, and that would then recur – after the great nineteenth-century bourgeois experience, distinguished by the solid traits of realism. and positivism – in the exclusively intellectual operation of the surrealists.[48]

In a certain sense, libertinism manifested itself as an atheistic form of asceticism, which was opposed, for example, in seventeenth-century France, to the religious asceticism of the Jansenists because «the former rejects obedience to nature by means of excess, the latter by means of abstention. They are both ways of living outside the norms of the world».[49]

Beyond their differences, Mannerist libertinism and Jansenism both try to go beyond nature, the natural world, by evading its commonplace regularity, which is a merely superficial regularity. Its true substance, which ultimately enhances the brief interlude of mankind's historical life, lies more profoundly in the viewpoints of both, retrievable far from public life.[50] All this seems to deepen the neat line of demarcation that the seventeenth century establishes between the existence of a transcendent *Veritas* and its concrete historical realization in the dimension of the political.

One can understand how the humanity that emerged from the libertine crisis could not grow in its 'external' dimension in a framework that saw History as Process, politics (the State) as a conventionalistic machine, and the natural world·as an immense system of wheels-and-cogs and self-propelled mechanisms. In its eyes, what was lacking was the objectively binding nature of the norm: the *katéchon*,[51] which in the past had made it possible to channel the vast network of legal and political experience by means of predictable conceptual models.

The doctrine of the seventeenth century Baroque really was, in this sense, a high point along the parabola of European nihilism: in it the form of thought called "political occasionalism" was characterized by the conscious, painful renunciation of a *katéchon* and the constant reference to a subjective *occasio* as the sole standard of judgment and arbitrary instrument of decision. With Walter Benjamin, we can say that «the Baroque knows no eschatology», but only «a mechanism by which all earthly things are gathered in together and exalted before being consigned to their end».[52] It is perhaps still indispensable to start from these significant and 'extreme' seventeenth-century spiritual positions in order to fully understand certain non-secondary aspects of contemporary political phenomenology.

II. *The Indecision of the Libertine.*
   History of Decisionistic Thought and Theory
   of the Modern State

1. *Sovereignty, history, decision.*

«The sovereign is the representative of history. He holds the course of history in his hand like a scepter. This view is by no means peculiar to the dramatists. It is based on certain constitutional notions».[1] This sentence of Walter Benjamin is perhaps the most appropriate starting point for understanding the enormous importance of the relationship between history and sovereignty in decisionistic juridical thought. For Benjamin the sovereign – as deciding will – appears in an image typical of Baroque iconography: as a resolving force for any ambiguous situation, a reality capable of introducing order in chaos, a temporary peace (*pax apparens*) in historical conflict, where the scepter testifies to the effective possession of legitimate violence.

Decisionism, actually the original mode, in Schmitt's sense, of legal thought, revolves around three key concepts: the first of them is *exception*, a genuinely meaningful phase of juridical knowledge, in which thought is driven afar from rule, towards a limit-concept, namely toward a «concept related to its outermost sphere».[2] The second is the concept of *dictatorship*, as a scheme for implementing the "substance" of the law in a concrete situation (*Rechtsverwirklichung*), in a provisional suspension of the legal form.[3] The third is the concept of *history* as a secularized space – but still such as to allow a glimpse of an obscure impending divinity – which the sovereign will is called on to decide in the last instance.[4]

Unlike any form of juridical-political thought still within idealism or rationalist metaphysical voids, which sustain the prevalence of a disembodied 'value' on the positivity of historical mediation, the three concepts described do not admit the pre-existence of a criterion or unit of measure (*Maßstab*) capable of superimposing a harmonious rationality on the difficult game of the 'political.' The state of exception is instead the "incommensurable", what is completely incomprehensible to normativistic doctrines of the State.[5] It should be recalled how the "incommensurable" profoundly characterizes the Mannerist and Baroque sensibility – a sensibility that marks the genetic moment, between the late sixteenth and early seventeenth century, of the experience of European juridical decisionism. It is significant that the end of the latter, far from idealistic optimism, is to penetrate the chiaroscuro of political existence, its perennial position – the central aspect of Baroque *Trauerspiel* – on the brink of the abyss of civil war.[6]

What theological and historical characteristics fostered Mannerist-Baroque decisionism? First, the fact that in it mankind was bound to its earthly existence, as its prisoner, with no hope of escape: the sacred/profane dialectic didn't open any eschatological perspective, and any "liberation" was excluded. The situation was as Benjamin again described it with expressive force:

> the hereafter is emptied of everything which contains the slightest breath of this world, and from it the Baroque extracts a profusion of things which customarily escaped the grasp of artistic formulation and, at its high point, brings them violently into the light of day, in order to clear an ultimate heaven, enabling it, as a vacuum, one day to destroy the world with catastrophic violence.[7]

Benjamin translates into linguistic form the characteristic tones of a Baroque painting, where the idea of death and corruption of the flesh is also valid as an allegory of the precariousness of the historical-political world, which sees "crisis" as an absolutely inevitable reality. This allegory can be recognized, for example, behind the problem of the void, which dominates not only the most restless spirit of the seventeenth century – from the interpretations of Baroque figurative art to Pascal – but also in the 'constructive' spirit of Descartes. The European Mannerist and Baroque sensibility offers no sign of hope beyond the profane and constantly returns to its initial condition, that of the reality of a world ruled exclusively by power relations and the resolving capabilities of the sovereign's political decisions. Decisionist thought thus appears as the sign of an accomplished nihilistic-libertine theory, entirely within the intellectual sphere of 'modernity' as an *"anti-Prinzip Hoffnung"*. Decisionism indeed holds up, 'occurs', only where Bloch's hope-principle, the generous and restless natural law-revolutionary tension has by now decayed, and where no supersensible value or idea any longer deceives historical man by fluttering before him the phantom of "liberation".

The seventeenth-century libertine is the intellectual elitist who theorizes this disillusionment to an extreme and replaces the hope-principle with the pleasure-principle, in the mechanistic explanation of the laws that govern the categories of the 'political.' The «*Abgrund / political elitism*» theoretical context, which Roman Schnur[8] mentions, acquires here its most apt meaning. The libertine political elites – creators and exploiters of the knowledge-making power that makes it possible to govern the masses – sense the presence, at the bottom (*Abgrund*) of human existence, of dark, powerful forces that are the true principles of political anthropology. The thirst for pleasure, the will to power, in all their multiple ambiguous implications, appear as an irrational nucleus, irreducible to conceptual forms but in-stead rich in references to the unexplored territory of political myth. This irrational *Abgrund* must be controlled and directed by man with rational criteria of action as to purpose. No rationality as a metaphysical idea can intervene and actively influence this process. The use of *myth* for political purposes is in fact exclusively instrumental, emancipated from Value and aimed at satisfying the 'powerful' will. This is the "daimon" of the Baroque Reason of State, acutely identified by Enrico Castelli,[9] envisaged however not so much in the – external – terms of the history of political doctrines, namely the 'public' ideologies presented to justify human behaviors, as in the 'internal' terms of political anthropology.

The descent into the *Abgrund* of the 'political' passes through an infinite number of stratifications, which can be archaeologically reconstructed by directing our analysis behind the flashy variegation of ideologies and utterances of political doctrines, down to the subterranean trends that anthropologically motivate political action –: from the libertine theoreticians to Hobbes, first of all the pleasure-principle and the will to power. These are strands constantly pushed into the shadows by nineteenth-twentieth century European idealistic investigation, rooted – albeit with results of considerable value – in the "natural law *vs* historicism" dilemma. Roman Schnur makes, in the opening pages of his work, a brief point on the vast research conducted in the areas of the history of ideas. It was in fact from the overall interference of research perspectives that one could deduce the consolidation of an area of analysis till then consigned to the vague *felicitas* of interdisciplinary temptations: this area, as Schnur maintained, referring to Gehlen,[10] had as its object the anthropology of the political in intellectual history, and was in its method more closely linked to Foucault's archeology than to the shallow map of the history of idealist doctrines.

Walter Benjamin and Carl Schmitt are in this sense two especially meaningful names. Our thoughts go first of all to the first chapter – which we've mentioned – *Trauerspiel und Tragödie des Ursprung*: it contains illuminating insights shedding real glimpses of light on the "inside" history of the theory of sovereignty. Topics such as «The inability to decide», «The tyrant as martyr, the martyr as a tyrant», «Play and reflection», «The King as creature»,[11] dealing with the shadowy side of the Baroque 'political,' make up the opposite slope of the idealist investigation and are treatise types totally unrelated to the traditional history of ideas, typical of the murky side of Benjamin's style, which couldn't possibly be understood by the linear-minded Panofsky.[12]

Schmitt's thought moves in the same direction, constantly evincing his jurist's personality even when his treatment seems to stray furthest from the "center" of his topics: the history and fate of the *jus publicum Europaeum*. Reference should be made to Schmitt's analyses, whose indelible mark we feel in the best pages of Schnur,[13] in order to fully understand also the inherent *limits* of decisionist thought. Decision, in order to be the true resolution point of 'extreme situations' and to thus be able to radically influence the political structure, must spring from a profound dialectic with the forces acting in society, without which it is rejected, and its lack of effectiveness is overtaken anew by a blind conflict of unguided powers – civil war in the name of idealistically founded 'values'.[14] We can say that the Baroque *Trauerspiel* registers this extreme difficulty encountered by sovereign decision, and perhaps the crucial moment of decisionism:

> The prince, who is responsible for making the decision to proclaim the state of emergency, reveals, at the first opportunity, that he is almost incapable of making a decision. Just as compositions with restful lighting are virtually unknown in Mannerist pain-

ting, so it is that the theatrical figures of this epoch always appear in the harsh light of their changing resolve.[15]

It is in the paintings of El Greco that this alarming situation is made visible.[16] The need to decide presents itself in parallel with the 'paralysis' of decision, determined by the risk of its inefficacy and by the uncertainty produced by the skeptical critique of values that should motivate it.[17] Traditional theological-political analyses of the concept of decision are well-known.[18] It is impossible not to detect their remarkable intelligence (always accompanied by a no less intelligent masking of reality) in delving into the real reasons for the ungovernability of mankind, starting from that rich historical and conceptual paradigm which is the seventeenth century European Baroque. The fact is that – as Benjamin states – human beings are not determined ultimately by thoughts, but rather by discontinuous physical impulses,[19] which prove to be unavoidable factors of conflict and struggle. Therefore conflict certainly can never be eliminated, but only held in check, transformed with the typically political tools of the will of decision.

2. *Political subjectivity from individualism to absolutism.*

We can rediscover in Schnur's essay *Individualismus und Absolutismus* two fundamental thematic threads, to which even its minor topics (though none the less important, if it is true, with Valéry, that «il n'y a point de détails dans l'exécution») make implicit reference.

The first thread consists of an in-depth theorization, which Schnur pays special attention to in his work, of the opposition that exists between the juridical-political categories of *absolutism* and *totalitarianism*. Absolutism affirms itself as a technical need and a choice necessitated by that individualism, which intends to avoid the perfectly desperate outcomes of anarchic radicalism (i.e. the other possible outlet of individualism). Hobbes in this regard places in a well-constructed systematic framework embryos of already widespread libertine and *politique* culture. As Schnur notes in referring to Buchheim's clarifying work,[20] no "conceptual confusion" is allowed anymore between authoritarian thought and totalitarian thought, the former a much-needed product (and one profoundly 'suffered' by the intellectual elites) of *subjectivity* confronting the danger of its own annihilation in civil war; the latter unanimizing and with no consideration for thought that grows *in interiore hominum sphaera*.[21]

«A mechanism can never be all-encompassing. It is something external, i.e. usable for obtaining an external obedience from citizens without ever touching their inner selves, their consciences».[22] Neither Mersenne nor libertine cynicism nor Descartes – nor, probably, Hobbes – can therefore be inclined toward interpretations hinting in the least at «totalitarian outcomes». Not Hobbes, even though here we come up against the formidable issue of Schmitt's interpretation of *Leviathan*, which tends to consider «a dangerous admission» Hobbes' indifference toward the inner convictions of citizens expressed by the *savoir/pouvoir* of the State.[23] As Franz Neumann maintains,

> where, as in an absolute monarchy, power is mainly exercised through traditional bureaucratic tools of coercion, its use is governed by abstract, predictable rules, even though they can be applied arbitrarily. Therefore, absolutism already contains the institutional principles of modern liberalism; on the other hand, totalitarian dictatorship is the absolute negation of these principles, since its main repressive agents are not courts and administrative bodies, but the secret police and the party.[24]

But it should be recognized that Neumann – in attributing too easily, in this context, the phenomenon of dictatorship to the principle of totalitarianism[25] – fails to clarify any further the conceptual complexity implicit in Schmitt's interpretation. The temporary "suspension" of the law as a prelude to the establishment of a new order – a "sovereign" and not a "commissarial" dictatorship – does not necessarily oppose the inner development of subjectivity, but only limits its *critical* range, preventing its *crisis* effect on the institutional order and thus circumventing the dangers that one of its emergences into the open would necessarily involve.[26]

What opens up here is a crossroads that leads to the second fundamental thematic thread of *Individualismus und Absolutismus*, to which we've referred. It's the relationship that Schnur detects between "suspension" (of values, in the wake of relativistic scepsis; of law, in the wake of decisionistic modes of issuing from civil wars of religion) and the "attempt of a Mannerist order" (*manieristischer Ordnungsversuch*). How, in fact, can the subjectivist suspension of values be reconciled with the need for an institutional order? How, in other words, can a *conventional* political order be established while avoiding a "critique/crisis" short circuit? Schnur shows how the theoreticians of political Mannerism – especially the seventeenth century French libertines – already had an inkling of the true extent of this problem.

At the point where extremist Mannerist subjectivism discovered the *need for an order* (though still an order emerging from traditional-bequeathed criticism) there began to take shape the slow *Bildung* that accompanied, on the side of bourgeois interiority, the existence of the modern State. It consisted mainly in a secularized version of the *renunciation* (to the immediate satisfaction of individual and social needs) of *education* and *civilization* as functional repression and channeling of vital instincts.

This problem, well embedded in the European intellectual history of the seventeenth century, of the pursuit of the "inner form" of bourgeois consciousness – i.e. of its contemporary functional modeling at the emergence of the huge critical potential of morality (Koselleck) – helps us to understand on what actual basis the transition took place, which Schnur never tires of seeking in the footsteps of Hocke,[27] from the Mannerist to the Baroque world. It can be said in this regard that where subjectivist extremism was still condemned to an obsessive repetition and deprived of the innovation of one's behavior, political mannerism had not yet reached its most mature stage, which would be marked by the subsequent "attempt at a Mannerist order", understood as an ideological form of transition to the Baroque Reason of State.

Hobbes was in this sense the first to systematize a fully Baroque political theory: in him the unwillingness toward *Wertobjektivismus* could not be more complete: sensory dispersion is in fact the expression of a complete microcosmic anarchy that neither admits exceptions nor finds within itself correctives. The truth of belief is nonsense, illusion, deception, superstition or madness; what any contemporary of ours would call "value" is conventional and, moreover, conditioned by the purpose for which it is believed as such. Nothing, therefore, is acceptable, if it doesn't respond to the concrete usefulness of those who accept it.

Schnur's essay *Individualismus und Absolutismus* ends where Hobbes' arguments begin to gain critical mass. Schnur has the merit, however, to lead the reader exactly onto the threshold of it, allowing a glimpse of the crucial importance of Hobbes' opposition to "conformism/anticonformism" for the purpose of establishing the new world order, a matter that – one might think – couldn't be clarified without a close analysis of Hobbes' relationship with the Catholic Counter-Reformation (Hobbes - Bellarmino?).[28] Nevertheless, there are already in Hocke substantial indications for a study in this regard:

> The general phenomenon of the "Baroque" takes its place in a new cultural and political aspiration of order," influenced by the consequences of the Counter-Reformation and by the conventions of absolutist culture, which at that time was taking shape, and of the society of the three estates [...]. Mannerism, which continues to flourish beside it, within and beneath the "Baroque", remains ever subjective, unorthodox, unconventional. The Baroque spirit aspires, often with expressive Mannerist means, to objective orders (Society, philosophy, Church, State), namely to their representation.[29]

"Mannerist subjectivism" and "classic elements" mingled with the concept of Baroque order therefore, in spite of appearances, have the selfsame root: an individual, after having experienced the extremist pleasure of the libertine and Mannerist intellect, cannot endure the continuous agitation and therefore seeks order, which he can accept this time only in hypothetical and conventional form, reserving the right of membership – in interiority – "in another world." Conversely, however, the order must be usable by the "deciding will" of the political elite, which will increasingly take on the character of "interpreter" and" "filter" of the needs of the dominated. The very formalized rules of order – albeit used according to their own logic, according to the internal sense of the "game" they belong to – will constantly be inclined toward the *life* of those who possess them, since they are privy to their function.

3. *The allegory of the scales.*

Once again, what re-emerged here, among the fundamental principles of *savoir/pouvoir* characteristic of the Baroque theory of the State, was the original element of the "deciding will." But this theory of power was consciously free of any triumphalism: the already mentioned limits of decision appeared from every standpoint insurmountable, nor could the *pax apparens*, as an image devoid of any value content and "modernly" eradicated ontologically, fully replace the function once per-formed by the theological-political *pax vera* myth.[30] It had to be acknowledged that some values, even if rendered – after the libertine-nihilistic scepsis – "unprovable," and purified of any traditional "aura," still continued to strongly facilitate (a libertine would say: like as many political "myths") achieving social integration. Therefore, the "compromise" enacted between the realistic Baroque Reason of State and the idealist-classicist need for an "extreme value" surely intended, on a metatheoretical level, to eliminate naive cognitivism, but also – in practical terms – to preserve part of the ethics of values as an indispensable function of government and an ultimate check on the emotions of the dominated mass.

If therefore in his heart a political Mannerist smiled at any idea of Value, which he had far exceeded, his smile was joyless, because Behemoth could also overwhelm him. This appears among other things the political meaning of the *Melancholia* of which Benjamin speaks. The allegory of the scales – agnostic historicism eternally undecided, in practice, between the two weights of "residual humanism" and "complete nihilism" – testified to the depth of the dilemma between a disenchanted detachment by idealistic natural law and the continued abidance of a political theology.[31] It's easy to see how this dilemma possessed, in the critical phase of modernity in which our historical experience resides (quite clearly attributable to Nietzschean-Heideggerian *Zwischenzeit*), an extreme vital significance of its own.

III. *A Baroque Creature*

The conclusion of the second *Faust* has a strange seventeenth-century sound to it: «Alles Vergängliche ist nur ein Gleichnis»,[1] which embodies the creatural problem – the creatural as problem. Perhaps because of its relevance to the fundamental themes of the great European *Trauerspiel*, though perhaps – even more – because what might be called a theory of *Gleichnis* – i.e. of the strained metaphorical relationship or referral from the creature to the creator – is a real key for understanding the relationship that seventeenth-century man has with the metaphysical problem of transcendence.

In this chapter I will limit myself to making a few observations on the Baroque representation of the creatural world, and therefore on what I would call "techniques of constructive illusion" (the art of dissembling, forgetting, of the "little death") formulated by the seventeenth-century intellect for "shaping" the spirituality of their time, filling, by means of artifices, the vacuum following the post-scholastic dissolution of the traditional concept of "truth".

1. *Phenomenology of Gleichnis.*

It has been called: «Baroque as a creatural world without a creator». In fact, compared to the problem of the link that relates the creature to the creator, the Baroque intellect proceeded in an ambiguous manner, for the most part by criticizing the assumptions of classical onto-theology.[2] Spirituality loved to express itself rather as *mystical experience*,[3] renunciation of the power of speech (in the sense it had already been for John of the Cross and Teresa of Avila), or as *metaphor*, via imagery, figurative speech on *Veritas* (no longer through medieval Christian *symbol*, but through the modern use of the *allegory*),[4] always with the knowledge that *Veritas* tolerates no 'direct' discourse on itself.

It should be noted that this metaphorical-allegorical activity – revered by all of seventeenth-century Europe and in particular by those who, like Baltasar Gracián, radicalized the expressive forms of that century – didn't ignore mysticism, and while placing itself on a different plane from it, agreed with the choice of contemplative silence.[5] What was the case of both – as philosophical historiography shows – mostly placed behind them, was fundamental-metaphysical knowledge, the philosophical system that claimed to accurately classify every *ens* as singular being, *per relationem* and finalistically –: onto-theology in its Aristotelian-Thomist version.

The latter – having already substantially lost, in the wake of the overall medieval solutions, serious tension, bearer of *thaumázein*, toward being – had become a reassuring descriptive ontic, capable of summarizing miracle (which in the Baroque went back to being complete mystery) in the neutral tones of an objective statistic. No more surprises from it, and therefore maximum doubt about its ability to oppose the moment of truth, which was atheism's real metaphysical awakening.

The expression that defines the seventeenth-century world, dominated by Baroque spiritual forms, as a creatural world "without a creator" should therefore be taken as a reaction to complete describability of the creatural world, supported by traditional onto-theological knowledge. In any case, it must be understood not just in the atheistic sense of conscious (libertine?) denial (but the relationship between libertinism and the Baroque should in turn be better investigated) of God, but in the sense of a certified, pained "emptying out" of the divine in earthly matters. Divine *Veritas* exists: what eludes (and perhaps cannot exist) is the *cognitive relationship* to it, the formal utterability of this link. This means that – at least dominantly – with the exclusion of the path of total contemplative detachment from the world (but one thinks of the complexity of this issue in the context of speculative Jansenism!), Baroque man, who does not easily give up his rootedness in the profane, is left with just the *virtuosity of transiency* – an ontologically 'unserious' choice precisely because it is 'virtuosity,' but capable of ennobling when (and the more that) the profane points to the brink of the abyss that is able to cancel it, revealing the "game-like" nature of life in the world. This virtuosity, which is the Baroque guise of *Gleichnis*, is clearly visible in the paintings of Velázquez and de La Tour. I'll try to better define its outlines on a theoretical level.

2. *Sensible form and intelligible essence.*

The schema that relates *sensible form* to its *intelligible essence* is typically Neoplatonist. It seems to express the most complete theorization of the superiority of the latter over the former, and – simultaneously – the inevitability, for thinking that gets to the bottom of things, of considering any form or sensible form *sub specie intelligibili.*

One must however recognize behind the terms of this Neoplatonic formulation the presence of a more articulated theoretical mechanism – a mechanism whose dyadic sensible/intelligible schema appears to be only its simplified core and allusion. Placing the sensible form of things in connection with something that 'lies beyond' doesn't mean depriving it of all value, but *saving phenomena* by transposing them to a purer sphere. (One thinks here of Husserl's approach, and the implicit Platonism that a scholar of the Baroque such as Benjamin noted in it in the *Gnoseological foreword* to his book on *Trauerspiel*). Phenomena are 'saved' because they are recognized in their indispensable or incurable profaneness, which lends a degree of autonomy to their appearance.

To clarify this I should perhaps reconnect the question also to the way in which this Neoplatonic theme was historically taken and enacted in the sixteenth and seventeenth centuries, during which – as has been convincingly argued[6] – it was given the highest critical attention. In that period there was a tendency to reduce the power exerted by the intelligible: now the areas of knowledge and action which, like ethics and politics, were more tied to the sensible aspect of phenomena, human behavior in its external capacity, definitely patterned themselves in accordance with a statute of (relative) autonomy. In stressing, more than in the past, their character as *art* (in the sense of artificiality, affectation, or even artifice), the Baroque highlighted the sensible element which made them specific. The albeit Platonic cast within the Baroque (here is the point that needs to be emphasized) *didn't devalue* the seeming form of reality in recognizing it as mere illusion. Though considering reality limited and illusory, at the same time illusoriness gained a positive and constructive function, made it a technique and an art aimed at collecting and ripening the 'creatural' fruits of the vital-sensible.

Illusion therefore, as awareness of transience-vanity of the sensible form, but constructive because since capable of provisionally 'saving,' almost retaining the transiency (*das Vergängliche*) of phenomena and the entire profane area of appearance: the presence a person's 'political' acts, in a word, his or her life amidst other persons. The paradoxical nature of this seventeenth-century theory of 'constructive' illusion lies principally in the fact that, while lying within the modern nihilistic devaluation of classical ontological issues, didn't give up trying to build in the positivity of illusion something capable of substituting, *par provision*, its recognized inaccessible foundation.

3. *Lost foundation, constructive illusion and Michelstaedter.*

But how to configure these 'brakes' which, as Baroque spirituality understood it, should have eased the despair over transience; and – even before that – how to make intersubjectively obvious this need for constructive illusion, given that any explicit discourse, any open questioning about it, risked the impossibility of being understood, through the constant 'concealment strategy' imposed on it in Western thought? It will be opportune, in this sense, to always keep alive the reference to those authors who – directly or indirectly, as genuine exceptions over the course of the development of philosophical and moral reflection – have dealt with this neglected side of the European spirit. I think first of Baltasar Gracián and Nietzsche, the relationship between whom – Schopenhauer being their *geistesgeschichtlich* mediator – has already been successfully highlighted,[7] and of those other 'untimely' considerations regarding voluntary illusion – defined as *rhetorical* – carried out under the influence of Nietzsche by Michelstaedter, which proceed at a very high level of thought, transposing one's attention to the transient essence of the creatural world typical of the Baroque into a very different way of thinking. But let's proceed in an orderly fashion.

To endure living in the world, an utterable link is needed between the profane and God: this is the reason that makes 'necessary' the Baroque theory of illusion. But is it really necessary? In other words, is it really necessary, in order to survive, to be reduced to substituting ineffable *Veritas* with a fake certainty, good for *Allzumenschliches*: a *rhetoric* that claims to replace unattainable *persuasion*?[8] Michelstaedter, who in every sense is still very timely, faced these issues with inhuman clarity, and provided an answer that set him precisely at the antipodes of Baroque spirituality, whose interrogatives, however, he shared.

There should be no illusion. This was Michelstaedter's answer. Nothing should disguise, conceal the reality of the uprootal. The uprootal – ineffability of the link and perhaps its very absence – had to be experienced and suffered to the dregs. A desert of ice devoid of ornament – even a minimal ornament, which the demand for heat, hope and consolation, i.e. mankind's weakness, would disastrously lead to.[9] Even the mystical solution – as Michelstaedter claims – doesn't promise stability or suggest 'illusions'. While Isaiah and Ecclesiastes dwell on the vanity of the world and on the *attention* (*prosoché*) to an inexpressible God, yet it is true that the attention isn't useful for forming a stable bond, a positive *'religion'* that promises a connection between irremediably distinct and separated planes. It is instead a miraculous moment and a tension that reaches the breaking point.

All this when instead the Baroque – in taking on the same problem – constructively thrived on the tension (which, however, remained unresolved) between the two planes, 'created discourses' on it. The Counter-Reformation allegories still preserved in that a great deal of medieval *symbolism*.

4. *Unnaturalness of existence.*

The Baroque art of dissimulation took a middle-of-the-road course, rejecting both the 'ancient' clarity of onto-theology and the unmasking response of Michelstaedter. It nevertheless developed extensive varieties of knowledge and vast areas of harmony and complementarity with these clear answers. In taking, for example, death as the only serious topic of speculation, in the proliferation of treatises *de arte bene moriendi* the Baroque glorified the limitation and vanity of the world, the contingency of every event and enterprise. If *simulating* meant exhibiting what was not, hence building a social ethic *sobre la rena* of a world of false relationships (Gracián), dis-simulating meant concealing what was, namely the reality that human life was a necessary path towards death, the only certain and significant event behind the screen of the naturalness of existence.

Thus Christianity was taken as the example of a grandiose, comforting illusion and dispenser of hope, whose Counter-Reformist ethics of situation and casuistry were just its colorful, flashy, expressive guise. Wanting to deceive oneself as to the naturalness of living in the world is necessary for ordinary survival. Already in the radical ethical crisis of the seventeenth century, in the 'Catholic' Gracián who however "has no *spontaneous* love for mankind", it is clear that whoever intends to fully expose the non-naturalness of human life, the terrible enmity of nature, or worse its lethal indifference, sooner or later pays dearly for his Gnostic vice: destined to wander among the things that have become inanimate *only for him*, while life creates a desert all around him, his destiny is total isolation. This is the destiny of Nietzsche, as it appears in the poetry of Umberto Saba.[10]

This sense of isolation is reflected in the suffering, typical of the Baroque, due to the detachment of historical existence from every still 'natural' area. Yet it's true that the isolation was also necessary, because man – as the radical spirit of the seventeenth century knew (and the perfect knowledge of Hobbes was just the visible tip of a vast iceberg) – lay in the 'bestial brute' part of its nature; in it dominated the ferocity and the will to dominate for self-preservation. (And this stage wasn't a wreck cropping up from the prehistory of the species: on the contrary, it appropriated those layers of culture that had been considered initially an effective antidote).

Again, with Hobbes, culture and Christianity are seen, however, in the end as the winning expression of natural law (*lex naturalis*, natural law) against arbitrary freedom and natural ferocity (*jus naturale*, natural right). And in effect civil religion and *Bildung* are needed for collective existence: seventeenth-century social ethics share the view that if there were no God, he'd have to be invented. God-want, God-need. But is all this really – as you might think – mere hypocrisy of public faith, *confession* against the *faith*, in Hobbesian terms? Or mightn't it point to something deeper: the possibility for man to have only confession to deal with (or with artificial truths, *tailor-made* for man) before the impossibility of faith, which in its purity is cold light, uninhabitable by man?

Confession (in Hobbesian sense) may perhaps be only a fruit 'necessitated' by hypocrisy, for the realization of a social ethic, but then – no differently – all the other basic formulations of primal knowledge, the axioms of scientific knowledge, must be recognized not as already true, but only as desired to be true by men to assure themselves about the naturalness and ultimate intelligibility of their existence.

5. *A philosophy of oblivion.*

Salvation lies thus entirely in contrivance: in *forgetting* the ground-lessness and non-naturalness of the phenomena that make up the life of man. Hence the typically Baroque operation (in the sense in which we speak of a 'surgical operation') – and glorified by that neglected side, within Counter-Reformist Christianity, which is the 'worldly' knowledge of the Jesuits – their «procured oblivion» and «little death». These subtle processes of inner transformation were related to the great change that took place on the epistemological level at the start of the seventeenth century, with *phenomenalism.*

Phenomenalistic epistemology dissolves any realistic conception of substance and forcefully introduces subjectivism – the arbitrary weight of unrelated perceptions – in every facet of cognitive activity. What ended up prevailing over the Truth of God as guarantor of the objectivity of knowledge was the old hallucination of Descartes (belonging to the Baroque side of his soul) that made him doubt whether the people who passed under his window were really *res cogitantes* or rather "men of glass", mannequins and machines in the human appearance of garments and the cloaks.[11] Anyone interested in the origins of the phenomenalist current in epistemology can't fail to be impressed by the striking similarities, under the sign of the Baroque, between the pure theoretician Descartes and the virtuoso of the imagination Gracián when one reads historiographic reconstructions like this:

> The perceptions of natural phenomena and the behaviors of other men became places in which each was a private and different world from all the others. Everyone was not a universe, but sensory data, private perceptual atoms inaccessible to anyone else, since no one could live another's perceptual experience [...]. One began to wonder if *the minds of others* existed, about what foundations and probative reasons one had to harmonize feelings, sensations, in short an inner world, with any other man. The philosophical schools of phenomenalism, from the seventeenth century until today, have posed the problems of the perception of the external world in terms of private, inaccessible *sense-data, Erlebnisse,* the knowledge of "other minds" on the basis of differences that, yet before entering philosophy, had entered the social imagination and shaped people's lives.[12]

Well then, the Baroque – which after the sixteenth Mannerist disorder again sought a form of order and, in its way, of 'classicism' – pro-posed not to deny, but only to *forget* the reality of this huge uncertainty, this 'simulation of truth' that undermined the metaphysical value and validity of human life. With Klossowski: if oblivion didn't hide from man the simulatory character of all actions, would he have the strength to go on living?[13] But Klossowski then exaggerates in maintaining – according to his thesis notes – the resolutely anti-metaphysical (and denial of any dualism) character intrinsic to this problematic Baroque position, in saying that «even if oblivion gives man the illusion of living and fulfilling in an original and authentic way what instead is a simulacrum, the copy of a copy, every dualism of representation is here suppressed; but not because it presents and displays itself as anything original, but on the contrary because the image refers dizzyingly to another image, without enabling one to ever find a prototype. The concept of copy is abolished because the model doesn't exist».[14] The 'philosophy of oblivion,' in maintaining that *one mustn't remember*, and that in any case what the Neoplatonists believed to be memory is ontologically false, it would therefore seem – in Klossowski's interpretation – the perfect opposite of anamnesis.

6. *Little death and nihilism.*

But how can the simulatory, fictitious character of living in the world be forgotten once this nihilistic awareness has been reached? How can a life project with the acceptance of its groundlessness and vanity be reconciled?

Through a mental reservation. In the mental reservation that accepts the ultimate vanity of every worldly activity and every vitalistic desire for self-assertion lies the Baroque's "little death," which isn't yet a mere flight into asceticism but, on the contrary, a drive to live with equal determination, after having assimilated *in interiore homine* the vanity of events.

Paradoxically, the actions committed by those who live in the natural life and those committed by those who live in the small death are, in their outward appearance, identical. It is only their *internal transfiguration* that, in the second case, profoundly changes their value. Rilke is the poet closest to us who was capable of embracing this difficult attitude in all its seriousness. Transfiguring the world is the only way to give meaning to it, because there was no pre-existent meaning. Meaning is par excellence 'non-natural'.

Events occur, time passes. Can we still 'plan' when the shadow of transience has definitively overshadowed every *Prinzip Hoffnung*? When, given the merely contingent value of occurrences, can we expect nothing from them? The most ethically meaningful response contained in controversial Baroque nihilism is precisely this: 'to immobilize' things in the moment of their decline (see Gracián, *Oráculo manual*, aphorism 39), to exploit the superiority provided by the human awareness of illusion. Actually, it seems that we can seriously plan only when we're lucidly desperate.[15]

How can we fail to grasp in that some affinity with Heidegger's analysis of the concept of 'project' (*Entwurf*)? Its understanding of nihilism is that it forces us to continue to plan in the context of the 'death of God,' and – I might add, beyond Heidegger – in the context of the 'death of experience'.[16] Such a world would be the exact inverse of the one – described by Max Weber in *Wissenschaft als Beruf* – in which the old biblical ploughman lived, who at the end of his day (and life) could claim to have had enough. The death of God on the other hand, by dissolving the originality of every occurrence and reducing experience to mere repetition, replaced sufficiency with fatigue.

It is perhaps a condition that can't be overcome (and perhaps we really must resign ourselves to seeing the noble gesture with which Zarathustra 'sent into retirement' the old Pontifex consumed in a thousand ways and in a thousand farcical repetitions by the nihilism of the masses). But it is in the light of this condition that the Baroque theories of dissimulation become once again particularly significant, by once more imposing on the attention of thought the subtle wisdom of the "little death" and of other seventeenth-century techniques of transformative illusion. These have the effect of demonstrating with increasingly greater clarity the grotesque aspect of the multitude of those who, falsely whole, believe themselves to be *only* living, and only natural inhabitants of this world.

Part II

Pathways beyond Decision

IV. Ekstatische Sozietät.
Robert Musil's "The Man without Qualities"

The specific problem of this chapter is the philosophical-political meaning of that immense network of metaphors which forms *The Man without Qualities*.[1] Early twentieth-century Europe experienced a profound social crisis that affected its entire range of values. In this context, bourgeois political subjectivity was dissociating, doubting the compactness of its bodily action, the unity of its points of reference – the necessary basis of a political theory. That of the logical possibility of an unchallenged relationship with the world was now a very far-off myth. At times it inspired, reproposing itself, tones of deep nostalgia, over which, however, there prevailed an awareness of the impossibility – or possibility only on the plane of an open utopia[2] – of seeking a nexus of rational unity, 'exact' control over the social world.

The thesis argued here is that the complex problem of *The Man without Qualities* can be interpreted as a significant metaphor of this political reality. Musil's singular intuitions point forcefully *beyond* the immediate meaning of their discursive field, to become serious expressive elements of the framework in which the European philosophical-political crisis is situated.[3] In this regard, I believe in particular that, once the dense fabric of Musil's images is somewhat reduced, the symbol of the *Ekstatische Sozietät* that dominates Ulrich's and Agathe's last experience can be understood as a lively allusion to the twilight of the 'liberal' individualistic-possessive sphere – an authentic ascetic transposition of this twilight.

The philosophical-political characteristics of Musil's universe are therefore defined[4]: we see that this universe has acquired such and so many elements of complexity with respect to the classical world of bourgeois affirmation, as to be completely illegible in any surviving 'Goethian' perspective – to the point of no longer knowing any accuracy besides the functional one of 'measurability'. Moreover, the sociological roots of the whole problem will be fully illuminated as Ulrich's bodily experience – which unfolds throughout the first volume of the novel of which *Seinesgleichen* and 'Parallel Action' are effective conceptual *nuclei*[5] – is viewed in the impressive process of the massification (*Vergesellschaftung*) of the scientific and philosophical horizon.

1. *Subject/object. 'Kakanien' as a philosophical-political microcosm.*

How does the subject-object relationship – traditional *Hauptproblem* of theoretical reason – compare to the project of man's bodily (and therefore also political, juridical) domination of the world? This is the question – posed in all its complexity – that forcibly nourishes, albeit implicitly, the very fecund Mitteleuropean cultural problem typical of the early twentieth century.[6]

It should be emphasized that, at the roots of this problem, the enlightenment *ratio* still displays itself alive and recognizable, reaching, in the literature of crisis, to the last experiences of the sign's insignificance. In Hofmannsthal, for example, at the extreme margin of the subject-object relationship, the perception of a dismay that is certainly not just linguistic-existential, but which is above all in a strong sense 'political' and practical, completes itself: Lord Chandos – the last incarnation of an 'I'-substance whose self-affirmative project dissolves into the impenetrable objective world – limits himself to saying quite simply:

> My situation, in short, is this: I have lost every faculty of thinking or speaking coherently on any topic.[7]

Thus it must be said that, from a philosophical-political point of view, the ultimate success of every bodily project of the 'I'-substance – of every power of signification of the object in the social realm – turns out to be more remote and utopian the more the properly post-romantic and 'post-heroic' character that nourishes the twentieth-century consciousness comes alive.[8] It must be noted how, in representing this, the long process of historical-political decay of a *Selbstbehauptung* founded *on individual bases*, of a self-affirmative fullness of the bodily 'I' bearing in itself the character of rationality, definitively comes to pass.

However, now with the European crisis, the subject's practical self-affirmation paid in full for its inability to build on what had once been considered the universal principles of rationality, while the old – never sedated – dualism of Reason and Individuality re-emerged everywhere more forcibly, questioning every 'reconciled' hypothesis, every hypothesis that carried within itself the imprint of individual sacrifice in the trans-subjective dimension.

Nevertheless, we must not think that the German cultural climate of the early twentieth century clearly and unequivocally expressed every-where its renunciation of synthesis as a metaphysical value, that is, that it experienced the definitive end of the idealistic hope of seeing, in the social synthesis, the historical projection of an absolute value; rather, the synthetic principle in its generality – as an ideological finality, a practical objective to be achieved in history – would not cease to repropose itself, on the level of ethical representations, in the variously renewed forms of natural law value.

Yet, contrary to this incompletely suppressed metaphysical perma-nence, a new theoretical perspective crept into the framework of Mittel-european neo-positivism – the ultimate fruit of contemporary 'radical' reflection. This perspective would culminate in an awareness of the im-possibility of a transposition of the ethical *Ordnung* into immanence. Now value is, in other words, unattainable as a foundational ethical ab-solute; it cannot dwell in history, «but it must be outside of the world»,[9] and all systematic efforts to 'understand-together' Reason and Indivi-duality from within, in a permanently recovered ethical form, remain futile.

The 'here' of history cannot be now, in Wittgenstein's perspecti-ve, which is clearly separated from the 'ethical' sphere of value, which places its *Ordnung* outside of what is communicable and outside of the world, since «as the world is, it is entirely indifferent concerning what is higher», and value «does not reveal itself in the world». As for the subject, «where in the world is there a metaphysical subject to be seen?»; it «does not belong to the world, but is a limitation of the world». By perishing as an «extended bodily reality», it is transformed into a point-like essence that transmits its own "silence" to everything known.[10]

It was thus that, on the road that marks the perception of the impossibility of an ethical *Ordnung*, the individual Ulrich-Robert

Musil proceeded in his determination to live out the latest events of the twentieth century's end of value. The parabola that *The Man without Qualities* describes – from Parallel Action to Ecstatic Society – sees the incessant shadows of the breakdown of Austrian society, of a golden-black Kakanien that can no longer offer a 'livable' model for worldly action.[11] It is in the face of this that Ulrich and Agathe experience – for a few instants – the fullness of unity, which nullifies any relationship in nullifying the object within it. But a harsh counterpoint to this is the impossibility of communicating *beyond* their small circle, of grounding a behavior that is also directed outwards towards trans-subjectivity, of dissolving in love the barrier of possession. Corporeity requires typicality, consolidation, while «in these nights the self holds nothing back, there is no condensation of possession on the self's surface». But precisely in this *absence of possession*, «the night embraces all contradictions in its shimmering maternal arms» and «every imparting is a parting without envy».[12]

Failure to achieve a stable relationship with the object, understood as irreducible bodily estrangement, soon turns into complete dissociation – or perhaps, even more, 'diffuseness' – of subjectivity. The two stages are inseparable. Ulrich says: «There is no longer a whole man confronting a whole world, only a human something moving about in a general culture-medium».[13] In him this diffuse subjectivity "does not act" but limits itself to living in possibility. The sense of complexity is in fact ethically paralyzing: «Every action and its opposite are accompanied by the subtlest arguments, which can be defended or attacked with equal ease. How on the earth can you champion such a state of affairs?».[14] Walter, the Wagnerian, protests, but Ulrich shrugs, rejecting any mechanical restoration of value. For him it is not so much a question of somehow 'justifying' the death of the Goethean individual, but rather of resolutely 'departing from it' towards other horizons.

Even the story of mad Moosbrugger reflects the shattered image of what had once been "free will".[15] The *personality* of criminal law crumbles under the weight of irony in a renewed *Götzendämmerung*,[16] whose alternative is now placed directly between Moosbrugger and the *Übermensch* – the only 'plausible' subjects – literally bypassing the concept of 'integral human individuality,' which dissolves under the lens of a powerful microscope and is reduced to mere impossibility. But the mature Musil avoids any complacency in this regard. He does not dwell on any sensational description of dissociation. On the contrary, this 'expressionistic' weakness – some traces of which are still present in the early drafts of the novel – appears to him in the long run as a sort of simplistic demystification. Also for this reason, despite his initial transport, with the passing of time he does not re-solve to free Moosbrugger, but rather, with extreme irony, already «in conversation with Walter and Clarisse, Ulrich turns out to be reactionary».[17]

But the eruption of the irrational is a harsh reality that cannot be ignored, even if – and here lies the fundamental difficulty – there is nothing to gain by considering it. The consideration of irrational reality suggests no behavior, but vice versa – pushed to its extreme logic – relegates everything to the fluctuating atmosphere of a dream-like society, in which there is no «real common world to share».[18] In this sense, it can really be said that, in the face of this, for Musil and Hofmannsthal there seems to be only one law: that by which the increase of life's multidimensional spaces, the multiplication of complexity, *sharing* wastes away.[19] Thus in Hofmannsthal's *Andreas* the forced absence of a regulated materiality (so to speak: 'juridically' re-gulated) will prevent each event, leaving space only for the allusion of symbols and analogies.[20] In *The Man without Qualities* itself, this is the lot of the communicative sphere: to be reduced to the mere *form* of a relationship, without knowing how to qualify the *content* of a communicative relationship as possession, or rather rootedness in the body.

Establishing in the social dimension the exact laws of bodily action (the laws of 'exact' bodily action): this seems to be the ambitious project of the initial Ulrich – and indeed the only theoretical condition capable of giving meaning to a Parallel Action. This would then be understood, in this sense, as a symbol not of a forbidden 'Austrian' restoration of value, but as a metaphor of an effective mundane *operation* placed under new historical conditions: those very conditions that a society in the process of massification necessarily presents.

It is certainly not – and here Musil's irony is evident – a matter of looking to the *Volk*, as Count Leinsdorf's old Austria believes, for a single and necessary Value; because the *Volksgeist* can only prove to be shattered, contradictory and – in its 'generality' – mute.[21] Within it, only its 'particularity' is shown to be meaningful. On the contrary, it would be necessary to define again – and this time starting at the sociological level of the relayed *Vergesellschaftung* – the "exact" modes of bodily affirmation of the self.[22] The fundamental problem of the 'pre-ascetic' Ulrich – an object of continual metaphorical allusion – is, in this, that of a 'powerful' individuality, one that is oriented towards bodily power (*zur Macht*, in the Nietzschean sense), yet that knows how to found *on exact bases* its own *Selbstbehauptung*. But it is precisely here that the greatest difficulties lie.[23] Precisely on this point does the awareness of the mounting force of irrationality – in nature as in history – become evident, while the great systems of rationalist philosophy are themselves tormented by what cannot in the end be reconstructed into forms.

The philosophical-moral and philosophical-political reflection that proceeds from Schopenhauer to Nietzsche and beyond Nietzsche is vigorously rooted under this issue, which witnesses the destruction of the image of an integral and self-sufficient individuality, capable in a Kantian sense of acting *alone and freely* in the world. Now, on the ashes of every rationalistic optimism, the symbol of Zarathustra mocks the poor political subjectivity belonging to the *Allzumenschliches*, and despises its impotence with regard to the impenetrable massified world, a subject-privative cosmos. The wretchedness of being on an individual scale, the impotence of its immediately bodily action, open onto the reality of an alien world which seems to go off on its own.[24]

> It seemed as though the age was beginning to devalue individual life without being able to make up the loss through new collective achievements [...] One had to find the cause of this, the secret mechanism behind it![25]

Ulrich concludes, referring to the contradictions experienced by worldly action on an individual scale. Thus, once «we started from the uselessness of sublime expectations and it seemed to us that it was an evil mystery», there is a strong temptation to bow to the enormous violence of the irrational and to call chance into play, since «everything is as possible as anything else» and «its unfolding is abandoned to itself, not subject to ordering spiritual laws».[26]

But despite this impenetrability of mundane "unfolding", this vivid perception of the lack of "ordering spiritual laws", the perspective of *The Man without Qualities* will be pushed towards the limit of its own "utterable" experience. And for a few moments the miracle of fullness will be experienced: one's relationship with the world will tend to reflect something of its central ecstatic core, of Ulrich and Agathe's achieved unity. But in reality the trans-subjective communication of the *unio mystica*, the relationship between *unio mystica* and the world, will remain constantly elusive[27], and along with them the hope of reuniting in the stability of the real world, under the laws of bodily action, which is regulated 'juridically' by *detachment* and *separation*.[28]

2. *The demise of possessive individualism. A man "without properties".*

> *Because our soul was created for whatever repeats itself over, and not for what lies outside the order of things.*
>
> (MwQ II: 118 6)

But if utopian synthesis, transparency, perfect cohesion all occur in the unrepeatable, dissension and separation certainly seem to appear where «the same things recur», or with the *typicality* of events.[29] This is the situation that the great Kakanien experiences for the first time, recognizing itself as the metaphorical space of a radically new social phenomenology as regards historical subjects and proportions. Possessive political individuality constitutes in the conflict the dominant sociological datum: the possessive self must openly accept this if it intends to perpetuate itself *as such* outside of utopia, in the pure mode of the 'private law of exclusive goods'; in fact, where the world is understood as the object of man's domination, for any individual the other is just a competitor in mastering the world, an alienation that tendentially eludes any synthesis.

But the new historical-economic phase of 'labor cooperation' – better: the general socialization of material relations, which in the early decades of the twentieth century was already looming on an institutional level – far from attenuating, heightened this perennial conflictual condition, founded on the shattering of possessive individualities, projecting it onto massed dimensions. The 'culture of contention' struck its roots more firmly into this new social substratum, which had its economic referent in the monopoly structure.

It is therefore necessary to recognize that the old culture of Count Leinsdorf, still formally at the helm of the State, remains at length disoriented in the face of this sudden and massive twentieth-century explosion of social and political difficulties:

> Of course I know everything», Count Leinsdorf said patiently. «But what I still don't understand is this: That people should love each other, and that it takes a firm hand in government to make them do it, is nothing new. So why should it suddenly be a case of either/or?[30]

Count Leinsdorf conceives it as a 'love-cohesion' *on command*, endowed with a strict sanction, which lives its happy mythical condition of being considered simultaneously, and without intimate opposition, a natural and a state value: a true 'ethical' expression of enlightened Austrian despotism. And now it was falling apart under the weight of twentieth-century political feeling, which, by placing itself from the 'extremist' point of view of subjective interest, literally blew up the old ethical-political *Ordnung*. But in particular, it coalesces around the individual figures of Count Leinsdorf, Arnheim, Walter and Clarisse, who seem to concentrate in themselves the most obvious hints of an immediately social character present in the entire *Seinesgleichen* event. These figures can all be considered under the thematic symbol of *Vergesellschaftung*, or process of massification of the old European universe.

Let us observe Count Leinsdorf, with his fan-shaped Wallenstein beard, a «non-mediated count» and «nothing but a patriot» in Catholic Austria. His motto is «Culture and capital», but his intimate suffering is linked to the process of deterioration suffered by the theological-political concept of sovereignty. By this he places himself to all effects between feudalism and capitalism, and his very dwelling is a symbol of this condition:

> it was considered [...] as the first attempt to stretch the skin of a large and comfortable country castle on the bourgeoisly reduced armature of a townhouse, and therefore one of the most important examples of the transition from feudal splendor to the bourgeois democratic style.[31]

In Leinsdorf the *Vergesellschaftung* presents itself as a problem in a particular form: it shows itself interwoven with the remaining possibilities of justification for aristocratic power.[32] In the end, Leinsdorf detests more the bourgeoisie which is gradually taking possession of the state than he does socialism, which in many ways he is in agreement with. After all, both for him and for «the true high nobility, there was really no very great difference between a middle-class factory owner and his workers».[33] His concept of Christianity as a political doctrine is filtered through his blue-blooded attitude toward nobility and is fully glorified only by the civilizing mission of the Austrian state, to which he devotes his every effort. To the extent that it is directed 'outside', towards the institutions, this concept is quite different from that forced ethic of inner equilibrium (which can be called pedantically Christian-Kantian) embodied by the compassionate Lindner.[34]

Arnheim, on the other hand, *is* the *Vergesellschaftung*. Rendi's monograph[35] documents how Musil modelled this figure on Walter Rathenau, hero of the economic and social history of the Weimar Republic. Ulrich-Musil has no sympathy for Arnheim-Rathenau: Arnheim is «only of this world»; «for him it was never a matter of spiritual renewal, of subversion of principles; his only problems were to infiltrate what already exists, *to take possession*».[36] Rathenau's books – and among them seemingly even the most disparate: *Die neue Wirtschaft* as much as *Zur Mechanik des Geistes oder vom Reich der Seele*[37] effectively sum up their era by interpreting facts exclusively through their «sense of reality», to use Musil's expression. Arnheim's conversations with Diotima offer enlightening insights into the *Vergesellschaftung*; in them the meaning of Musil's metaphors of "complexity" becomes more transparent:

> Once a business expanded to the degree reached only by the very few I speak of, there is hardly anything in life it is not somehow involved with. It is a little cosmos. You would be amazed if you knew what seemingly quite uncommercial problems – artistic, moral, political – I sometimes have to bring up in conferring with my managing director...[38]

But it is perhaps with Walter and Clarisse, absorbed in the music of Beethoven's Hymn to Joy,[39] that Musil speaks to us more forcefully – albeit obliquely, indirectly – of the *Vergesellschaftung* and of the complementary shattering of individual action. Let us try to interpret in this key Walter and Clarisse as seen by Ulrich:

«From them radiated an ever renewed feeling in the immense individual tumult». It is on this 'individual' that the accent heavily falls. The two are undoubtedly yet another 'possibility', but this possibility is locked up in a narrow space: it is still the old *Individualität* born from the liberal humanistic political universe.

Walter and Clarisse, despite themselves, carefully record the decadence of this universe, carrying it within them in the disordered wealth of an irrationalistic feeling. Ulrich – compared to them – is already beyond that: while Clarisse intends to literally embody the Nietzsche-possibility, for Ulrich the disturbing element is precisely the literalness of this interpretation. Walter and Clarisse's interpretation is to be considered, in other words, too easy an 'execution,' since it is the spontaneous reaction of those who experience the disintegration of their time *from within*, of those who struggle within the narrow confines of individual heroism (which is the only *conceded* form of participation in the death of the liberal humanistic political universe).

But since "in Kakanien there was also speed, but not too much" and therefore also the consciousness of historical development proceeded between brusque accelerations and equally brusque arrests, even Ulrich – it must be said – does not go beyond the simple intuition of the *Vergesellschaftung*. Despite this limitation, it will be right in the face of his criticism that the extreme impotence of Walter's music will stand out,[40] «impalpable ashes of sounds that, a few hundred yards away, fell to the ground without even reaching the hill».[41] And so Walter and Clarisse's piano – a real megaphone of destroyed individuality – continues to produce noise, «befuddling the house». Now, to all effects, we realize that the shattering of individual existences, living in separation, are the only thing that can be heard behind the desperate sound of the piano: in Walter's music «the soul cries in the uni-verse like a deer in heat, without any other answer than the identical emulating shouts of a thousand other souls who yearn in the great whole», all of them reaching out – without hope – towards the *Ohnmacht*.

In the face of all this looms «the firm position of Ulrich»: he defines music as «an impotence of the will and a perturbation of the heart»,[42] recognizing that by now action alone reproduces, in its 'weightlessness', the slight futility of music. The individual's condition is now definitively that of being submerged by a dense interweaving of events at the head of which there is no directorial spirituality.[43]

However, for Ulrich, the consciousness of 'being here' – in the endured *Vergesellschaftung* – is everything, and there lacks all further desire to achieve more fitting cognitive forms of the new social phenomenology.[44]

But let us return for a moment to the initial problem of the *Ekstatische Sozietät*, where possession does not exist and «every concept is intertwined in a thousand ways with the night's poignancy».[45] Here Ulrich can truly be called a man *without properties*: he knows that only love without possession, transposed out of the world as mere thinkability, could aspire to full unification, to the *unio mystica*. Instead, in the world «the dream of being two creatures and a single one» is immediately degraded into sentimental fantasies, colliding with the solid status of reality: «it was above all *the uncontestable structure of bodies* that pushed feeling back into reality»: «It is an intolerable thing that one cannot really be part of one's beloved, though it is so simple...».[46]

We must therefore ask ourselves – once it is recognized how perfect transparency lives in the space of mere thinkability, of pure reflection on the limits of bodily action: what are the presuppositions that drove Musil, as influenced by Mach, towards «a mysticism as clear as day», leading him to buffet 'from within' against the confines imposed by worldly communication? Moreover: is what nourishes this experience of music really – as it may seem – an irrationalistic inspiration or do we not face the extreme enlightenment boundary of Western self-criticism, the last vivisection of reality, made unrecognizable perhaps precisely by its willful approach to the limits of effability? In this direction – which should ideally find its way to the relationship between Musil and Wittgenstein[47] – our analysis will continue.

3. *An ecstatic society. The decay of the time of corporeity.*

> *Saul did not make good each single consequence*
> *of his previous sins, he turned into Paul!*
>
> (*MwQ II*: 945-6)

Musil unceasingly seeks a higher and more complete level of 'exactness', deepening his awareness of the limitations inherent in Mach's Neokantianism. The 'other state' (*anderer Zustand*) presents itself here as a metaphor of the exact world, as spatiality of which 'non-appetitive' man finds himself the hero. He tends to recognize in corporeity the place in which he has suffered crisis and defeat, as a political subjectivity that no longer knows how to reassemble the world and the social arrangements in a unified way, starting from himself. The complex relationship between a possessive/appetitive man and a contemplative/non appetitive man thus reflects in Musil a very vital, sensitive problem in European culture, translating itself immediately into an urgent need to reshape the concepts of *exactness* and *life*, in the constant search for a synthesis – albeit temporary – between the two alternative poles. In the hypothesis of the *Zwilling-schwester*[48] itself one feels a not insignificant trace of all this. We should add, however, that Musil, far from taking the millennial Kingdom as a pure 'rediscovered metaphysics,' will always regard it with a final grain of rationalistic distrust. The concept Ulrich has of it will be no less problematic than the original situation of cognitive dismemberment that needs to be healed.

So if, as I have said, the Millennial Kingdom – and in it the idea of an Ecstatic Society – does not achieve (fails to achieve) the stability typical of a retrieved metaphysics, it nevertheless arouses deep enchantments. Musil, as Mittner observes, is not Proust, and «the experiment fails, because no definitive state is achieved, but only individual moments of fullness».[49] But this does not prevent the reader from falling under the spell of an undeniable fascination for a 'problematic universe revolving around the other state,' for Musil's myth of a concave world that – always hidden, never elevated to a synthesis[50] – lives «in a solitude and an immobility full of continual events of pure crystal».

We are faced with a radical change in the meaning conferred on *things themselves*: the 'contemplative' subject operates a *Sinnesänderung* which is based on an awareness of the limits of knowledge and the projection of these limits on everything in the world, taken as an object of knowledge. This also seems to be the meaning of the quotation of the 'visionary' Swedenborg, made in a non-definitive chapter of the novel that bears the indicative title of «*Ulrich and the two worlds of sentiment*». In this sense Musil is at the antipodes of any Proustian "definitive state", whose emanations extend to the self as epiphanies of essence[51]: in Musil the halo of light that the 'mystical' situation projects on things, starts from the subject itself (a subject that still coincides with the enlightenment totality of the actor principle, but which simultaneously perceives the unstoppable and by now advanced process of its own disintegration), which receives no light from any pre-existing externality,[52] from any essence to be reintegrated.

Thus, already in a fundamental point of *Törless*, the young Musil described this cognitive experience in psychological terms, and its many elements foreshadow his later concept of *anderer Zustand.*

> ... not those things live, not Basini has two sides; but I had a second sight and saw all this not with the eyes of reason. As I feel an idea come to life in my mind, so I also feel that something lives in me at the sight of things, when thoughts are silent. Under all my thoughts, I have something dark in me that I cannot measure rationally, a life that cannot be ex-pressed in words and yet it is my life...[53]

It remains to be noted here that the images of the 'appetitive-possessive' man and the 'non-appetitive-contemplative' man appearing in the last chapters of *The Man without Qualities* are actually hypostatizations from the same type of Western man. That is to say: there certainly does not exist any appetitive man separated from a non-appetitive man, but only a man by turns appetitive and not appetitive, who sometimes sees these own attributes overlapping in the same activity.[54] The 'I' is a "force field" of appetitive/non-appetitive events estranged from itself.

But the very time of 'corporeity', which Musil makes an implicit reference to in theorizing the 'possessive' part of the 'I', is double within itself and hides a profound ambiguity in this dual nature. We seem to distinguish in it two things. On the one hand, there is a "time of formation," in the sense of classical *Bildung,* the reflection carried out by the Western spirit on its own activity (of which Hegel's *Phenomenology of the Spirit* and Goethe's *Wilhelm Meister* were the maximum theoretical interpretations). And on the other hand, there is a "technical," dehistoricized time, always equal to itself as a projection of the units of measurement of the global working process.[55]

In this way, on the horizon of the appetitive man, two very different meanings of the same concept are condensed, that of *bodily work with respect to a need,* of acting in a "predatory" manner to satisfy an original impulse.[56] It can be said that while Goethe's formation time corresponds to a level of reflection that still implies an individualistic relationship between man and nature, "technical" or "technical-work" time marks the complete domination of 'collective' man over nature. On it is founded the rule of an action that is placed within a system of massified and "spiritually impenetrable" needs: the "sociological" problem the early Ulrich had to face.

As for the peculiar character of Musil's contemplative 'I' – which discovers the irrational at the extreme limit of a still 'enlightened' cognitive process – this is even clearer in contrast to the irrationalist philosopher Klages. In Klages' vitalism the spirit is considered a simple destructive negation, both as *worldly bodily work*, and even as *pure reflection*. In both cases it would deny the immediate assumption of the vital flow.[57] The beginning of history is the end of the primeval 'Pelasgian man,' living in a natural universe full of symbolic images – and at the same time it is the advent of 'Herculean man,' «in his two forms: as a mere theoretical negation of the life which appears in the East in Buddhism and Taoism, or as the will of spiritual power, active practicality, which triumphs in Western civilization».[58] Thus Klages considers not only technology, but any activity of the spirit as a crime against life: this is the assumption that underlies his concept of 'indicative thought'.[59] Paradoxically, work and renunciation, bodily work and ascetic contemplation live together – at the same pole of opposition – in the face of immediate, orgiastic, blind living, alien from any 'knowing how to live,' but assumed as an exclusive value.

Thus the reasons for Musil's 'resistance' to Klages appear clear, as Gustav Donath, the Walter of *The Man without Qualities*,[60] refers to them. Musil in no way repudiates the line traced by the Western speculative experience – what Klages roughly defines as *Geist*.[61] Even though it is true that the Geist «kills life», it is not by seeking new and problematic means of expression (of «expressive knowledge») that life is epiphanized. (And here the reasons for Musil's lack of interest in the 'new' techniques of literary expression appear even clearer).[62]

Musil knows that mysticism does not own the world, but has only one 'state' for itself. And this *anderer Zustand* confers the sense of limitation to worldly questions, that scientific realm of 'question' which, not by chance, extends only to those spaces «where something can be said».[63] Therefore we should not attribute to the *anderer Zustand* functions of positive, albeit ideal, fulfillment of the novel's events.[64]

This alone can be said: that with it we are at the last stage of a quest that the young Musil had begun on Mach's path, the object of which were the conditions of possibility of a *life* (therefore of a becoming, a flow of the irrational) that was also *exact* (hence deducible, calculable, measurable by the mind). Mach had made the young Musil glimpse at the chance for an existence supported predominantly by the intellect and *yet* of great significance. Surely no irrationalist illusion in all this, but also – at the same time – no 'fear' in the contact with the irrational, the 'absolute black' of Western thought. Always and everywhere, the attempt to carry out to the end the *alt-europäisch* speculative heritage, without facile flights to the Orient. «We do not have too much intellect and too little soul, but too little intellect in the things of the soul».[65]

As further confirmation of the impossibility, in the novel, of a final dimension definitively reached, there is the «*Journey to Paradise*». The «*Journey to Paradise*» – as an impossible answer to an impossible question – can perhaps be read in terms of verifying a *Satz* of the *Tractatus*: «... even once all the possible scientific questions have been answered, our vital problems have not yet been touched. Of course then there is no longer any question; and this is precisely the answer».[66]

To the 'question,' in fact, of a positive denouement of the story – which is attempted by Anders and Agathe, despite nothing more succeeded in being said – the answer is a harsh alternative: either live outside of language, excluding yourself from the trans-subjective world, experiencing what can never be expressed, also remaining in the happiness of those who do not cherish the hope of any power or influence over the world; or else remain in the sphere of 'science' and strictly respect the confines of formulation of each question. This second horn of the alternative is *the path of Society*, in which reality is constituted by the answer to all possible questions, and the condemnation, accepted with courage, to remain ignorant of «what counts most».

So, once again, the «*Journey to Paradise*» cannot but remain detached from the novel. No recourse to the mythical-inexpressible is allowed. Anders is not Ulrich: it is only a remote chance of his that is 'historically' unfeasible. History knows only mediations and the purity of the journey to paradise, the consummated incest, the last reunification of the constituent parts of the 'I' that were dispersed or forgotten. It cannot be founded positively in the trans-subjective structure, but is destined to remain «only for a few» entirely within the *modus amoris*.[67]

4. *The problem of the good life and the nostalgia for the essence.*

> *What is the objective character of a happy, harmonious life? Here too it is clear that there cannot be such a character that can be described.*
>
> *... and the good life is the world seen* sub specie aeternitatis.
>
> (L. Wittgenstein, *Diaries 1914-1916*, July 30, 1916;
> October 7, 1916)

Musil tends to think of the Millennial Kingdom as a regulated spatiality whose rule cannot be stated, whose law cannot be expressed, whose *Ordnung* cannot be described[68], whose boundary, which prevents the 'thinkable' – the ecstatic condition of the *modus amoris*[69] – to become a source of value and meaning, with easy consolatory effects, cannot be crossed. In reality, in the meantime, there continues to be an urgency to order physical particularities that are necessarily 'buffeting' and clashing among themselves. Thus the *Stilleben* ('still life'), mentioned in one of the last chapters,[70] is very significant in this regard: it alludes to the fact that the *Ordnung* would be practically possible only if everything remained firm, in a mythical world in which human society did not yet exist. The concept of *Stilleben* introduces us to a timeless world, or better, one without an inner perception of time: «All still lifes really paint the world at the sixth day of creation, when God and the world were still by themselves, with no people!».[71] An allusion (nostalgic and ironic at the same time) to a level where the problem is not yet presented: this seems to be the paradoxical meaning hidden in the still life metaphor, a world in which the possessive self – architect of the conflict – is not yet arisen.

The symbol of a world *without social action* – much more than total human absence – is therefore the image of a still life. In it, matter, in its fixity, is absolute 'use value', an assumed given in its bodily immediacy outside of every 'social exchange,' of any conceptual abstraction addressed to practical-operational ends. To say that "man has not yet appeared" is equivalent, in the metaphor, to supposing a human figure totally immersed in natural material and undifferentiated from it, a "profile built of fruits" like an Arcimboldo's Summer[72] – voracity without mediation in the eclipse of historical time.

Instead, after the happy immobility of the sixth day of creation, social action introduces bodily possession, and bodily possession in turn provokes the establishment of a possessive-appetitive anthropological form, which

> urges to action, to motion, to enjoyment; through its effect, emotion is transformed into a work, or into an idea and conviction, [...] or it encapsulates itself in this success and transforms its vital energy into stored energy.[73]

Apart from any other consideration, it is worth restating here that the possessive-appropriative universe, resulting in the area in which the conceptual knowledge of nature, oriented to technical-practical purposes, develops par excellence, can only be tendentially all-encompassing, that is, it cannot but turn to itself – where it is affirmed – any cognitive tension, subordinating the *uti* and the bodily *frui* to the universal mediation furnished by the practice of work.[74]

So, from Musil's perspective, the fundamental problem seems to become rather another. Considering that in the possessive universe knowledge, precisely because it is instrumental, is forced to conform to the outward appearance of physical relationships – to construct language according to the exigencies of external domination – it follows that the confines of describability will inevitably be delineated so as to reproduce the necessary logical structure of the existent, in the impossibility of 'naming' that which does not fall because of its material tension in this project of domination.[75]

This is the condition encountered by Musil's speculation. Faced with the solid status of language, he avoids interpreting what it cannot express as an open way to metaphysics, almost an extreme legitimization of this as *Lebensphilosophie*.[76] It has already been noted earlier that Musil's other 'state' is a metaphorical image of the *need for a deeper knowledge* of the unlimited variety of experience, as a field of that contemplative tension which is addressed – to say it with Mittner – towards a vast «universe without God».[77] The meaning of Musil's intuition is also confirmed by the recovery and reinterpretation that are made of the topic belonging to traditional mystical literature (Plotinus, Meister Eckhart, Jakob Böhme). Likewise, mystics are read as symptoms of the deep penetrating tension directed towards the hidden side of experience, as questions not resolved on that face of things which is perennially pushed into the shadows. And here, with regard to the ecstatic society, we are not convinced by Rendi's cut and dry affirmation that in Musil

> the mystical element does not want to be what Wittgenstein speaks of, in sharp opposition with communicable experience; the 'inexpressible' by definition wants to be expressible as an essential part of human life.[78]

In the novel the perception of silence in Wittgenstein's sense causes Ulrich and Agathe, two subjectivities that have experienced the crisis of value to the full, ultimately to come to meet with the need to place themselves 'beyond ethics,' recognizing the unspeakable character of a life that is at the same time *exact* and *silent* – in other words, of an ecstatic dimension.

The story of Ulrich and Agathe proceeds wholly in this direction. It is in this sense of the presence and also the ineffability of the 'rule' – that Mittner speaks, in reference to the last part of *The Man without Qualities*, of «hope for a great mystical achievement that neither hero nor author can achieve»,[79] a glimpsed and ever fleeting achievement, like the material of dreams. It is significant in this regard that Musil leaves the idea of the barely sketched ecstatic society, consigned to a few diary notes.[80] There is no doubt it was from the 'lack,' the ultimate indefiniteness of this idea, that the subsequent spiritual development of Ulrich is negatively illuminated: his definite perception of the 'silence' of things, relegated to an ascetic place (*Ort*). The spatiality of knowing and acting (so-called 'active' spatiality) on one hand, and ecstatic spatiality on the other, would no longer be separable even logically, but the mystical dimension opened up by the latter would constitute the extreme limit to which any rational activity inevitably leads.

As Heidegger observes about Trakl,[81] *Ort* is originally a spear tip, the 'point' par excellence, the 'place' in which spatiality culminates, in whose direction any vital flow is conveyed. Thus ecstatic society – this delimited place, whose confines indicate the arrest of any 'discourse' on the perceived – is glorified by the existence of a pole, a symbolic nucleus of attraction. It is the Ulrich-Agathe nucleus that, to use out of context another image of Mittner's, can be defined as *témenos* with respect to the world, an irradiating nucleus but at the same time aware of the limits of its flow, detectable in that barrier of communication, opacity of intersubjective relations, which divided from other men.

But what can we say, at this point, about the problem we first moved from: that of Ulrich and his bodily world, or – even more – that of Robert Musil and the inability to fix, in his own age, the laws of an exact acting? It would be wrong if – observing the ascetic distance in which the novel's events tend to fade – the mystical solution were considered in a literal and univocal sense, almost as if any possibility were denied of seizing from it significant allusions concerning the historical world, the roots of the *Seinesgleichen*. On the other hand, we have seen Ulrich's path full of metaphorical indications, clearly detectable for an interpretation that does not neglect the philosophical-political side of the novel.

It has been said that Ulrich transfers the tormented story of the modern crisis of subjectivity into an ascetic utopia. We can now certify that it is not a question of utopia but of being aware of the indescribability of the extreme limit of knowledge, where the ecstatic society stands as a 'place' in which this extreme limit is revealed. But the non-transparency, the negation of the uncontested character of worldly possession, is a painful reality. If the world becomes an enigma, and the relationship between the individual and society is a reflection of impenetrable nodes in the eyes of the individual, then the isolated individual will discover himself prone to flights, exposed to «nostalgia for the essence», to the tragic quest for the unity of the world[82] – aware, despite everything, of always having to stop a few steps short of the utopian reappraisal of value.

V. *Moosbrugger and the Law*

In Moosbrugger, the "mad killer" of *The Man without Qualities*, Musil depicts with extreme simplicity the gap – always tending to become polar opposition – between *life*, seen as a set of subjective situations in continuous evolution, and the modes of life's intelligibility and organization, as they arise in the various segments of Western knowledge (natural science, morality, law, etc.). I will try here to highlight some meanings present in the Moosbrugger allegory that are perhaps not quite immediately evident.

1. *Ulrich, science and Moosbrugger.*

How is it still possible to maintain a *continuum* between life and the knowledge of life today, when the orders of human existence have been segmented and subdivided into separate microcosms that only specialized forms of knowledge – and certainly not an all-embracing metaphysical principle – are able to faithfully reproduce the fragments, but without adding anything about 'how' to accurately address behavior? The price of the accuracy of scientific knowledge is its fragmentary nature, that is, its renunciation of the restitution of a meta-principle capable of orienting and giving meaning to local forms of knowledge.

The sentimentality and approximation inevitably contained in *moral theory*, which had been the great response of Western classical metaphysics – from Plato through Christianity up to Kant and beyond – are looked upon with impatience by those, like Musil, who have passed through Mach's skepticism and, not being satisfied with it, have come to recognize in the «Godless mysticism»[1] of the Millennial Kingdom the place in which to pose the problem of the soul and the 'good life.' This problem – a true, constant presence, although sometimes obscured, in the history of the spirit – deserves to be considered an ontological problem, even if, for anyone who cares to deal with it, it is no longer a traditionally understood "science of morality".

The issue of truth and the 'good life' is too serious to be satis-fied with the inevitable approximation of a *Massenmoral*. As for Ulrich,

> he despised those who could not follow Nietzsche's dictum to "let the soul starve for the truth's sake", those who turn back, the fainthearted, the softheaded who comfort their souls with spiritual nonsense and feed it – because reason allegedly gives it stones instead of bread – on religious, metaphysical, and fictitious pap, like rolls soaked in milk. It was his opinion that in this century, together with everything human, one was on an expedition, which required as a matter of pride that one cut off all useless questions with a 'not yet', and that life be conducted on a provisional basis [...]. The fact is, science has developed a concept of hard, sober intelligence that makes the old metaphysical and moral ideas of the human race simply intolerable, even though all it has to put in their place is the hope that a distant day will come when a race of intellectual conquerors will descend into the valleys of spiritual fruitfulness.[2]

So the nonsense of morality, imbued with religious and philosophical sentimentalism, is no longer (if it ever was) the appropriate language in which to pose the problem of 'exact' behavior, namely of the just life. Where life becomes more complex and impenetrable, science comes up against its limits and its power ceases. Moosbrugger, placed at the boundaries of rules and norms, is emblematic of this situation. Moosbrugger is the essence that refuses to be systematized, the external limit of every formalism (including legal formalism, as we shall see). For this reason, more than for any possible romantic sort of *Monsieur-le-vivisecteur* type motive, Ulrich notes that «for some unknown reason Moosbrugger concerned him more deeply than the life he himself was leading. Moosbrugger seized him like an obscure poem which everything is slightly distorted and displaced, and reveals a drifting meaning fragmented in the depths of the mind».[3]

Ulrich still considers this closeness to Moosbrugger as dictated by an "unknown reason" and in some moments he rebels with an enlightenment spirit against this "ambiguous" inclination:

Thrill-seeking! […] To be fascinated with the gruesome or the taboo, in the admissible form of dreams and neuroses, see-med quite in character for the people of the bourgeois age. «Either/or!» he thought. «Either I like you or I don't. Either I defend you, freakishness and all, or I ought to punch myself in the jaw for playing around with this monstrosity!»[4]

But this reduction of the problem to terms of the alternative is destined not to hold up for long, since the formalism of reason is unable to restore any matter to itself without residue. Moreover, at another point Ulrich says: «If mankind could dream as a whole, that dream would be Moosbrugger».[5] Moosbrugger is in fact oneiric force, imagination, passion, free association of ideas in their larval state. And all this of course against the concept (the heavy *Begrifflichkeit*) of conscious, 'waking' intersubjective communication. So no easy romantic interpretation, just this question: who is Moosbrugger and what language does he use?

2. *Moosbrugger's language.*

Moosbrugger has started out in life as a poor devil, an orphan shepherd boy in a hamlet so small that it did not even dared speak to a girl. Girls were something he could always only look at, even later on when he became an apprentice and then when he was a traveling journeyman. One only need imagine what it must mean when something one craves as naturally as bread or water can only be looked at. After a while one desires it unnaturally. It walks past, skirts swaying around its calves. It climbs over a stile and it is visible up to the knees. One looks into its eyes, and they turn opaque. One hears it laugh and turns around quickly, only the look into a face as immovably round as a hole in the ground into which a mouse has just slipped.[6]

Moosbrugger experiences the strong sensations of his inner world as something inimical that imprisons him and makes him grotesque in the eyes of all as soon as he tries to speak, to externalize himself, so as to justify himself. Because Moosbrugger must always justify himself, 'plead his case' and cloak his behavior with rectitude (an attitude he is the first to see as false), his position is always one of weakness, and not only towards psychiatrists and investigative jurists, but also in his own head, where he painfully sees every 'logical' mechanism overwhelmed by the power of associations. For Moosbrugger this causes extreme suffering, because he knows that every association he conducts (as he is led to do) beyond the limits of what is 'allowed' is destined to be punished, sooner or later, with total confusion and the darkening of his conscience.

> But oh, how curious the psychiatrists got when they showed him a picture of a squirrel and he said: 'That's a fox, I guess, or it could be a hare, or maybe a cat or something. [...] Moosbrugger's experience and conviction were that no thing could be singled out by itself, because things hang together. [...] Life forms a surface that acts as if it could not be otherwise, but under its skin things are pounding and pulsing. Moosbrugger always kept his legs solidly planted on real earth, holding them together, sensibly trying to avoid whatever might confuse him. But sometimes a word burst in his mouth, and what a revolution, what a dream of things then welled up out of such a cold, burned-out double word as tree kitten or rose lips! [...] The reasons, the considerations he could remember, he had already stated in court anyway. But what had really happened seemed to him as if he had suddenly said fluently in a foreign language something that made him feel good but that he could no longer repeat.[7]

Moosbrugger's language is one of solitude, seen as the only 'true' condition: anarchists, his virtual brothers, he defines as «the false ones»[8] because they gather in leagues and are gregarious. Justice for Moosbrugger: «Even as an apprentice he had once broken the fingers of one master who tried to beat him. He ran away from another with the master's money – in simple justice, as he said».[9] And further on: «Injustice must be the basis of my brutality, I have stood before the court, a simple man, and thought Your Honors must know everything anyway. But you have let me down!».[10]

Moosbrugger's world recalls indirectly – by opposition – the world of law, towards which he is, in terms of phenomenological structure, in continuous, open conflict. But how can we define in its essence the world of law and, *contrarily*, the world of unconscious life, Moosbrugger's world?

3. *Phenomenology of law and the world of life.*

Law is an objective, collectively shared social technique, a place of conscious, rationalized relation tending to ensure a character of 'predictability,' the elimination of ambiguity. A phenomenological analysis confirms this representation: according to some,[11] we can define a series of statements that help to establish a priori, on an ontological level, the law and, in general, the broadest field of legal formalism. Let us list some data, based on Gardies' "axioms":

a) law needs to presuppose a *plurality of personal subjects*, that is a world whose subjects are *persons*;

b) communication between persons is endowed with a *meaning*, a *single direction*: the complexity of life's relationships, in order to be interpreted (filtered) juridically, must be 'reduced,' purified of so-called 'multivalences' – certainly theoretically impoverished, and in any case traced back to sectorial sense elements, each of which is – *per fictionem* – individually analyzable;

c) personal subjects are conscious of being themselves, as subjects, *objects for others*;

d) personal subjects are aware of existing in an *intersubjective time*;

e) personal subjects are endowed with an *imperfect memory*: once time has been postulated, one cannot think of a right without at the same time postulating a minimum of this ability to 'evoke the past' by recognizing it as past in relation to the present in which is evoked. In short, both *mentes perfectae* and *mentes momentaneae* are excluded: the former would make the law useless (a prime example of which is testimony), the latter impossible;

f) in intersubjective experience, side by side with subjects, we have *objects*, or rather independent realities with respect to the point of view that each subject has on them, and enduring over time. These objects are liable to *attribution*, and subjects in turn are capable of *possession*.

The set of these utterances (or "axioms") listed so far seems to me fairly well reflected in the character of Ulrich's father, who embodies the psychological framework of the "old jurist," personifying it. One recalls the passage in which he appears:

> He himself had started out as a tutor in the houses of the
> high aristocracy while still working for his degree, and he
> had continued tutoring even as a young law clerk – not
> really from necessity, for his father was quite well off. But
> those *carefully* nurtured connections paid off later on when
> he became a university lecturer and law professor, and they
> led to his gradually rising to become the legal adviser to
> almost all the feudal nobility in the country. [...] Even after
> retiring from this practice, the old scholar who had achie-
> ved distinction made a *careful* catalog of of every event con-
> cerning his circle of former patrons, extended *with great
> precision* from fathers to sons to grandsons. [...] He received
> just as promptly in return brief letters of acknowledgments,
> which thanked the dear friend and esteemed scholar.[12]

The picture described is without doubt deliberately grotesque, but
the psychological elements that appear in it go beyond the description
of a calcified individual psychology, to delineate certain constant features: diligence, accuracy, exactness, punctuality, predictability are the
subjective side of law seen as a technique of communication and objective organization.

The axioms stated at the outset constitute – to better say it – the
a priori conditions of thinkability of the law-phenomenon: let us
compare them with what emerges from the 'pure' model of unconscious life as reflected in Moosbrugger:

a') in Moosbrugger the plurality of humans is not one of personal
subjects: every human is the result of a bundle of sensations detached
from each other, of which it is, actively, the artificer and, passively, the
projection. The murdered woman is the prototype of the non-person:
every humanistic personalism is dissolved by the powerful microscope of the unconscious in steps like this:

> As he wandered on through the villages, or even on the
> deserted roads, Moosbrugger would encounter whole pro-
> cessions of women. [...] These females had inspired only
> feelings of aversion in him. [...] There is in this attitude to-
> ward the living, moving, silently rolling or flitting fellow
> creature enjoying its own existence something that suggests
> a deep innate aversion to it. And then what could one do

when she started screaming? One could only come to one's senses, or else, if one simply couldn't do that, press her face to the ground and stuff earth into her mouth.[13]

b') in Moosbrugger there is no single univocity in the direction of meaning: in him what is complex avoids the 'reduction' into simple or sectorial elements. Moosbrugger 'identifies himself' with things, while things 'come alive' in him:

> The table was Moosbrugger. The chair was Moosbrugger. The barred window and the bolted door were himself. There was nothing at all crazy or out of ordinary in what he meant. It was just that the rubber bands were gone. Behind every thing or creature, when it tries to get really close to another, is a rubber band, pulling. Otherwise, things might finally go right through one another. Every movement is reined in by a rubber band that won't let a person do quite what he wants. Now, suddenly, all those rubber bands were gone. [...] Maybe one just can't cut it so fine?[14]

c') in Moosbrugger there is a harshness, a lack of flexibility, which means that he cannot voluntarily dominate his own 'making himself an object' for others. Moosbrugger is always, literally, an object for others, in a perennial state of exception. It follows that, because of his reification, he cannot set his own actions for intersubjective projects.

d') not even time can have an intersubjective meaning in Moosbrugger. Moosbrugger's time is generated by his solipsism and in turn generates in him a profound sense of guilt: Moosbrugger feels guilty precisely because he does not live in an intersubjective time. That is: his exclusion from intersubjective time is a symbol of his 'fall' into the original guilt desired not by himself (Moosbrugger does not hold himself responsible), but by an incumbent 'destiny' of which he is the victim.

e') Moosbrugger is *mens momentanea, individuum ineffabile*. His separation from the world provokes the negation of any possible link of temporal causality. Instead, public conscience – in which communication between people endowed with 'imperfect memory' is situated – is for Moosbrugger merely «a wide area of overlapping general notions, like the gray shimmer in a telescope focused at too great a distance».[15]

f) Moosbrugger does not 'possess' anything, nor is he able to grasp anything. Strictly speaking, he is the true *Mann ohne Eigenschaften*, a man without properties paralyzed by his own plural world, which precludes him from being in contact with (= appropriation of) real objects.

So how can we conclude from this a discourse on the representation of law and justice in the paradoxical Moosbrugger's character?

4. *Justice, responsibility, disruption of order.*

I think it is impossible to conclude without bearing in mind that at least three other concepts deserve to be recalled, because they can add some additional elements to the comparison between the two antagonistic worlds of *technique* (legal technique, law as an objectifying function) and *life* (that is, what we called 'Moosbrugger's world'). These are the concepts of 'justice,' 'responsibility,' 'order' and its (necessary) upheaval.

The discussion, even summary, of the issues that. these concepts raise would obviously require a far more extensive and articulated development than what is permitted here. I will therefore confine myself to laying out the essential core of them, above all by recalling the steps of *The Man without Qualities* that concern them, and letting the reader complete the thought that Musil alludes to in his metaphors.

a) On *justice* :

«My right» – he thought, drawing the word out as long as he could, to realize this concept, and thought, as if he were speaking to someone –: «it's when you haven't done anything wrong, or something, like that, isn't it?» Suddenly he had it: «Right is justice». That was it. His right was his justice! He looked at his wood-plank bed in order to sit on it, turned awkwardly around to tug at it – in vain, as it was screwed to the floor – then slowly sat down. He had been cheated of his justice! [...] That was how they made a mockery and a shambles of his right, and he took to the road again. Can a man find his rights on the road? All the women were already somebody else's right, and so were all the apples and all the beds. And the police and the judges were worse than the dogs.[16]

b) On *responsibility*:

> Legally, Moosbrugger's case could be summed up in a sentence. He was one of those borderline cases in law and forensic medicine known even to the layman as a case of diminished responsibility. These unfortunates typically suffer not only substandard health but also have a substandard disease. Nature has a peculiar preference for producing such people in droves. *Natura non facit saltus*, she makes no jumps but prefers gradual transitions; even on the grand scale she keeps the world in a transitional state between imbecility and sanity. But the law takes no notice of this. It says: *Non datur tertium sive medium inter duo contradictoria*, or in plain language, a person is either capable or not capable of breaking the law; between two contraries there is no third or middle state. It is this ability to choose that makes a person liable to punishment. His liability to punishment makes him legally a person, and as a person in the legal sense he shares in the suprapersonal benefaction of the law.[17]

And again:

> Of course, there was not a single person in that vast crowded courtroom, the doctors included, who was not convinced that Moosbrugger was insane, one way or another; but it was not a way that corresponded to the conditions of insanity laid down by the law, so this insanity could not be acknowledged by conscientious minds. For if one is in part insane, one is also, juridically, partly sane, and if one is partly sane one is at least partly responsible for one's actions, and if one is partly responsible one is wholly responsible; for responsibility is, as they say, that state in which the individual has the power to devote himself to a specific purpose of his own free will, independently of any compelling necessity, and one cannot simultaneously possess and lack such self-determination.[18]

Faced with all this, Moosbrugger could not but resign himself:

> Ulrich well understood the deep resignation with which Moosbrugger at such moments lamented his lack of an education, which left him helpless to undo the knots in this net

woven of incomprehension. The judge translated this into an emphatic reproof: 'You always find a way to shift the blame to others!' – This judge added it all up, starting with the police record and the vagrancy, and presented it as Moosbrugger's guilt, while to Moosbrugger it was a series of completely separate incidents having nothing to do with one another, each of which had a different cause that lay outside Moosbrugger somewhere in the world as a whole. In the judge's eyes, Moosbrugger was the source of his acts; in Moosbrugger's eyes they had perched on him like birds that had flown in from somewhere or other. To the judge, Moosbrugger was a special case; for himself he was an universe, and it was very hard to say something convincing about an universe. Two strategies were here locked in combat, two integral positions, two sets of logical consistency. But Moosbrugger had the less favorable position; even a much cleverer man could not have expressed the strange, shadowy reasonings of his mind. They rose directly out of the confused isolation of his life, and while all other lives exist in hundreds of ways – perceived the same way by those who lead them and by all others, who confirm them – his own true life existed only for him. It was a vapor, always losing and changing shape. He might, of course, have asked his judges whether their lives were essentially different. But he thought no such thing. Standing before the court, everything that had happened so naturally in sequence was now senselessly jumbled up inside him, and he made the greatest efforts to make such sense of it as would be no less worthy than the arguments of his distinguished opponents.[19]

c) On *order* and its 'necessary' upheaval:

Clarisse was gnawing at the root of love. It is a forked root, with kisses and bites, glances clinging and a tormented last-minute aversion of the gaze. "Does getting alone well together lead to hate?" she wondered. "Does a decent life crave brutality? Does peacefulness need cruelty? Does orderliness long to be torn apart?" Such were, and were not, the thoughts provoked by Moosbrugger.[20]

Perhaps, if thought deeply, the metaphysical concept of order must always be placed before the possibility of its transgression, its actual upheaval. Order does not show, in other words, the true image of itself in its norm, its rule (the visible element by which it is constituted), but in its exception, in the extreme case that threatens to make it collapse. (Walter Benjamin wrote unforgettable pages on this point).

Will it not be so: that the harmonious face of order, its *mathematica facies*, can express itself with greater completeness in those who are objectively called on to endanger it – by transgressing it with suffering, as Moosbrugger does – precisely to make it clear to the multitude of men, to point out, with a long series of visible subversions, its ultimately indescribable character? That of Moosbrugger – a sacrificed individuality that accepts seeing his own sacrifice thus used – would then be fully Ulrich's "other name". Is it really just paradoxical to interpret in this sense the thoughts of Clarisse (but also those of Ulrich) on the Moosbrugger-metaphor?

VI. *Divine Violence and Disruption of the Theological Form. On the young Walter Benjamin*

1. *The 'liberal' concept of language.*

"... Die eigentliche Sphäre der Verständigung,
die Sprache."

(W. Benjamin, *Zur Kritik der Gewalt*)

In all likelihood, an impression may ultimately arise from the re-reading of the writings of Walter Benjamin's philosophy of history[1]: it concerns the uncertain centrality of the mythical element in historical immanence, and – even more – the particular theological-political use that is made of myth in history.

All this is not without relevance for the philosophy of law and political theory. It is possible to note apropos of this how the ultimately rationalistic[2] interest, which manifested itself in German culture immediately after World War I in the 'mythical' aspects of the theory of power (*Macht*), often led to a perspective that emphasized the traits of *Gewalt*, resulting in an approach to the problem of power that, in terms of political doctrine, did not hesitate to label itself as 'anti-liberal'. Underlying this approach, held in common during the Weimar years by disparate theoretical positions (it suffices to recall, on the one hand, the utopian current that Ernst Bloch and Walter Benjamin belonged to, and, on the other, Carl Schmitt's realist theory of the 'political'), I think we can acknowledge the awareness and criticism of an old liberal deformation, according to which language is able *to talk about everything*. Language would neutralize *in toto* the space of violence, transgression and the possibility of an 'absolutely other/absolutely hostile', by functionally using their practical categories: exchange, discussion, informative and non violent conversation. The essence of the unspeakable because not recomposable would already be canceled as possibility: everything could be 'spoken of' and, in so being spoken, everything could be mediated.

The matter of controversy of the young Benjamin presents, at least in this respect, a number of analogies with what is typical of Carl Schmitt: Benjamin's will to liberation is the *Dezisionismus* corresponding and opposed to the will to rationalize the ambiguous concept of *Gewalt* (and *Herrschaft*) which is Schmitt's. It must therefore be emphasized that the difference in the subjective intentions expressed by these cultural threads of common ancestry in Weimar Germany, already defined very roughly as 'anti-liberal', is accompanied by an objective convergence in identifying the problem, through a lively inquiry – that the *rationalistic* sense pervades the internal structure of their philosophical-political argumentation – as to the ultimate meaning of the 'irrational' phenomenon of myth.[3] For our purposes we will have to hold firm from the very start to the belief that the young Benjamin's thought should in no way be separated from the spiritual and ideological context that distinguished the Weimar environment of the 1920's – an environment that recognized within itself, as its never altogether conceptually resolved core problem, the persistence in the structure of the 'political' of the last repercussion of a *theologia politica perennis*.

2. *Critique of Violence*.

His *Critique of Violence* – an essay that already in its title echoes the themes of Georges Sorel[4] – is perhaps among Benjamin's early works the one that, both for its subject and its particular style of discussion,[5] realizes in a more immediate way the German political atmosphere attracted by the myth of a 'redemptive revolution'. The political events of this period are, in other words, all implicit in the discourse that is developed in Benjamin's essay. This is so even if the author maintains his analysis at a high level of abstraction, aiming more at an in-depth speculation on the philosophical connections among the concepts examined than at a historical description of the novelty of the new political-constitutional facts on which his critical discourse is based.[6] So it is significant that the essay opens on a still wholly de-historicized concept of violence – understood as a *means* toward just or unjust ends and in its relationship with the spheres of law and justice.[7]

Benjamin introduces, in other words, only in a marginal way the historiographically more meaningful elements, in the light of which his discourse could be quite differently reinterpreted (e.g., the right to strike, the evolution/involution of representative power, the State, etc.). These appear, when they arise in the discussion, almost dematerialized, and in any case employed to confirm theses already established metaphysically. In short, his approach from the very start makes it clear how his focus on the soteriological end in the young Benjamin is destined to intertwine with his interest in the concrete-historical aspect of the political concepts taken into examination, frequently prevailing over them. But leaving aside, for now, any further critical point of more general import, it is essential to follow the main features of the discourse undertaken by this 'minor' Benjamin.

Benjamin's problem initially regards the theoretical foundation of his critique, which he establishes by first conceptually situating violence in a means/end relationship, defined as «the most basic and elementary relationship of any legal system».[8] His quest for the decisive criterion for the critique of violence starts from the observation that it belongs only to the realm of means, and not to that of ends. And here natural law, which questions whether violence is a means toward just or unjust ends, already betrays Benjamin's critical insufficiency, since it does not pose any problem in the use – in fact deemed 'physiologically' natural [«*Nach seiner Anschauung,* [...] *Gewalt ein Naturprodukt, gleichsam ein Rohstoff»*] – of violent means, provided that they are directed toward just ends (think, beyond Benjamin's example of the Terror in the French Revolution, of the theories of the monarchomachs regarding tyrannicide in the historic period of early modernity), and forcibly avoids any critique of violence in terms of the concept itself, in its 'essential' sense – a critique that is exerted *solely at the level of means,* neglecting as 'inessential' the question of the rightness of the ends to which these means refer.

But, like natural law, not even (so much the less) positive law succeeds in establishing a strong critical perspective, characterized as it is by its focus on 'historically developed' power [*historische Gewordenheit*] , or on its historical source of legitimation (the State), taken as the exclusive criterion for assessing violence.

> Just as natural law can judge any existing law only in the critique of its ends, so positive law can judge the development of any law only in the critique of its means.[9]

In any case for Benjamin

> both schools meet in the common basic dogma: just ends can be attained by justified means, justified means used for just ends. Natural law attempts, by the justness of ends, to 'justify' [*rechtfertigen*] the means, positive law to 'guarantee' [*garantieren* the justness of the ends through the justification of the means.[10]

Given the terms so far observed, a simultaneous separation/integration between *rechtfertigen-Gerechtigkeit* (to justify-Justice) and *garantieren-Rechtmäßigkeit* (to guarantee-Legality), for Benjamin there can be no way out of the deadlock in which his quest for a fundamental criterion for the critique of violence inevitably ends up falling, unless one abandons the field of the philosophy of law as such – whether positive or natural, it does not matter – and penetrates the still poorly defined borders of a philosophy of history.[11]

Benjamin's discourse on violence deepens only when he focuses on the problem of the relationship between the State's power to legitimate force (so consider Max Weber) on the one hand, and juridically considered subjectivity, on the other. His analysis of the limits placed 'legally' on individual violence (violence «that present-day law is seeking in all areas of activity to deny the individual»[12] leads Benjamin to observe how force, when it is not in possession of law as it exists at any given moment, represents a threat not because of the ends which it pursues, but because of its mere existence outside the law [*durch ihr bloßes Dasein außerhalb des Rechts*].

Where the salient data are: (*a*) the statement in itself delegitimizing inherent in potentially violent individual interest; (*b*) the consequent need for the legal system to know how to apportion – by fittingly alternating limitations and expansions, repression and recognition – the range of individual rights, these being understood as like portions of transpositions into the reassuring sphere of the 'legality' of so-called *natural ends* [*Naturzwecke*] , of interests and needs – otherwise identifiable only negatively as conflicting entities – of the individual. Legalization contains within itself a radical neutralization of the violent exteriority inherent in the 'natural order', that resists such legalization:

> it can be formulated as a general maxim of present-day European legislation that all the natural ends of individuals must

collide with legal ends if pursued with a greater or lesser degree of violence.[13]

Therefore, the significant reverse of the legal recognition of 'natural ends' lies in the regulation of violence, that is, of the way, which is typical of the law and the State, to consider «violence in the hands of a single person as a risk or a threat to subvert the legal system».[14] It must therefore be acknowledged that there is still a great deal of Sorel behind his notations on strike violence – rather, on the strike as a form of violent action – that runs through Ben-jamin's early essay. Here indeed distinctions are still made, in the footsteps of the anarchism of the *Réflexions*, between 'general poli-tical' strike forms and 'general proletarian' strike forms, which Ben-jamin defines as «antithetical also in relation to violence» («*so ist die zweite als ein reines Mittel gewaltlos*»].[15]

Of course, the concept of 'pure means' is, in this context, very problematic. It seems in any case to disregard – in order to distance itself from any ruinously bloody reality – any possible 'catastrophic consequences' that may factually occur during their manifestation, since «the violence of an action can be judged as little by its effects [*Wirkungen*] as by its purpose [*Zwecke*], but only by the law of its means» (*ibid.*). And in terms of means, the only action that is violent in its essence is that of a power which, by betraying justice, «is either law-making or law-preserving [*rechtsetzend oder rechtserhaltend*],[16] which means that it helps to restore and reinforce an intimately coercive legal situation.

The anarchic-naïve component of the young Benjamin's thought is enhanced in his critique of the law of the police,[17] from which context, despite its pervasive emotional tension, there emerges a remarkable ability of speculative insight into what the debate within the *Staatslehre* of the 1920's had shown to be the aporias that liberal democratic thought inevitably develops in coming to grips with the problem of the 'law enforcement' [*Rechtsverwirklichung*].[18]

The police, Benjamin observes,

> is violence for legal ends (it includes the right of disposition), but with the simultaneous authority to decide these ends within wide limits (it includes the right to decree) [...]
> In this authority the separation of law-making and law-pre-

serving violence is suspended, so that it cannot finally be denied that in absolute monarchy, in which legislative and executive power are united, violence is less devastating than in democracies, where its existence bears witness to the greatest conceivable degeneration of violence.[19]

In any case, the young Benjamin's critique – even in its utopianism – never loses itself in the moralistic disapproval of coercive reality which characterizes social relations, but seeks to formulate more clearly its own philosophical concept of 'pure means', to the point of wondering openly: «In general, is the non violent regulation of conflict possible?».[20] Benjamin at once answers this question in a positive way:

> The relationships among private persons are full of examples of this. Nonviolent agreement is possible wherever a civilized outlook [*die Kultur des Herzens*] allows the use of unalloyed means of agreement [*reine Mittel der Übereinkunft*]. Legal and illegal means of every kind that are all the same violent may be confronted with pure, nonviolent ones as unalloyed means. Courtesy, sympathy, peaceableness, trust and whatever else might be mentioned are their subjective preconditions [...]. Its profoundest example is perhaps the conference [*Unterredung*], considered as a technique of civil agreement [...]. This makes clear that there is a sphere of human agreement that is nonviolent to the extent that it is wholly inaccessible to violence: the true sphere of 'understanding', language.[21]

But certainly – Benjamin acknowledges – if at one time, in a more primitive stage of the expansion of social communication and, complementarily, at an archaic level of development of law, this area of language could be thought of as a space of 'pure means' – freed of violence and almost cut off from the vast reality of conflict – subsequently the legal sanction has also penetrated into this sphere, dissolving it from the within. Proof of this – Benjamin goes on to say – can be found in the transition from the impunity of lies (or from the legal irrelevance, typical of archaic systems, of the act by which language disregards its social function of the communication of 'truth') to the punishability of deceit (or to its subsumption into the area of legal sanction of the effects of the 'false' use of a non violent means).

Moreover, legal communication, considered as a technique and as social mediation, cannot but presuppose a mechanism of protection of common recognition of its rules (and, at its root, a mechanism of political legitimation of its rules' production). For Benjamin, this mechanism can only consist at bottom in absolute *Gewalt*.[22]

3. *Law as myth.*

Now, in spite of all this – going back to the initial questions – I believe that Benjamin's Sorelian component ought not to be over-estimated. If in his *Critique of Violence*, despite its vigorous polemic against *politiciens*, a Sorelian interpretation seems highly restrictive, this interpretation seems even groundless with regard to Benjamin's immediately subsequent work. One theoretical root lies in the very different theoretical considerations against the "constructive ambiguity" of law at the conclusion of his essay on Karl Kraus.[23] In this essay Kraus, the combative publicist who from the columns of *Die Fackel* never tired of striking out with his white-hot articles against the literary fashions of early 20th-century Vienna, stands outside of time (and this in a particular metaphorical sense, namely: anachronistically) as a destructive, purifying force, giving Benjamin the opportunity to subject to merciless criticism the ideology of the flatly and positivistically creative 'average European':

> For too long the accent was placed on creativity. People are only creative to the extent that they avoid tasks and super-vision. Work as a supervised task – its model being political and technical work – is attended by dirt and detritus, intrudes destructively into matter, is abrasive to what is already achieved and critical toward its conditions, and is in all this opposite to the work of the dilettante luxuriating in creation. His work is innocent and pure, consuming and purifying master-liness. And therefore the monster stands among us as the messenger of a more real humanism. He is the conqueror of the empty phrase. He feels solidarity not with the slender pine but with the plane that devours it, not with the precious ore but with the blast furnace that purifies it. The average European has not succeeded in uniting his life with technology, because he has clung to the fetish of creative existence.[24]

Quite something else is the theoretical background which Benjamin refers to in this Kraus-like message of his, of purifying destruction: he now forms a web of allusions that refers beyond his Sorel-like vagueness of the *Critique of Violence*:

> One must have followed Loos in his struggle with the dragon 'ornament', heard the stellar Esperanto of Scheerbart's creation, or seen Klee's *New Angel* (who preferred to free men by taking from them, rather than make them happy by giving to them) to understand a humanity that proves itself by destruction.[25]

Yet, precisely here a thematic element continues to unite the two essays – *Critique of Violence* and *Karl Kraus* – by establishing between them a logical relationship that somehow bridges the decade between them. It is the element of "destroying to purify", the possibility of recognizing in Kraus's tragically helpless voice the imitation of that of the *Angelus Novus*, as far from any historicist myth of continuity and progress as it is close to the liberating use of violence, to the justice of the Old Testament God. Divine violence posits itself more than ever, in the Benjamin of the 1920's (and therefore already two decades before *On the Concept of History*) as the last *appearance* of the will of the terrible Old Testament God[26] – as appearing in history, through the conflicts of the 'political', but resolutely outside of the 'juridical' and its forms, of the signs of a *toto coelo* external will.

External: because the divine will destroys any law – any 'internal' coercive one – in carrying out his own justice. Therein lies his rule *als waltende Gewalt*: in the fact that he acts in a state of permanent extralegal *exception*; while the law is in essence *rule*, issuing from a mythical incumbent principle, the consequence of a separate and infinitely powerful inimical fate. The carrying out of divine justice – symbolized by God's judgment over the tribe of Korah[27] – occurs outside of the law and rule, and not as an extreme case of the rule. More than a carrying out, it is a manifestation: his appearance, far from constructing any sort of system, nullifies any system established by mythical violence.[28] Let us consider in this regard the concluding part of the essay:

> Once again all the eternal forms are open to pure divine violence, which myth bastardized with law. It may manifest

itself in a true war exactly as in the divine judgment of the multitude on a criminal. But all mythical, lawmaking violence, which we may call executive, is pernicious. Pernicious, too, is the law-preserving, administrative violence that serves it. Divine violence, which is the sign and seal but never the means of sacred execution, may be called sovereign violence [*waltende*].[29]

The sources of legitimation ('Law' *vs* 'Divine judgment'; 'mythical violence' *vs* 'divine violence') oppose each other at this point. In whoever recognizes the supreme authority of divine violence – violence «that governs» – there is implied the desire to delegitimize any enactment of the legal system, any reality that envisions law as myth. Divine violence – the external manifestation of the terrible presence of God – thus leads necessarily to the concept of *revolution against law*. No interaction is allowed between the two nuclei: concepts not clearly referring to either of these two groups of legitimacy would be nothing but contradictory. Where the young Benjamin emphasizes the fight against law as the supreme realization of divine justice, tradition rejoins revolutionary Utopia, thus dovetailing directly into the vein of the nihilistic culture of the early 20th-century, to whose deep ideal charisma the young Benjamin is attuned.

4. *Fate, guilt, law. The* Theological-Political Fragment *and the symbol of Kafka.*

But the nature of Benjamin's nihilism would still be insufficiently identified if another fundamental concept of the *Critique of Violence* remained unprobed: the concept of fate. 'Fate' [*Schicksal*], which is always «at the basis of legal power»,[30] has its roots in a mythical time, in a time in which the Hebrew universe reveals its true signs: the separateness [*Trennung*], the never reconciled estrangement of God and the very image of God as a place of absolutely objective relationships that bear down mightily on man.

Bare natural life thus reveals itself as a «mute prop of guilt».[31] The myth of Niobe is witness of this in the classical mythological universe, and this is so even if the living – conceptually distinct from bare life – is innocent. Guilt falls objectively on mankind, on the living innocent, and – if blood is the symbol of bare life – liberation from this guilt has to pass through blood purification (*ibid.*), capable of demanding recourse to the violence of man against man, and even killing, which is still sometimes legitimate, since the fifth commandment «is not a criterion of judgment [*Maßstab des Urteils*], but a standard of action [*Richtschnur des Handelns*]» for the acting person or community, which must deal with it alone, and take, in extraordinary cases, the responsibility of disregarding it.

The feeling of guilt and of fate seems here to lead back to Kafka's *The Trial*, interpreted this time «without Kafkaisms» (Ladislao Mittner) and bearing in mind a famous quote by Hermann Cohen that Benjamin uses in his essay on Kafka,[32] according to which «a knowledge which is inescapable» is that which indicates how the very structure of fate must «originate and produce» their own violation, their own deviation: which is just what, in other words, takes place «for the justice that proceeds against K.».[33] It is the mythic structure of the law that makes the sentence precede the crime, independently of the materialization of human guilt, but only after the terrible, paradoxical intervention – because seemingly free – of the law. The (necessarily inadvertent) violation of the unwritten law does not lead therefore to a penalty [*Strafe*], but to a punishment ßühne]. «But regardless of how cruelly it strikes the unwitting, its intervention is not, in terms of the law, a chance occurrence, but fate».[34] Neither separation nor guilt nor punishment is to be understood as a unique concept of the Jewish cosmos: their meaning is universal; in them the trace of Heidegger's 'fugitive gods' endures and emerges, a condition faithully reflected in nature's hostile, confused estrangement.

But, in view of all this, how can it be called conceptually fate? Benjamin somewhere else[35] gives acute indications (based on equally felicitous insights) on the relationship that links what is 'destined' to what is 'historic', comparable in many ways to what Heidegger says about the ontological nexus between *Geschick* and *Geschichte*. Thus Benjamin writes:

> The laws of fate, unhappiness and guilt are defined by the law as criteria of the person [...]. Fate shows itself, in the view of life, as condemned, *as having essentialy first been condemned, and then became guilty* [...]. Law condemns not to punishment, but to guilt. *Fate is the guilty context of the living* [«*der des Schuldzusammenhang Lebendigen*»].[36]

But if fate and guilt are inextricably linked to each other, no relationship can exist – precisely because of this inseparable connection – between fate and happiness: «beneath the heavy sphere of fate every happiness is guilt», where the dominion is that of «a scale on which happiness and innocence are too light and soar aloft. This scale is the scale of the law».[37]

Precisely against the 'fate - guilt - law' context man's struggle for happiness asserts itself as the foundation and ultimate goal toward which the 'secular order' [*Ordnung des Profanen*][38] strives. The kingdom of God is certainly a result, in the etymological sense of the term (*exitus, ex-eo*), the final outcome (in Benjamin *Ende*, not *Ziel*) with respect to which the secular course of history posits itself as something totally unrelated, radically different. Nonetheless, this 'secular' quest for happiness, despite its estrangement from the flow of messianism, far from contradicting it, may instead facilitate the messianic realization. In happiness, in fact, the layman aspires «to his own decline, but it is only in happiness that he can find his own decline».[39] Can it perhaps be said that the secular struggle for happiness is the condition of the kingdom of God: in this sense the epigraph from Hegel placed by Benjamin in his fourth thesis of the philosophy of history, «Seek ye first food and raiment; and the kingdom of God will come of itself».[40] Mankind's immediate material quest for happiness and satisfaction is, in other words, a celebration of placated need and, simultaneously, a recognition that behind it «is a struggle for rude material things, without which the finer spiritual things do not exist» (*ibid.*).

But the struggle for happiness is also a struggle for the reappropriation of the 'past': a topic that returns insistently in the essay *On the Concept of History*, in which the discontinuity of history – the exception that disrupts the possibility of a form, always refers to something beyond, against all progressive/historicist assumptions. Here is the core of Benjamin's philosophical utopia in the *Theses*: in his polemic directed entirely against the transcendental *Historismus* embraced by German Social Democracy against the concept by which time is presented as a "straight and empty" path, without qualitative leaps and unrepeatable emergencies.

Such a concept of temporality always equal to itself has perhaps its most typical manifestations in Kantian theory of law, where the world of norms is conceived as a network of forms capable of firmly sealing social being [*Sein*] by placing oneself on a transcendental plane in relation to it [duty, *Sollen*]. In this universe of formal relationships there would no longer be any room for leaps, discontinuities – to wit, for "exceptions", "states of emergency" or "necessities": all concepts of legal-philosophical origin, which appear as the devil to cast away and for which there is not even a language capable of representation. Such concepts in fact tend toward the outermost limits of knowledge, alluding to an 'outside' that still has repercussions on the events of historical existence, which in his *Theologico-Political Fragment* Benjamin declares to be 'secular'.

In a formalist universe the exception is madness: its *signs* must be allowed to fall into the void, muffled and neutralized in the infinite deafness of the historical continuum. Thus the image that might be invoked in this regard is that of a fabric, weak but whole, made up of small rings – the molecules of the history, all equal among them because perfectly formalized – which reinforce one another by forming a continuum. This is the image that, in Benjamin, the philosopher of history (a perfect antithesis in every point of the historian of *Historismus*) is called to shatter at all costs. Thus the titanic, angelic thought of the philosopher of history wants to regain the past for himself, purified of the *acedia* of historicist historiography, of the intimate sadness of an interpretation that is based on self-identification with the past. *Jetztzeit* is the time in which the thought of the *Angelus Novus* lives, opposing itself to the false unity of a «homogeneous, empty» era, manifesting itself allegorically as true divine violence in a biblical instant.[41] But the time of 'significant moments' cannot but refer to a reality from which the present moment was generated and realized, to a mother-continent which is the theological dimension of the long periods of the ages. And here it must be recalled that 'thinking by eras' is what Benjamin recognizes as most typical in Kafka.

The critique of violence thus ends up in Benjamin's analysis at the symbol of Kafka. In it a significant role is played by the characteristics mentioned at the start: a lucid awareness of not being able to describe everything through the myth of an omnipotent language, as well as not being able to mediate everything by a liberal masking of conflict. Kafka expresses acutely, as Benjamin does not fail to note, the necessary reality, in radical twentieth-century thought, of an area that transcends language and social communication, of a 'beyond' of which (or from which we originate) only disjointed, contradictory, formally non-reconstructible signs appear. These are the signs that animate his critique of myth and law, the latter naively understood in Benjamin as a 'mythical product'. Kafka's students themselves are signs,[42] men who do not recognize their own voices, the unredeemed.

Benjamin observes how the world, alienated of mythical presence, finds its most effective allegory in a juxtaposition with prehistoric times: in prehistory, with the species' memory blacked out,[43] oblivion expropriates man even of his past. Prehistory, far from being meaningless for the present, is a living legend, a symbolic place of reification. «That this period should be forgotten does not mean that it will not resurface in the present. Indeed, it does so precisely because of this oblivion».[44] The critique of the violence of myth is, therefore, for the 'expropriated' man, above all in a tension of enormous potential that is released in terms of justice to lead outside of 'pre-historic' estrangement. Here the perspective of the *Critique of Violence* re-emerges with clarity in what we might call the naive and fragile (but also acute and paradoxical) natural law without law (or against law) of the young Benjamin. Benjamin says, referring to a statement by Werner Kraft: «The word 'Justice' [...] is not employed by Kafka; yet it is from justice that the critique of myth here takes place».[45]

Benjamin, as interpreter of Kafka and as Kafka's double, sees in divine justice the allegory of a world in which the complete neutralization of the 'other' is mere impracticable ideology: thus just divine violence *als waltende Gewalt* seems not to exclude the possibility of an interpretation that sees it as allegorically aimed at annihilating this ideology. The violence of the 'other', which according to Benjamin emerges from liberal discourse, from the dark sides of language, implicitly indicates the need for a thought that reflects and makes visible the contradictions arising from the 'unredeemed specificity' outside of any now only regressive attempt to operate on them, through omnipotent language, a definitive synthesis and a mythical *reductio ad unum*.

VII. *Naphta, or a* katéchon *for Europe*

1. *A strange Jesuit.*

Who is Naphta? The question just framed abandons the evocative role of literary allegory to invest the essential nuclei of Western political thought. Along with it we must likely undertake an investigation into the history of European culture at a non-superficial level of analysis.

Naphta is the most ambiguous character of Mann's *The Magic Mountain*, the Jesuit whose unusual and paradoxical thought bursts the democratic banalities of the Enlightenment figure Settembrini. Yvon Bourdet in the central essay of his book[1] attempts a problematic identification of Naphta with György Lukács, presenting as his clinching argument the 'mystery' of the later Lukács' *sacrificium intellectus* – his 'Jesuitical' submission to the authority of Communist orthodoxy, embodied in the 'good' totality of the Party.

But the superficiality and reductive criterion of Bourdet's arguments leave something to be desired. Trying to guess *whom* Thomas Mann had in mind in creating Naphta has little sense and risks being misleading. What matters is what Naphta objectively ends up signifying, regardless of Mann's subjective choice of models. In other words, we need to let Naphta speak for himself, listening to his speech in all its murky complexity. In the chapter where Naphta first appears, the classical themes of *jus publicum Europaeum*, the state of nature, war, arbitration, are all laid out and articulated in an already surprisingly anti-liberal perspective – the same perspective that unmistakably defines Naphta: at the same time collectivistic and within the *jus divinum*, communist and advocate of theocratic solutions to the central problems of *Weltpolitik*.

> Herr Settembrini has omitted to add – broke in Naphta –
> that Rousseau' idyll is a sophisticated transmogrification of the
> Church's doctrine of man's original free and sinless state, his

primal nearness and filial relation to God; to which state he must finally return. But the re-establishment of the City of God, after the dissolution of all earthly forms, lies at the meeting-place of the earthly and the heavenly, the material and the spiritual; redemption is transcendental – and as for your capitalistic world-republic, [...] your mania for nationalism obviously shrinks from the world-conquering cosmopolitanism of the Church. Still, I cannot see how you reconcile your nationalism with your horror of the war.[2]

As for bourgeois morality,

civilian society doesn't know what it wants. It shouts for a campaign against the fall in the birth-rate, it demands a reduction in the cost of bringing up children and training them to a profession – and meanwhile men are herded like cattle, and all the trades and professions are so overcrowded that the fight round the feeding-trough puts in the shade the horrors of past wars.[3]

Justice is reunited with "exactness" only if thought in relation to transcendence:

Permit me to remark that any system of pains ans penalties which is not based upon belief in a hereafter is simply a bestial stupidity. And as for the degradation of humanity, the history of his course is precisely synchronous with the growth of the bourgeois spirit. Renaissance, age of enlightenment, the natural sciences and economics of the nineteenth century, have left nothing undone or untaught which could forward this degradation. Modern astronomy, for example, has converted the earth, the center of the All, the lofty theater of the struggle between God and the Devil for the possession of a creature burningly covered by each, into a different little planet.[4]

It is interesting to note how this spiritualistic and theocentric perspective gets entangled with a voluntarism that, in concerning itself with the theory of knowledge, tends to become nihilism. Indeed, Naphta maintains «with disagreeable composure»:

My good sir, there is no such thing as pure knowledge. The validity of Church's teaching on the subject of science, which can be summed up in the phrase of Saint Augustine:

> *Credo, ut intelligam*: I believe, in order that I may understand, is
> absolutely incontrovertible. [...] Whatever profits man, that is
> the truth.[5]

Especially in these last passages the shadow of nihilism is projected on pronouncements dictated by a nominalism of just seemingly spiritualistic inspiration. It is a situation that leads back to Nietzsche, the «coarse confusion» generated by the belief that, through direct knowledge of things, the *simplex sigillum veri* can be grasped.

> From where is it known, that the true nature of things
> lies in *this* relationship with our intellect? Is it not possible
> that the situation is different? That the hypothesis that best
> gives it a sense of power and safety comes from it as maxi-
> mally *preferred, appreciated and therefore termed true*?[6]

To compare with Naphta:

> Do you believe in truth, in objective, scientific truth, to
> strive after the attainment of which is the highest law of all
> morality, and whose triumphs over authority form the most
> glorious page in the history of the human spirit? [...] it is
> this unconditioned, this a-philosophical natural science that
> always has led and ever will lead men into darkness.[7]

Utilitarianism, pragmatism («Your pragmatism», Settembrini responded, «needs only be translated into terms of politics for it to display its pernicious character in full force»),[8] a theory of knowledge and politics seemingly *auf Gott*, but substantially *auf Nichts gestellt*. All this is combined with a theology of history whose objectivism can only be explained by thinking of the radically egalitarian condition which – from the Christian point of view, which Naphta esoterically alludes to – is intrinsic to all human beings before the problem of salvation .

But even if his assertions are dogmatically unimpeachable («Man is the measure of all things, and his welfare is the sole and single criterion of truth. Any theoretic science which is without practical application to man's salvation is as such without significance, and we are commanded to reject it»; «Lactantius, who was chosen by Constantine the Great as tutor to his son, put the position very clearly when he asked in so many words what heavenly bliss he could attain by knowing the sources of the Nile, or the twaddle of the physicists anent the heavenly bodies. Answer him, if you can!»; «Let me assure you that mankind is about to find its way back to this point of view. Mankind will soon perceive that it is not the task of true science to run after godless understanding, but to reject utterly all that is harmful, yes, even all that ideally speaking is without significance, in favour of instinct, measure, choice»),[9] despite the perfect orthodoxy of these statements, the suspicion remains, urged by his fundamental ambiguity, that in Naphta the assumption of salvation as the ultimate criterion of evaluation of things may be completely hypothetical, conventional.

The criterion of evaluation, its measurement (*Maßstab*) may in other words turn out to be an empty shell that could be filled as much by the idea of God and salvation (but in any case the general theology would be subordinated to political theology) as by Nothing. Only a *conventional decision* would cause things to be ordered according to a certain scale of evaluations rather than to another.

Hans Castorp wonders:

> A proper Jesuit! But what I mean is, he a real, actual Jesuit? [...] He said certain things – you know the ones I mean – about modern communism, and the religious zeal of the proletariat, and not withholding its hand from bloodshed [...]. Is that allowed?[10]

And Settembrini adds:

> Herr Naphta is [...] a man of intellect – or I should not be seeking his society – and as such he is always searching for new combinations, new associations ad adaptations, new shades of meaning proper to the time.[11]

Moreover, on the relationship between lax morality and nihilist decisionism, Hocke's observations are particularly valid:

> Casuistic probability – this theological-individual ancestor of existentialism – leads to a far more complete dissolution of all values and laws than what we encounter in the developments of the so-called 'modern' art of yesterday and today. The juridical order of mankind, its primitive security in the law, in short its vital, empirical security, are undermined and irremediably relativized. The result of this doctrine is and must be not only aesthetic subjectivism, but ethical nihilism, *total subjectivist free-*

dom of decision before laws, norms and conventions of all kinds, even in a game of hide-and-seek behind eternal screens.[12]

So is there any contradiction between the extreme spiritualistic voluntarism of *credo ut intelligam* and the nihilism promoted by a collectivist metaphysics that sees in the proletarian mass movements «a temporary abrogation of the contradiction between spirit and force, in the sense of overcoming the world by mastering him, in a transcendental, a transitional sense, in the sense of the Kingdom»?[13] Contradictions, Naphta would answer, can be harmonized. What could never be admitted is Settembrini's middle-of-the-road, mediocre individualism, which takes a bit of this and a bit of that, a bit of a liberal state and a bit of Christianity, without getting to the core of any of those concepts. But are we not then in the midst of the neo-authoritarian critique of empty nineteenth-century liberal formalism? Do we not seem, at least at this point, to hear Carl Schmitt speaking against Krabbe, Kelsen and Wolzendorff? The decisionist-conventionalist arguments we alluded to above would confirm it, but there are several other elements of consonance, further homologies within the discourse, that are worth examining.

First, the strictly *dualistic* structure of Naphta's thought recalls fairly clearly the articulations – made up of lights and shadows, completely alien from the 'grays' of Enlightenment monism – of the neo-authoritarian and nihilistic arguments of certain theoretical, post-Weimar currents. Schmitt's *Freund/Feind* dualism is the best example of this. «Spirit is dualistic [...]. Dualism, antithesis, is the moving, the passionate, the dialectic principle of all Spirit. To see the world as cleft int two opposing poles – that is Spirit. All monism is tedious».[14] The «asceticism and sovereignty program» [*Askese und Herrschaft*] that (in a way homologous to Schmitt's *Ausnahmezustand*) temporarily suspends the dualism of spirit and power,[15] has such a small place in Lukács' 'praxism,' which knowingly ignores the problem of asceticism (the extremely lucid pages of Schopenhauer's criticism of Hegel would be useful here), that one cannot escape the impression of a constant straining by Bourdet to validate his interpretive hypothesis.

Second (apart from the strange character – if we should accept the identification with Lukács proposed by Bourdet – of a "Catholic thinker" Hegel that Naphta supports),[16] how could his emphatically reactionary critique of the French Revolution be explained, "unpleasant accident of history," as any radically critical voice of *Zivilisation* in a manner consistent with his point of view defines it? As Naphta tells Settembrini:

> We part company here. All power and all control was originally vested in the people, who made it over, together with the right to make laws, to their princes. But from this your school deduces in the first instance the right of the people to revolt from the monarchy. Whereas we, on the contrary...[17]

> What had been the net result of the vainglorious French Revolution – what but the capitalistic bourgeois State? [...] And one it was hoped to improve upon, forsooth, by making the horror universal! [...] Progress? It was the cry of the patient who constantly changes his position thinking each new one will bring relief".[18]

Donoso Cortés (following in Schmitt's footsteps) could have been the author of Naphta's statements concerning the indissoluble entwinement of Catholicism and politics, where "*katholikòs*" ("universal") refers to the concept of *Weltpolitik*, 'great' politics:

> Politics and Catholicism were, as conceptions, psychologically akin, both of them belonging to a category which embraced all that was objective, feasible, empirical, with an issue into active life. Opposed to it stood the Protestant, the pietistic sphere, which had its origin in mysticism.[19]

Consider the provocation: Leo Naphta is Carl Schmitt. As Dallmayr acutely noted, Schmitt «saw (or believed he saw) what consequences inevitably lead to a rigorous moral and political relativism. The problem that determined the whole course of his thought is this: where can we find an objective unifying element in the midst of moral and political dissolution?».[20] For both Naphta and Schmitt the spirit seeks a refuge, a difficult *ubi consistam* in institutional reality, such as to keep humanity safe from the tendency to disintegration, which is at the same time a dangerous and an inviting abyss. Certainly no 'depoliticization' is present in Naphta. Indeed, in him we espy (as from what he says about the problem of mass nihilism, whose supporters are the movements of proletarian internationalism), a scant awareness of political reality, as well as the posing – which we could not fail to define in some Schmittian way – of a fundamental question.

How to create a brake, re-establish a limit and therefore an obligation, after the descent into nihilism has corroded at the base all the previous possibilities of metaphysically establishing a principle of cohabitation? We no longer know whether it is Schmitt or Naphta (in any case certainly not Lukács) who answers: «Without an idea of *katéchon*, Europe is lost».[21]

2. *Naphta, Schmitt and the European crisis.*

Leo Naphta, Carl Schmitt. In the background the historical drama of Europe. The juxtaposition is not new. Some good reasons for at least a partial identification between the two characters were already adduced in an old essay by Delio Cantimori,[22] an essay cited recently in this very regard and perhaps not accidentally, by some Italian scholars.[23] Naphta and Schmitt mark off the real problem, which is that of a *katéchon* for Europe. But, one may ask, what *katéchon*, since there is no chance of achieving any *form*? European history proves itself 'shapeless', and the attempt by the visionary Spengler is perfectly desperate and backward – dense with shrill anguish, in a gloomy nonsense – to delineate, right around the years of the *Zauberberg*, a "morphology of world history."[24] Nevertheless Spenglerism arrived – because of its allusive capacity to indicate real problems of meaning (see: "the mass is the end, it is the radical nothing," as Spengler expresses) – at the height of his fortune: 1920 saw the 'recognition' given by the academic review *Logos*, which offered an interesting *Spenglerheft*.[25]

The picture is therefore that of a Europe crisscrossed by vitalistic ferments pressuring to reinterpret the political dimension in terms of «demonic reason of state», in clear contrast to the classical and formal claim contained in humanist ethics. This claim is expressed in the need for clear conceptual distinctions: humanist classicism is in this sense wholly 'striving towards the concept'. We recall that it was in these very years that Mann's *Gedanken im Kriege* saw the light, and in particular his writings *Von deutscher Republik* (1922) and *Pariser Rechenschaft* (1926),[26] full of meaning and impotence in their non-political *Humanität*. As Mann himself observed, «the stimulus that gave birth to them was not in reality political, but fully spiritual».[27] It was the bitter sundering between these two poles of experience, traceable to Meinecke's distinction between *kratos* and *ethos*, which pervades the sensibility of Europe's 'free spirits' – not «philosophers and journalists», as Delio Cantimori noted, but «that narrow international cultured world for which Mann and Huizinga, Curtius and Unamuno spoke; and then, citing at random, Salvador de Madariaga, Ortega y Gasset, Benda and Lucien Febvre; Stefan Zweig and also Ehrenburg (in writings such as *Julio Jurenito* and *D.E.* [*Destroying Europe*]), a *respublica* of 'free spirits' above the fray. The list could go on with more or less illustrious names: Thibaudet, Cajumi, Drieu la Rochelle, Bernanos, Gide, Valéry, Adriano Tilgher, and so on, in a strange potpourri».[28]

The crisis of nationalities – the nation states that turned out to be mere managers of legitimate violence – had the effect of nurturing intelligent skepticism, in this small republic of educated Europe, on the 'public' values of politics. Their skepticism was valuable because it is always healthy to unmask. But their spiritual crisis also expressed other concerns: the Naphta metaphor, in addition to Schmitt, can be linked to Jünger, especially in passages like this one:

> The present age requires above all a single virtue: decision. What matters is being able to want and to believe, regardless of the contents that this wanting and this believing yield [...]. We worked for a few years in rigid nihilism with dynamite. We also gave up the slightest fig leaf of a real problem, razing the XIXth century to the ground with our artillery: we ourselves. [...] We declared war around a roulette table, which had only one color – zero, which always guarantees the croupier will win. We Germans had not given Europe any chance of losing. But by removing any chance of losing, in effect we didn't even give it anything to gain: we played against the bank with its own chips [...]. From this position one can work very well. This taking the norm from the mysterious first meter of civilization, preserved in Paris – for us it means completing our defeat [...]. Our march has long been directed towards a magical zero limit, beyond which only those who have other invisible sources of energy will survive. Our hope depends on what remains, since it can't be measured on Europe, but it itself is a creator of measurement.[29]

The European paradox in the pages of Jünger (a "lucid visionary" like Spengler) becomes evident: *the creator of the measurement is nothingness*. Karl Löwith, the "Fiala" who quotes these passages of Jünger's, comments: «Jünger knows that this conscious nihilism is one with resolute anarchy, which acts alone and closed in on itself».[30] Jünger's disjoining (which however we hesitate to define as 'nihilistic') of the criteria of judgment from the natural law rationality proper to the European philosophical tradition explains why he seemed unpopular to men with an open intellect like Mittner,[31] as in his day he was frowned upon by the dialectical idealist Marcuse, who however at various points in his critique seemed to repeat the 'progressive' prejudices of the Enlightenment figure Settembrini.[32]

It is certainly illusory to conceive of nothingness as a «measurement maker» and indirect *katéchon* maker. The activism of these «resolute but indecisive» men – as Cantimori observed – did not produce a new order, and all the less managed to free Europe from the tyranny of value.[33] The discussion of value – though ineliminable from European critical consciousness – cannot however arrive at a *form*, transform the chaotic material of history according to an ordering model. In fact, the transformations of the political depend, more than on a *ratio*, on an *auctoritatis interpositio*, and theory ends up forcibly refraining from establishing "what is" *das Rettende*, what in a Heideggerian sense could "save". Before this reality there seems to be no favorable destiny for Europe, no historically feasible solution. Western knowledge cannot reconstruct form, reassemble the 'phial' or container used by the scientist in his laboratory, in which – when it was still possible to proceed with univocal and 'classical' conceptual distinctions such as between ordering and ordered, form and matter – the formless liquid, the carbide, the 'naphta' was decanted. The transparency of the glass was deceptive as to the possibility of a detached observation of phenomena.

To believe that a form pre-exists: this was the supposition that sustained the lost natural law-metaphor of the 'phial'. Related to this, even today Delio Cantimori's lapsus appears extremely significant.

Part III

Reconstructing the Concept of Ethical Form

VIII. *A Critique of Normative Ethics.*
Some motifs in Schopenhauer's Philosophy of Law

1. *Kant's cannula.*

In his essay *The Basis of Morality*, the lucid criticism that Schopenhauer employs against rationalism and formalism in Kantian ethics appears to the reader as a consequent appendix to the argument with which Schopenhauer himself comes to deny free will. The common argument is that, although apparently free to do what he wants, man is not free – given the original conformation of his being – *not* to want what he wants.[1]

In fact, if man's moral value is realized once and for all in the original conformation of his being, and if for that reason man cannot help but act upon what he is, it therefore follows that virtue becomes a simple *predisposition*: virtue is not learned, but is something for which one is somehow predestined. *Velle non discitur*, Schopenhauer often repeats: «We should therefore be just as foolish to expect that our moral systems and ethics would create virtuous, noble, and holy men, as that our aesthetics would produce poets, painters and musicians».[2] On this point reality and experience always clash victoriously with the premises of formalistic and abstractly normative ethics, which are characterized by the desire to improve man's morality and intent on talking about progress in the field of virtue, almost as if there were to be an inexorable tendency to «progress towards the good». In reality, in order to improve man, we would have to recreate him *from scratch*, and «the turning round of a man's heart in is body, the remoulding of his very being», while all that can be done in the light of ethical rationalism «is to clear the intellect, correct the judgment, and so bring him to a better comprehension of the objective realities and actual relations of life».[3] Formalistic ethics do not reach beyond, and "their limits are quickly discovered».[4]

The interest that *The Basis of Morality* has aroused is no doubt derived from those pages, inspired by consistency, in which Schopenhauer demonstrates how normative morality represents nothing more than a methodical, well-intentioned and falsely farsighted "philistinism". Moreover, this interest comes from those other pre-Nietzschean pages in which the *vis* of controversy takes hold, revealing how the mystifying outcomes, the artificiality, and the inconsistency of rationalistic morality are ultimately nothing more than the logical consequence of all those systems, built upon an apparent idealism, which replace the knowledge of reality with a pre-constructed image of existence particularly suitable for religious and political compromises (including those dictated by the «religion of progress»).[5]

Not surprisingly, Schopenhauer's critique of Kantian morality opens with a concept that Kant elaborates in his *Groundwork of the Metaphysic of Morals*: the concept of a practical philosophy whose task is not to clarify the reasons for what happens, but to formulate the laws of what *must* happen, *even if it never happens*. In this definition, Schopenhauer immediately sees a resounding *petitio principii*, which does not hesitate to define the *proton pseudon* of Kant:

> Who tells you that there are laws to which our conduct *ought to* be subject? Who tells you that *that ought to take place, which in fact never does take place*? What justification have you for making this assumption at the outset, and consequently for forcing upon us, as the only possible one, a system of ethics conched in the imperative terms of legislation?[6]

It can be seen as a law in the sense that it is precise and original, he warns, only a *civil law*, i.e. an institution created within a political system: never with regard to morality, that is the specific context within which the phenomena of the human will take place. Only in appearance the introduction of the concept of «moral law», upon which the entire structure of Kantian ethics rests, is formal and neutral: it is actually rooted in a theological morality, reflected in the methodological 'purity' of the criticism, and thus rendered unmentionable, if not at the price of foregoing that same purity. (According to Schopenhauer, as already known, Kant's intellectual decrepitude begins with the second 1787 edition of the *Critique of Pure Reason*, and the "unbearable" idealistic outcomes of the criticism are implicit at this juncture).

That which holds true for moral law also holds true for the "absolute duty" which is an essential principle of formalistic ethics: according Schopenhauer, however, it can only be conditioned in relation to a situation, and is never categorical. This, on the other hand, is the great limitation that philosophical normative ethics is inevitably destined to encounter when it assumes the tone of a theory of duties, as it is unable t render itself truly independent of puritan theological morality. According to Schopenhauer's radically critical and, once again, occasionally pre-Nietzschean argumentation, the puritan theological origins of Kantian morality also cannot be as truly *religious* origins. In fact, they are anti-religious, because, if every duty can only be linked to the situation, and related to rewards and punishments (as is the case in practice, in contrast to the angelism of Kant's "pure duty"), then obedience will either be «wise or foolish, according to circumstances», yet «always actuated by selfishness».[7] Anyway obedience will be inevitably based on selfish motivation and, most importantly, «on the greater or lesser amount of credulity evinced in each case».[8]

Finally, philosophical ethics does not draw upon the only value that was exclusive to theology, or rather the ability to boast at least a certain degree of practical effectiveness upon men.[9] Kantian formalism *demands too much of them*. In order to remain consistent with a concept of ethics free of any empiric residue and transcendentally founded at all costs, it demands that men – eternally guilty – strenuously tend to comply with an absolute duty. Yet, Schopenhauer retorts, «let us consider the full meaning of such a position. Human consciousness as well as the whole external world, together with all the experience and all the facts they comprise, are swept from under our feet. We have nothing to stand upon. And what have we got to hold to? Nothing but a few entirely abstract, entirely unsubstantial conceptions, floating in the air equally with ourselves».[10] Despite being very unlikely, we ought to expect that these concepts will provide us with the strength necessary to 'morally' counteract the gigantic dimensions of selfishness.

We ought furthermore to rely upon the hope that it will occur to men to live according to the imperative "take action based on the principle of that which you want to become universal law for all beings endowed with reason", which is devoid of content and entirely removed from the situation –: from any situation that is ethically interesting. The paradox is evident,

> for ethics has to do with actual human conduct, and not with the *a priori* building of card houses – a performance which yields results that no man would ever turn to in the stern stress and battle of life, and which, in face of the storm of our passions, would be about as serviceable as a syringe, or a *cannula* in a great fire.[11]

This total lack of content is further compounded by another aspect that makes Kantian morality "revolting" in the eyes of Schopenhauer: its puritan postulate, according to which an action owes its moral value exclusively to the fact that it is subject to the notion of duty. In fact, for Kant «duty for duty's sake» embodies a man's value, but for Schopenhauer this renders men prone to moral pedantry, predisposing them to bow before an empty fetish. And – worse yet – predisposing them to see a hypostatized reason as a "natural vehicle" capable of placing man in communication with the transcendent.

According to Schopenhauer's radical criticism of Kant, reason does not provide man with any guarantee of truth in either the theoretical or practical fields. With reason, man draws abstract concepts from intuitive concrete representations, and this ability gives rise to the fundamental prerogatives that elevate man above the animal state: the consciousness not only of the present, but also the future and the past, as well as planning, memory, and language. But it cannot be said, for this reason alone, that acting according to reason and acting virtuously (or rather not selfishly) are one and the same, nor have they ever been considered as such by any culture or any language: if anything, Schopenhauer points out that evil combined with reason, and altruism combined with unreasonableness, occur more frequently. Reason, therefore, is not a valid foundation for justice and philanthropy, and it only plays a secondary and subordinate function in human actions.

2. *Necessary selfishness and the invasions of the bodily sphere.*

The different moral doctrines only hit the mark if they do not begin with the prejudicial disavowal of the fact that selfishness is among the predispositions that determine the general condition of human nature. That which the will desires, Schopenhauer observes, is essentially life. This blind impetus gives rise to the struggle to achieve dominance over things and over men, whereby it is natural that war becomes one of the general forms of the will's objectification.[12] The human species can only maintain itself through disagreement and fighting, as an expression of the same conflict that tears apart the will from within, forcing it «sink its teeth into its own flesh», unaware that it is tearing itself apart. Unaware, because every man has a knowledge that's heavily biased by the *principium individuationis*, which makes him assertive. This is why «is essential to our consciousness that each person is himself the whole world»[13] : everyone can rightly say that his own death coincides with the death of the world – the world that exists only in so much as it is experienced by the individual that exists and that alone represents it.[14] An entire universe of experiences dies every minute, along with every individual man who has lived through them, and dies.

It is therefore clear that in such a situation, defined by Schopenhauer as «the natural point of view», for every man his own existence and his own preservation is more important than the existence and the preservation of all other beings, and it is also clear how he, *according to his natural tendency*, is led to believe that anyone who opposes his aspirations is deserving of his anger or even his hatred, arousing a more or less strong desire for annihilation within him. Within this antagonism formed between the self and the other lies the ontological cause of selfishness, which, in the philosophical discourse that Schopenhauer lays out for us, consists of a sort of *ethical solipsism* necessitated by the form itself in which the individual consciousness is effectively structured. In fact, it is here that we can observe the reference to Hobbes, made by Schopenhauer himself.[15] The metaphysical basis that Schopenhauer offers for selfishness and the resulting state of war between individuals is clearly structured according to the Hobbesian model, which describes the natural onset of violence and aggression among men. But it nevertheless also diverges considerably from this model, at least in the sense that, in the same natural state and on the basis of a *natural intuition* akin to scholastic synderesis, the will for individual assertion that, in overcoming one's own bodily sphere, invades that of others, is considered to be *unjust*.

It can therefore be said that Schopenhauer agrees with Hobbes' diagnosis regarding the selfishness underlying the natural life conditions of individuals and the resulting situation of widespread hostility, but also distances himself from Hobbes in the sense that he does not believe that selfishness and hostility have a merely empirical and exterior dimension, meaning that they are not reduced to mere facts, but also include a particular moral dimension that makes them evaluable from an axiological standpoint.

In short, what Schopenhauer refers to as "invasion", or rather the "intrusion" of one's will for assertion into the bodily sphere of the other,[16] is not reduced to a simple (and axiologically neutral) behavior, but implies a *moral significance* of which both the culprit and the victim of the invasion are certainly aware, describing it – even if sometimes only in the internalized form of feelings and not on the level of lucid awareness – as "unjust" behavior. In this manner, the victim experiences the invasion suffered as a moral pain, quite distinct from the physical suffering caused by the act itself or by the discomfort associated with the harm inflicted, while to the perpetrator of wrong «the knowledge presents itself that in himself he is the same will which appears also in that body, and affirms itself in the one phenomenon with such vehemence that, transgressing the limits of its own body and powers, it becomes the denial of this very will in the other person».[17]

The ontological and ethical concept of injustice, understood according to the abstract form described above, is specified and exemplified in § 62 of the *World*. The first example is that which is clearest and most theatrically evident: this is the phenomenon of cannibalism, in which the conflict established by the will to live and to oppress the other, incorporating (or literally, swallowing up) the bodily sphere of the other, is manifested without compromise, in the most atrocious manner possible. Equally significant in terms of the invasion of the other's bodily sphere, albeit with a somewhat lesser intensity, are homicide, personal injury, and the subjugation of the other to slavery, including in an extensive concept of slavery every situation in which a man is forced to employ his forces for the benefit of others rather than himself, and therefore simple deprivation as well.

Only slightly less severe among the various manifestations of injustice is the violation of another's property. On this point, Schopenhauer enters into yet another dispute with Kantian normative ethics, which view the origins of this right as the *taking of possession or first occupation*, arguing:

> How could the mere declaration of my will to exclude others from the use of a thing give me at once a *right* to it? Obviously the declaration itself requires a foundation of right, instead of Kant's assumption that it is one.[18]

Neither occupation nor simple use would suffice to morally justify a *ius excludendi*, because such a justification could only be reached by someone who has transfused his own forces into the thing to be appropriated, through his own work:

> All genuine, i.e. moral, right to property is originally based simply and solely on elaboration and adaptation, as was pretty generally assumed even before Kant, indeed as the oldest of all the codes of law clearly and finely expresses it: "Wise men who know olden times declare that a cultivated field is the property of him who cut down the wood and cleared and ploughed the land, just as an antelope belongs to the first hunter who mortally wounds it" (*Laws of Manu*, IX, 44). [...] A thing may be developed, improved, protected, and preserved from mishaps by the efforts and exertions of some other person, however small these may be. The person who seizes such a thing obviously deprives the other of the result of his labor expended on it. He makes the body of the other serve *his* will instead of the other's will.[19]

Furthermore, if the value or moral foundation of a similar right, as Schopenhauer intends, arises from having transposed one's own work into a certain thing, and consequently from having *included that thing within the area of assertion of one's own body*, then a right to that thing, no less extensive than that which each one of us directly boasts over our own body, will be justified on a moral level.

In the end, any phenomenal form of injustice can be committed through violence or fraud, whereby the choice of means is not influential in terms of morality. If injustice always consists of an enslavement of others for one's own purposes, by choosing violence one essentially chooses to resort to physical causation – direct coercion – to achieve that end, while by choosing fraud one communicates illusory reasons to the other: «fictitious motives on the strength of which he follows *my* will, while believing that he follows *his own*».[20]

If, in keeping with the above, injustice is an action detrimental to the other – or better yet *the other's natural sphere of assertion* – then it must be said that the concept of *justice* is a derived and negative concept with respect to the original and positive concept of injustice, or wrongfulness (*Unrecht*). This is one of the most widely-known parts of Schopenhauer's legal philosophy. Contrary to what one might assume with regard to the origins of the term, according to Schopenhauer the idea of injustice is not derived from idea of justice by negation, but the latter is instead derived from the idea of *non-injustice*. The concept of justice (and justness) therefore covers all actions that can be performed without harming others, or rather without doing them wrong.[21]

In fact, if you start from the preconceived opinion that the notion of justice, or right (*Recht*), should be positive, and try to define it in this manner, you will never succeed, because that concept contains a mere negation, the negation of the offense. Since everyone has the right to do anything that doesn't cause offense to others, then one also has the right to use force to fend off any offense attempted by others. The reaction to the injustice perpetrated by another cannot itself constitute an injustice, and it is therefore just; that is to say that it does nothing other than reestablish the boundaries violated by those who invaded *my* sphere of assertion, and consequently – although it could be considered as violence in itself, and as such would undoubtedly constitute an injustice – in the case in question it would be justified: it becomes a right *because of the motivation that caused it*.

The concepts of just and unjust are not merely conventional, and appreciable in the light of a pure normativism, but are rather moral determinations rooted in a situation: that is to say that they are valid due to the concrete existence of a particular human conduct, regardless of whether any political or social institution wants to regulate them in a positive way. However, Schopenhauer doesn't talk explicitly about *natural law* here. He doesn't talk about it, but he doesn't abstain from referring to what it might mean in terms of a real *moral right* (based merely on the senses and intuition, and not on a rationalistic natural law) *not to suffer injustice*, as a consequence of the elementary observation that

> it depends on everyone merely in every case to *do* no wrong, but by no means in every case to *suffer* no wrong, which depends on his accidental, external power.[22]

In other words, the concepts of just and unjust, while recognized as unconventional, are only applicable in the natural state as particular moral concepts, which are effective only in the interior domain, and valid «for the self-knowledge of the will in each of us».[23] Schopenhauer therefore asserts that there is a purely moral right, which is not referable to an universal law in Kantian sense, but is nevertheless particular and concrete: the doctrine of this pure (or natural) right thus ends up being a chapter of a neither formal nor normative morality regarding the exact determination of the *limits* that a particular individual cannot overcome without committing injustice, as well as the exact determination of the *actions* that – despite exceeding these limits, but carried out by the same particular individual with the aim of fending off a pre-existing injustice (e.g. cases regarding the right to exert resistance, or "self-defense") – cannot, in turn, be considered *unjust* in any way. The specific subject of this domain of morality, which Schopenhauer refers to as the philosophy of law (*Rechts-philosophie*), remains the action, or better yet the realm in which the correct judgment is made about acting justly (based on a right, *Recht*) and acting unjustly (based on a wrong, *Unrecht*). In this sense, philosophy of law is not a moral philosophy in the strict sense, although it cannot set aside the purely moral consideration of human action. Schopenhauer provides clarifications in this regard:

> Whoever [...] wishes to set aside the purely moral consideration of human conduct, or to deny it, and to consider conduct merely according to its external effect and the result thereof, can certainly, with Hobbes, declare right and wrong to be conventional determinations arbitrarily assumed, and thus not existing at all outside positive law; and we can never explain to him through external experience what does not belong to external experience.[24]

Therefore (and herein lies the fundamental difference between Schopenhauer and Hobbes), while Hobbes considers moral right, generated by the individual's particular intuition, to be devoid of any positivity, for Schopenhauer it represents the *ethical criterion* for evaluating positive law's consistency with justice. So while it is true that, in order for the law to exist, the rules merely need to be supported by a coercive power capable of enforcing them, likewise in order for this positive law not to lapse into positive injustice it mustn't deny the specific contents of morality dictated by the primitive intuition of wrong (*Unrecht*).

3. *Crutch, automaton, bitter laugh. The doctrine of positive law and its limitations.*

With regard to the functions of public authority and legislation, however, Schopenhauer reconverges with Hobbes, from whom he had strayed dealing with the concepts of just and unjust. Public authority arises from man's natural tendency to minimize, through a covenant, the amount of injustice that each individual must inevitably suffer due to the violent and arbitrary aspects present within the social dimension. The sphere of public authority is not intended to promote a normative morality claiming an universal rationality, but is rather justified – when it is justified – by the minimal task of limiting widespread social violence.

In short, the form of public authority typical of modern times – the State – is merely a historical phenomenon generated by practical interests, which – corrupted by the violent and abusive nature of its origins – nevertheless quite often results in the existence of what Schopenhauer eloquently describes as «a gathering of cheaters and their victims».[25] As a necessary evil, to the disenchanted observer the essence of the State consists of "a bitter laugh". That which betrays the near total absence in society of natural predispositions that allow for a positive morality is just this merely instrumental reality of the institution: «a crutch instead of a leg; an automaton instead of a person».[26]

These violent origins of the State also raise suspicions about the subsequent actions of the State itself. In fact, if morality only refers to the action (classified by inner judgment as either right or wrong, just or injust) and, with normative rules, establishes precise limits, nevertheless effective only against *those who have already decided not to commit injustice,* the legislation is conversely focused upon actions *publicly classified as unjust.* It must therefore be said – especially with regard to the most controversial public issues – that suspicions arise concerning the State's interests in guiding the judgment criteria governing that classification.

With regard to the right to punish, which classically constitutes the most evident outward mark of public power in its claim of sovereignty, Schopenhauer sees this as exclusively based on positive law, and indeed it is this foundation that makes the true purpose of punishment possible: to be effective at preventing and thwarting injustice. In other words, the community of individuals has no choice but to entrust an order of external laws with the task of discouraging anyone from violating the rights of others, through effective means of intimidation. Law, law enforcement, and penalties thus only target the future, and not the past. In other words, the penalty is only justified if one deviates from a *purely compensatory* concept, like that of Kant, which – being isolated from its preventive purpose – gets confused with revenge, as it consists of the desire to obtain satisfaction for a wrong suffered «with the spectacle inflicted by ourselves upon those who made us suffer it». But for Schopenhauer this is a «poorly founded and absurd» theory: «the *jus talionis,* set up as an independent, ultimate principle of the right to punish, is meaningless».[27]

The idea that punishment could serve as an *instrument for rehabilitation,* or even for man's inner improvement, seems equally absurd to him, and this can be seen in several eloquent passages like the following, which deserves to be quoted in full:

> The penitentiary system also seeks not so much to punish the deed as the man, in order to reform him. It thereby sets aside the real aim of punishment, determent from the deed, in order to attain the very problematic end of reformation. But it is always a doubtful thing to attempt to attain two different ends by one means: how much more so if the two are in any sense opposite ends. Education is a benefit, punishment ought to be an evil; The penitentiary prison is supposed to accomplish both at once. Moreover, however large a share untutored ignorance, combined with outward distress, may have in many crimes, yet we dare not regard these as their principal cause, for innumerable persons living in the same ignorance and under absolutely similar circumstances commit no crimes. [...] Therefore moral reformation is really not possible, but only determent from the deed through fear.[28]

Then, in conclusion:

> The theory of punishment here advanced, and immediately obvious to sound reason, is certainly in the main no new idea,

> but only one that was well-nigh supplanted by new errors; and to this extent its very clear statement was necessary. The same thing is contained essentially in what Pufendorf says about it in *De officio hominis et civis* (book II, chap. 13). Hobbes also agrees with it (*Leviathan*, ch. 15 and 28). It is well known that Feuerbach has upheld it in our own day [...].[29]

Punishment therefore has a purely dissuasive and intimidating function: it is neither merely compensatory, nor naively rehabilitative. But in reality, as Nietzsche later observed with harsh realism, punishment includes revenge as both a product of the self-preservation instinct, and as *restitution* for the pain and damage suffered. However, since in so-called 'civil' societies, dominated by the rule of law ideology, revenge as restitution is limited by predetermined schemes, it can be argued that preservation (of both individuals and society) tends to prevail over the desire for restitution of the injury, damage and pain suffered. But it is also true that the (anthropologically motivated) provision of revenge is ready to re-emerge at any time. It should be noted that, with regard to these points, in his later works, like in *A Genealogy of Morals* – in which his greatest divergence from Schopenhauer occurs – Nietzsche continues to declare himself a pupil of his ancient *Erzieher*, all of whose other points of view he will soon repudiate.

IX. *Paul Valéry's Plato*

What changes is unpredictable eros capable of causing, what stable arrangements in the world is it able to *build*? These questions evidently presume that the philosophical category of "constructive doing" (*poieîn*) does not come to an end in the simple area of the empirical and the measurable according to quantity, but that it requires a much more thorough analysis of its own metaphysical implications.

The thematic centre of these notes is therefore the concept of *poíesis* (hence "poietics", "poetics"), considered as a synonym – but perhaps not rightly so (see below, 2 *b*), – of "productive action", and distinguished from an Aristotelian standpoint from *praxis,* seen as "moral action" (*Top.*, Z VI, 145 and 16; *Metaph.*, E I, 1025 b 25; *Nic.. Eth.*, B I, 1103 a-b). The hypothesis from which we start considers the history of Western metaphysics after Plato, as a whole, as a lengthy obscuring of the original meaning of poietics. In other words, this meaning appears not to be fully pondered and to be confined far away, in a place which is invisible and unattainable by philosophical reflection, whose subsequent path – in both the onto-theological version of medieval Aristotelianism and in the "modern" Cartesian one – followed an increasingly divergent trajectory from the primitive intuitions of Greek wisdom.

This hypothesis is certainly not new. It can be considered linked to the well-known statements on the problem of the obscuring of being contained in Heidegger's essays (the "last" Heidegger) dedicated to technology and, more generally, to nihilism as the destiny of the West,[1] as well as to the works of Jean Beaufret and Emanuele Severino.[2] In spite of the indications on the link *eînai-poieîn*, undeniably present in such works, it must be acknowledged that a history regarding the obscuring of the concept of poietics, able to account for the various steps which have occurred, has yet to be written, and – above all – how this ontological obscuration has produced serious consequences in the single spheres of Western knowledge, forcing thought to elaborate an absolutely over-simplistic concept of "doing", has yet to be explained.

1. *Diotima's speech.*

I will assume as the main scene of Diotima's speech – the «foreign woman from Mantinea» who plays the role of Socrates' first interlocutor in relation to the mystery of *eros poietikós* – the following passage of Plato's *Symposium*:

> I hold it is for immortal distinction and for such illustrious renown [...] that they all do all they can,and so much the more in proportion to their excellence. They are in love with what is immortal and inspired by *pregnancy of soul* – for there are persons who in their souls still more than in their bodies conceive those things which are proper for soul to conceive and bring forth. And what are those things? Thought and virtue in general. And of these the begetters are all the poets and those craftsmen who are styled *"inventors"*. Now by far the highest and fairest part of virtue is that which concerns the *regulation of cities and habitations*, it is called wisdom and justice.[3]

In the final part of the passage, the link that binds *poíesis* to the construction-constitution of city-states (*póleon*) and houses (*oikéseon*) appears fully visible. This connection reveals the centrality of the *poieîn* category in order to understand the concept of *politeía*, or "constitution" of the city, understood not so much as a simple legal text – as even the best historiographical reconstructions of ancient constitutionalism (see among others McIlwain) tend to do –, but in its deeper *ontological-political* scope: as a material constitution, "substance" and "constancy" of the spatial arrangement, placed beyond the contingency and the pure being-so of any juridical (or formal) arrangement. In this regard, it should be noted once again how little centred, in relation to this section of problems, the category of *práttein* is, having, in the Western metaphysical tradition, almost exclusively moral-behavioural connotations, which separate it from the material root – in the sense of the *hyle* – of the 'corporeal' that the *poíesis*, instead, by its very nature, recalls.

However, before reaching this level of analysis, we should deal directly with the concept of *poíesis* and with the ultimate meaning of "poietics", both in relation to the concept of eros which sustains them, and in relation to the concept of *téchne* in which every "constructive doing" necessarily converges. I will therefore proceed by breaking down the analysis into three fundamental points:

a) the concept of *eros* as the root of *poíesis*,

b) *poíesis* and *téchne*,

c) the material constitution of States as the product of a *political poietics*.

a) First of all we must note – as Plato observes – an error in approaching the problems:

> But you should not wonder – Diotima said – for we have singled out a certain form of love *(Eros)*, and applying thereto the name of the whole, we call it love; and there are other names that we commonly abuse.[4]

The error is that according to which, moving from a gaze that limits itself to taking into consideration the sensitive appearance, philosophical reflection tends to ignore the *structural unity* of the poietic making sustained by eros. Because there are numerous names (*tà onómata*) through which the individual sectors of *poíesis* are distinguished from each other (poetics in the strict sense, music, architecture, politics and so on), but no real or ontological differentiation corresponds with the nominal one. On the contrary: such a differentiation, forwarded onto an ontological plane, would be nothing but hypostasis, illusion, *eídolon*.

The truth is that constructive doing is *unique* albeit in the various fields of application, in the various "arts" in which it manifests itself, inasmuch as eros is unique – the «intermediate form» (*metaxý ti*) which connects, as vital energy, the two worlds: that of *idea* on the one hand, and that of empirics, where the work produced as a sensitive object is located, on the other.

The following passage (205c) fully clarifies what we are saying:

> You know that poetry *is more than a single thing*. For of anything whatever that passes from not being into being the whole cause is composing or poetry; so that the productions of all *arts* (*technais*) are kinds of poetry, and their craftsmen (*demiourgói*) are *all poets* (*poietái*).

Here the meaning of poietics is really the most extensive among all the thinkable meanings: for it, *poíesis* indicates every act (or *aitía*, the Aristotelian «cause») through which we have a passage from non-being to being. And it is not certain that the subject of this «act», «action», «cause», should be man, as a reductive anthropomorphic theory of «doing» would appear to logically conclude. Consider also that already in the passage of the *Sophist* (219b) in which a first definition of the poietic process was given, its author-actor remained nameless: «When anyone brings into being something which did not previously exist, we say that he who brings it into being produces it (*poieîn*) and that which is brought into being is produced (*poieîsthai*)».

It is here that the Heideggerian interpretation intervenes, trying to make evident how *poíesis*, rather than the activity of a subject who "puts into being" something which was not before, indicates an *allowing to appear*, an unveiling process in its essence and in its visible form (= in one of its many possible visible forms) *what has always been there*. In short, it is a transformation, a change of *eîdos* by which the entity «comes into being», entering the circle of the visible, i.e. moving to appearing,[5] which only indirectly touches on the true sphere of the acting subject's wilfulness. *Poíesis* – we have said – is certainly the name of the action, of the «cause that makes things pass from non-being to being» (*ek toû mè ontos eis tò òn iónti otoûn aitía*). But man does not seem to be its direct author. It is therefore necessary to ask: who is the actual subject of *poíesis*?

To this question the *Symposium* gives an answer which is as clear as it is not always fully understood. The true, actual subject, by which man, only the apparent creator, is manipulated, is not the ego but the *eros*, the *daimon*,[6] of which the creative ego fleetingly re-presents the incarnation: in which the ego – as *inventor* of new forms – becomes incarnation thanks to Poros, the «personification of expediency». *Eros* here becomes a trans-subjective structure of the communication of forms (*eidē*) poietically constructed in participatory conformity (*méthexis*) with the immutable essences. It is not just an inspiring activity, but an activity that – connected to *logos* and by this strengthened[7] – *performs* the work in concrete terms, thus becoming the authentic ultimate root of creative work.

"Poietics" is thus any construction of new forms that is supported by *enérgeia*, i.e. by what we could define the actuality or "industriousness" of eros: "poetics" in the strict sense of the meaning, such as the constitution of States, the construction of houses and buildings (architecture) as well as the composition and execution of melodies and rhythms (music). In addition to the unitary structure of eros which pervades them, these activities are united by the equally unitary nature of *endeavour* (*ergon*), which only changes its guise in the various cases, but which draws upon the same qualitative essence.

Considered from a *poieîn* point of view, a literary work therefore possesses an ontological qualification which is not different to that belonging to a political constitution: the metaphysical gaze must not insist on the distinction between them, since both are highlighted as products or works which are *successful against time*, that is, against the power of disappearance, the disappearing itself as power. Rather, the distinction must be made between a work which is alive and one «born already dead», because it lacks eros or is technically poorly executed. The latter will not even have the typical traits of the *work*: duration in time and rooting in space. And the defect in eros will equal the importance of the defect in *téchne*, since it belongs to the low empirical world, therefore it is not even a "work", but simply a perishable product. Likewise one must not only consider the complex object (political constitution, building, poem, melody: the *ti polý* quoted in 205c) whose parts are, for example, connected unskilfully, but also – and perhaps above all – the object whose formation or individuation was not determined by an erotic tension based on the *necessity* of the event: a necessity in which justice seems to reside in more specifically, the *dikaiosýne* of *Symp.* 209a.

Such a product will not only be "eradicated", but "eradicating". The fruit of mere empiricism, it will move away from its idea until it loses this without trace. And naturally, the negative effects of such a product will be the larger the longer they last in time (not to be confused with the ontological duration), since the length of its duration will be accompanied by an equal eradication intensity. The man who will have lived for a long time (and, *a fortiori*, the man who will have been educated) according to this false construction (false because *ontologically* deficient, and not – let's be clear – morally, following a subjective judgment of value which has declared such an axiological *insufficiency*) will see the ability to achieve a creative experience move further and further away.[8]

It should be noted that this is the problem – a very contemporary one, but in reality outside all time – which Paul Valéry addresses in his aesthetics of *poíesis*, taking the classic theme of constructive doing as a formative experience as the target of his own investigation. So that it would be interesting to attempt a comparative reading of the *Symposium* (but also, as we shall see, of the tenth book of the *Republic*) with Valéry's fundamental texts on the theory of constructive doing, such as, in the first instance, the *Eupalinos, ou l'Architecte* dialogues and *L'âme et la danse*.[9]

The fullness of the experience lies entirely in the "taking care" of matter, of the solidity of bodies as living matter. Western metaphysics has lost the "corporeal" sense of building and with it, it has forgotten the scope of the analogy between philosophical thought and architecture, which only a clear theory of forms could still support. Thus speaks the Socrates of *Eupalinos*:

> Man, I assert, *fabricates by astraction*, ignoring and forgetting a great part of the qualities of what he uses, and concerning himself solely with clear and definite conditions, which can most often be simultaneously satisfied, not by a single material, but by several kinds. He drinks milk or wine or water or ale indifferently out of gold, lass, horn, or onyx; and whether the vase be wide or slender, or shaped like a leaf or a flower, or with a quaintly twisted foot, *the drinker considers the drinking alone*. Even he who made the cup was unable to do more than harmonize very roughly its *substance*, its *form*, and its *function*. For the intimate subordination of these three things and their profound interfusion could be but the work of Creative Nature herself. The artisan cannot do his work without violating or disarranging an order by the forces which he applies to matter in order to adapt it to the idea he wishes to imitate, and to the usage he intends. He is therefore inevitably led to produce objects of which the whole is always a degree below the level of their parts.[10]

The work (*opera*) is a combination of substance, form and function. At this point, the order of *physis* represents something other than a simple model to which a mimetic effort needs to be applied: it is not a question of "imitating" organic life, but of "generating" forms whose vitality *may not be inferior* to that of organic life. In fact, the "poietic way" in which eros manifests itself is precisely that of *generating* (*génesis* or *génnesis*: see *Symposium* 206c-d, 207d): a generation *en tais psychaîs* (209a), whose link with the body contemporary philosophy has unfortunately forgotten. «O matériaux, belles pierres! O trop légers que nous sommes devenus!».[11] Here, as concerns the sense of corporeity, it is above all Alain's thought that comes to mind: Alain, the interpreter of the *Charmes* but also of Plato, a soul subtly similar to Valéry, but more than Valéry a friend of the earth, optimistically open to man and a strong *rooting* element of life in the world. As Sergio Solmi expressed himself in relation to Alain's aesthetics, confirming kinship with Valéry on this point,

> art, after all, is nothing but the desire to give full existence to our insufficient inner life, and to ourselves, failed men and only half alive as every creature. In *Eupalinos'* dialogue, whilst comparing the colourful terrestrial world with the pale region of shadows, Socrates regrets with Phaedrus the refined columns which hold up the front of the temples and delineate the delicate air and the sky's light. An inhuman nostalgia of the impalpable shadows for that which has a weight and a dimension, which weighs on the earth and supports the stars, so that no shadow, no ghost will ever be worth what fully exists, since the kingdom of the dead is more fleeting than that of the living...[12]

Unlike Plato's, Valéry's Socrates is the soul of a dead person who remembers the earth. And remembers it with nostalgia, as is apparent from the very beginning of the dialogue with Phaedrus («Les vivants ont un corps qui leur permet de sortir de la connaissance et d'y rentrer. Ils sont faits d'une maison et d'une abeille»).[13] What, more than the concrete, "poietic" link with the body, should metaphysics have thematized, and how little, instead, has it in fact thematized other than mere rationalistic abstraction? In what Phaedrus calls «the beautiful prayer to the body» by architect Eupalinos, Eupalinos *speaks like Alain*. It is worth reporting his words in full:

> EUPALINOS: O Phaedrus, when I design a dwelling (whether it be for the gods, or for a man), and when I lovingly seek its form, studying to create an object that shall delight the view, that shall hold converse with the mind, that shall accord with

reason and the numerous proprieties... I confess how strange soever it may appear to you, *that it seems to me my body is playing its part in the game*... Let me explain. This body is an admirable instrument, of which I am sure that those who are alive and who all have it at their disposal do not make full use. They draw from it only pleasure, pain and indispensable acts, such as living. Sometimes they become identical with it; sometimes again they forget its existence for a space; and at one moment mere brutes, at another pure spirits, they know not what multi-tudinous bonds with all things they have in themselves, and of what a marvelous substance they are made.

[...]

O body of mine, that recallest to me at every moment this tempering of my tendencies, this equilibrium of thy organs, these true proportions of thy parts, which make thee to be and to stablish thyself ever anew in the very heart of moving things; keep watch over my work; teach me secretly the demands of nature, and impart to me that great art, with which thou art endowed even as by it thou art made, of surviving the seasons, and of saving thee from the incidents of chance. Grant me to find in thy alliance the feeling of what is true; temper, strengthen, and confirm my thoughts. Perishable as thou art, thou art far less so than my dreams. Thou endurest a little longer than a fancy; thou payest for my acts, and dost expiate my errors. Instrument, thou, of life, thou art for each one of us the sole being which can be compared with the universe. The entire sphere always has thee for a center. O mutual object of attention of all the starry heavens! Thou art indeed the measure of the world, of which my soul presents me with the shell alone. She knows it to be without depth, and knows it to so little purpose that she sometimes would class it among her dreams; she doubts the sun... Doting on her ephemeral fabrication, she thinks herself capable of an infinity of differents realities; she imagines that other worlds exist, but thou recallest her to thyself, as the anchor calls back the ship...[14]

This is Eupalinos' prayer to the body. Intellectual abstraction distances us from being; the body re-establishes the measure. All metaphysics should therefore contain a serious ontology of matter, and, in the first instance, of living matter, in order to restore to *eros poietikós* what is its due: the propulsive role in generating the work (*ergon*), from which *only conceptual* knowledge appears to have ousted it. And, furthermore, it is the *intermediate world* between matter (body) and intelligible idea which violently comes into play at this point, the *metaxý ti* which we have already seen distinguishing the *daimones*, the «intermediate forms» of the living being which «being midway between the two [elements] , bridge the gap, so that the whole is reunited with itself» (*Symp.* 202 e). An entire world of phantasmal forms runs between the two poles of being and guarantees the compactness of the cosmic structure, its «being as a whole». The analogy applies here (which Plato will resume in *Epinomis*, 984-5) between *kosmos* and *politeía*, with the latter – understood in its broadest sense – as a political *kosmos*, poietically constructed by a *eîdos ti metaxý*, the true *nomos* of the world, where *nomos* is not simply 'law', but the concrete order and the 'intermediate form' of the political organisation of life on earth.[15]

Valéry's Socrates regrets the original unity of *building* and *knowledge* of which the *eros poietikós*, always looking for its complementary principles in *logos* and in *téchne*, is the central mythical depiction. He views with nostalgia that other Socrates who once questioned, eager to learn, the foreign woman from Mantinea. An entire life has gone by, and the Socrates of *Eupalinos* despairs of being able to recompose what is now dissociated: the two poles of building the body and of intellectual knowledge. This dissociation is perhaps the destiny of Western metaphysics, its ultimate point of arrival:

> PHAEDRUS: I now understand how you could hesitate between *constructing* and *knowing*.
>
> SOCRATES: One has to choose between being a man and being a mind. Man can act only because he can ignore, and content himself with a part of this knowledge which is his peculiar extravagance, a knowledge that is somewhat more extensive than is necessary![16]

"Ignorance" as a condition of imperfect human action! In fact, with Socrates – I am now speaking of the historical Socrates –

the knowledge of *praxis* was born, and simultaneously the obscuration of that of *poíesis* began. But in Socrates the *daimon* of poietics, more than ever alive, always allowed awareness of the fact that the birth of the work is not a matter of *force* (even if only *moral force*), but rather of what every Greek would have called *knowledge*.[17] Hence the reaffirmation of the single root of knowing and doing, but also the regret for not having been able to concretely implement this unity - a regret that takes on a lyrical tone in the dialogue between the Socrates of *Eupalinos* and Phaedrus:

> SOCRATES: I should have built, sung... O thoughtful waste of my days! What an artist I have destroyed! What things have I scorned, and alas, what begotten!... I feel like the Judge of my own spiritual Netherworld pronouncing sentence against myself! Whilst the facility of my renowned sayings pursues and afflict me, here I am raising up as Eumenides my actions that did not take place, the works that were never born – those glaring voids, vague and enormous crimes that they were: those murders, the victims of which are imperishable things!...[18]

But it must be said that Valéry, when describing this Socrates, placed undoubtedly *after* the separation between intellectual knowledge and poietics, risks turning him into nothing more than a "modern man". In reality poietics, the constructive doing, of which the Greek concept of *téchne* is a manifestation, never ceases to be *epistéme* also, and in a strong sense. But what then is the relationship between the three concepts: *poíesis*, *téchne* and *epistéme*? And what is the additional relationship between this problem and the question of the intersubjective organisation of social life, of the construction of forms (*eîde*) in order to maintain it? (We recall here, among other things, how poietics, inasmuch as it is the art of "founding" city-states and of "creating" houses destined to be the home of men and families, constitutes one of the fundamental forms of *téchne*).

At this point it is necessary to further analyse the connection which links *téchne* (and, through this, political knowledge, *epistéme politiké*) to the horizon of poietics, of which we have so far shown the fundamental relationship with *eros*.

2. *Poietics and political knowledge.*

b) It is intuitive, and could perhaps be taken for granted, that *téchne* has very little in common with modern technology. What distinguishes the two phenomena first of all is the quality of the bond with *epistéme*, where *epistéme* is naturally something other than "science": the concept in fact rather indicates "reflected knowledge", "(theory of) "knowledge", the place of an intellectual activity which is somehow *external* in relation to the whole process of material production-reproduction of the entities. The fact is that all the entities, occupied by the whole "technology", can by now tolerate only one *epistéme* completely giving way to the technical organisation of existence. In this sense it can be said that the process that subordinates epistemology to "technology", seen as a horizon and as a whole, has now reached its full completion.

In fact, one may ask: which *epistéme* could rise out of "technology" as a whole? The question would appear to be pointless only by admitting the reduction with no residue of *epistéme* to a calculating intellect as an indisputable fact, but in this case keeping silent about the problem – which Heidegger himself, philosopher of technology, indicates with energy[19] – of meditating thought.

Now, necessarily leaving aside the complex problem – which would therefore begin to take shape – of the relationship between the world of technology and meditative thought, I think that in the first place it is necessary to consider how both technology and the original Greek concept of *téchne* cannot be bent to an interpretation which sees them reduced in an anthropomorphic (= man as actor-author of the technical process) and instrumental manner (= technology as a simple "neutral" relationship between medium and end), but rather they require to be subjected to an in-depth analysis on an ontological level, which can only be done through the comparison with the category of *poíesis*.

In *Die Frage nach der Technik*,[20] Heidegger openly claims that *poíesis* is not so much the mere productive action attributable to a subject-man, but rather the «bringing forth» (*Hervor-bringen*) something of the «unveiling manner (*Entbergen*) of its truth». This is the very essence of *poíesis* as technology, or technique: «Technology, therefore, is not simply a medium. Technology is one of the manners of the unveiling. If we focus on this fact, a completely different field opens up before us as regards the essence of technology. It is the scope of unveiling, i.e., of truth»[21] I wish to emphasise here how the problem of the essence of *poíesis* – for whose definition we have already found numerous and important traces in the passages of the *Symposium* examined so far – is compared by Heidegger with that of *truth* (*alétheia*) of the thing produced, which takes place in the manner of unveiling (from *a-lantháno*). (Stated in only apparently more radical terms: one of the central ways in which truth can be conceived passes through the medium of poietics. Truth itself is the peak of a *poietic construction* process).

Thus the theme of the *forms* (*eîde*) *of human doing* as *forms of truth* is fully presented. This theme is the object of the grand finale of Diotima's speech (*Symp.* 210a - 212b) and is also the inspiring principle of the *Seventh letter*, at the point where Plato, highlighting the nexus between logos (as *epistéme*) and eros (as mystical revelation), argues against the inability of the majority to recognise the *problem of truth* that lies behind every political construction, at every *téchne* of politics:

> This, however, I can declare of all those who have written or will write claiming to have clear what I am laboriously investigating [...]: it is not possible, in my opinion, that they have understood the meaning of these researches. On these subjects, on the contrary, there never has been and never will be something written by me. We should not speak of this as we do for other sciences (*rhetòn gar oudamôs estin ōs alla mathémata*), but when one is very familiar with these problems, when one lives with them, then the truth shines suddenly (*exaíphnes*) in the soul, like a flame from a spark, and of itself it feeds afterwards.[22]

According to Plato, the ethical forms reached by the contemplative person at the end of the long process described in the *Symposium*, 211c-d, would be endowed with a deeply rooting force: the thought which *builds to inhabit* would tend towards these, and therefore would not disperse the intensity of the vision, or *theoría*. For Heidegger, too, the essence of building is mainly "to inhabit". It is certainly not impossible to deepen the connection which links this

Heideggerian belief to the most genuine Platonic perspective, particularly when bearing in mind that it is precisely the essay *Bauen - Wohnen - Denken*[23] which gives us the best indications in this sense.[24]

That "building", as *téchne* of the *polis*, *political téchne*, is truly oriented towards rooting, towards man's "inhabiting", constitutes – as is without a doubt Plato's viewpoint, but also Heidegger's interpretation, – a cognitive or noetic *statement*: perhaps one of the most significant statements concerning man's "situation", understood as "collocation" or *Ortung*. It follows that *téchne* (unlike technology) is necessarily, and not accidentally, *rooting*. Hence its *politicisation*, since its «doing» is (and cannot be other than) «building for the *polis*». *Materially rooted* houses, dwellings, constitutions are its work (which is not simply its «product», as Jean Beaufret reminds us, quoting in this regard a regretful Balzac: «Nous avons des *produits,* nous n'avons plus *d'oeuvres!*»).[25] Well, houses, dwellings, constitutions, are – modelled and solidified forms – of *téchne*, not viewed mimetically-naturalistically as "art" (which is illusion, a "third-degree" detachment from nature itself,[26] but methexically as the direct participation in the ethical idea - where *méthexis* evidently refers to the *metaxý* of the *Symposium*.

I owe the observation of the necessary coexistence of a tension towards order within each *dérèglement* which is technically finalised (and finalised *in any direction*, including the one considered axiologically "evil"), to a brilliant essay by Luc Brisson.[27] I limit myself to pointing out that the symbolic image of *poietic order* tends normally to attract to itself that of *erotic disorder*. For the latter, indeed, it is difficult even to set up a corresponding symbolic image. The anthropological investigation shows us how we mostly resort to images of an extremely weakened or "diffuse" order from a Dionysus standpoint, but even Dionysus has *his own* order!

Eros too – the par excellence power that throws off balance, but also the generator of works and crafts, – has its own order. On the contrary, eros should possibly be understood as *the other aspect* of *téchne*, which – lying together with eros on the common horizon of *poíesis* – represents the latter's consolidation in terms of objective knowledge. At this point the emphasis has already clearly shifted to the moment of truth which characterizes *téchne* as knowledge of order, knowledge of the political order, *epistéme politiké*: even destruction, the «acting in negative» of the nihilist, requires the existence of a *téchne* for its effectivity, which therefore possesses – as a common language – an own involuntary constructive tension. This is because *téchne* can produce negative contents, but the act of producing necessarily originates from the negative, presenting itself as an unexpected communicative horizon and immediately placing the concrete contents of action in the background. (Thus Gide's Lafcade, in *Les caves du Vatican*, produces a gratuitous "act" which is simply the negative work in which his *poíesis* is consolidated).

It is clear that here the problem begins to become that – with a very difficult solution – of the ontological foundation of constructive doing. And the *téchne* affects, as *téchne tẽ politeías*, technique of the *polis*, the theme of the intersubjective constitution of a communicating community, as well as its concrete organisational forms. The formal foundation of a community has always been the central theme of politics and law; the relationship between these two entities, intended as categories, and poietics, i.e. the horizon of constructive doing as a metaphysical horizon, has almost never (or certainly never) appear to have been problematized. I will try to provide some elements of reflection in view of such a problematization in the following point.

c) Law is essentially constructive doing for the duration. The system is *man's home* in a hostile-propitious, alien-familiar, nature, ultimately a mystery. Within, man's home-right appears as the universal coherence of actions within the sphere of non-hostility. There is no humanisation without progressive, edifying time, a time which is at least to a minimum extent peaceful, an institutional time. It is therefore wrong to see justice as the legal value par excellence: in many systems it is secondary; the structural juridical value is perhaps rather the *continuity* (in space, in time) of actions, of human ideas.

'Duration' and 'institution' are the two poles around which law rotates in its constitutive function of a stable experience against the power of disappearance. Although not fully thematising the theoretical scope of this problem, the traditional institutional theories provide the most significant elements of analysis. It is the theme of *constitution* (understood, as we have said, not only in the normative-formal sense, but also in the juridical-material one) which centralises upon itself, in its pregnancy, the greatest number of theoretical deve-lopments: so for Hauriou

> institutions (constitutions) represent in law [...] the categories of duration, continuity and reality; they, in which the founda-tion of continuity in social things resides, [...] juridically occu-py the duration, and their solid concatenation intersects with the lighter fabric of transient juridical relations. [28]

As regards the constitutional order as an institution, Mortati speaks of an actual «ontological element of law», organised on the basis of supra- and sub-order positions, over which the will of a "founder" presides.[29] But what is more specifically, on a metaphysical level, *duration*, this concept that constitutes the real "fabric" of which the law structure is made, as an area of the human construct-to-inhabit concept? Once again, the jurist Mortati begins to define, in relation to the key concept of 'constitution', the hidden connection that exists between the technical-juridical analysis and the onto-pheno-menological analysis, attentive to what we might call the "eidetic" dimension of the law. I quote in full:

> The word 'constitution' [...], valid for every branch of know-ledge that seeks to investigate the intimate and truest essence of an entity, aims to designate that trait, or that set of traits, considered necessary to identify each of these entities, differentiating it from the others, and therefore intended to accompany it through-out its life cycle [...].
>
> Having thus considered the principle of order as imma-nent in the constitution of a body, one must consider as its necessary attributes: *a*) priority (logical, not temporal, given that the body begins to exist at the very same instant in which the principle becomes operative) in relation to the single parts or to the single manifestations of life; *b)* pre-eminence, which derives from the conditioning function of the concrete mani-festations of its activity; *c) permanence in time*, since the birth and extinction of the body itself is linked to it. [...] Unlike the natural order, the human one is not given but *constructed*, thus its existence is conditioned by the emergence of an element capable of asserting, beyond the oscillating and shifting wills of the individual members, the need for *constancy* in the beha-

viours necessary to keep the group united, for as long as is necessary for the satisfaction of human needs.[30]

Constitution, understood in the broadest sense – as a general way of human "establishing", and not as a specific act, – is linked to the desire for permanence-predictability and to the fixation of the becoming. Going back on a metaphysical plane, in other words constitution would therefore be nothing but a mechanism, produced by constructive doing for the duration, intended to "hold" what we could define as the metaphysical scandal of becoming: i.e. the fact that being exits itself and falls into time, which is disintegration. Aristotle had already observed how the ancients had always had a strange feeling, composed of indignation and derision, towards those who forwent building this shelter, presenting themselves as a creature «beyond the law», «which has no ties, and is like the piece of a game placed at random».[31] Thus, if it is true that «rule implies duration», inasmuch as law is a rule, it is marked by a necessary vocation towards overcoming the precept-based *pointillism* in the direction of constitution. The main difference between command and rule (usually neglected due to insensitivity towards the problem of time) lies in this: that the command requires fulfillment as a "now" (both in the present and in the future: do this *immediately*, do this *tomorrow*); whilst the rule requires it *forever*, or at least for a given *period of time*. Therefore, the action which conforms to the rule, becoming regular action, acquires duration. It is also *ascetic time*, the energy accumulator, which desires duration, and therefore enables the rooting *poieîn*. This is contrary to what occurs in what we might call the immediate perception of time, i.e. mystical *time*, which tends to be incarnated and exhausted in the moment of decision (think of the *Jetztzeit* described by Walter Benjamin), to grasp the *kairós*.

If the passing of moments is really transcended in duration, then it can be said with Bergson that duration is something that moves *inversely* in relation to time, as the negation (or at least the «slowing down») of the flow:

> our duration is just a moment that replaces a moment: thus, there would never be anything but the present, no prolongation of the past into the present, no evolution, no concrete duration. Duration is the continuous progress of the past which gnaws into the future and which swells as it advances.[32]

But Bergson ends up by providing an exclusively internalised, conscientious vision of the phenomena in which duration is shown, removing the concept from all possible applications in the field of a social ontology that wants to take into consideration poietic activity. I can only refer here to the analysis formulated on the subject by Eric Voegelin, who – despite other possible defects – still has the merit of keeping attention focused on the problem of the constitution of intersubjectivity, beyond any questionable metaphysics of the ego.[33]

In any case, the Greek *polis* remains the model of institution as regards duration, whose bases – which can only be sociologically "restricted" – allow the full development of spiritually formed individualities. Leo Strauss notes that

> when speaking of constitution, we think of government: we do not necessarily think of government when speaking of the way of life of a community. [...] But a city is a community commensurate with man's natural power of firsthand or direct knowledge. It is a community which can be taken in in one view, or in which a mature man can find his bearings through his own observation, without having to rely habitually on indirect information in matters of vital importance. *For direct knowledge of men can safely be replaced by indirect knowledge only so far as the individuals who make up the political multitude are uniform or "mass-men"* [...]. Just as man's natural power of firsthand knowledge, so power of love or of factive concern, is by nature limited; *the limits of the city coincide with the range of man's active concern with non anonymous individuals.*[34]

It must be recognised that the Popper myth of open society did not capture this dimension, optimistically glossing over the harsh observation of the fact that

> an open or all-comprehensive society would consist of many societies which are on vastly different levels of political maturity, and the chances are overwhelming that the lower societies would drag down the higher ones. *An open or all-comprehensive society will exist on a lower level of humanity than a closed society, which, through generations, has made a supreme effort toward human perfection.* The prospects for the existence of a good society are

therefore greater if there is a *multitude of independent societies* than if there is only one independent society.[35]

We often risk forgetting that the forms of constitution of social existence aimed at a goal of spiritual development of individuals are the fruit of 'constructive doing', or poietic art, which corresponds to a precise level of political knowledge (*politiké epistéme*). The question that must be posed is therefore: how can we identify the forms of intersubjective organisation that most allow the development of ʹconstructive doingʹ as an indispensable creative experience for man? How can we promote these forms? These fundamental questions should be answered by a non-reductive science of politics capable of intelligently deciphering the voice of Diotima, transferring what she expresses about the problem of the essence of *eros poietikós* to the level where the other problem is located – not so unconnected therefore, as we have seen, – concerning a *poietics of politics*.

I believe that the themes we have touched on last will allow us to return to the passage of the *Symposium* from which we started (209a) and perhaps, to read it differently.

X. Outlines of Conventionalist Ethics

> *There is no truth upon which to construct one's*
> *own behavior. In order to keep the society of mankind*
> *on its feet, however, it is necessary to behave as if this*
> *truth (God?) were to exist. This is the convention that*
> *renders ethics possible. And this –a snake biting its*
> *own tail – is perhaps the only truth applicable for*
> *mankind.*
>
> The New Aenesidemus

> *The rosary of thirteen beads –my father answered*
> *–has the weight of all the heads I have already cut off*
> *in its defense.*
>
> A. de Saint-Exupéry, *Citadelle*, III.

According to the conventionalist epistemology that has developed starting from the reflection contained in the Nietzschean *Posthumous Fragments*, it is well-known that ideas cannot be considered 'true' if not to the extent that they are somehow 'experienced', or rather embodied in some specific way of life.[1] This is not a simple matter of individual morality (reconciling one's own views with one's own actions), but a theoretical utterance: there is no truth beyond that which is embodied; that is to say that there is no appreciable reality in human terms beyond that which is effectively experienced by an individual and by that individual's way of life. This gives rise to a consistently anti-intellectual position, according to which life is always worth more than an idea or than any ethical dimension of value, having character pre-eminence over the intellect, image pre-eminence over the concept, and sensitivity pre-eminence over analysis.

Ideas are therefore not the terrain in which the decisions and choices that really matter for the behavior of mankind flourish: an idea is not a substance that contains its own 'truth'.[2] The fundamental principle of a conventionalist epistemology is that no postulate establishing a system of values can be subject to any criterion of truth. The 'truth' of a system of values can be established instead starting with the acceptance of certain postulates, but only in a pragmatic manner, remaining within the system of communication established between those who choose to recognize these postulates.

The 'truth' underlying scientific knowledge does not escape from this rule: the scientific perspective is nothing more than one perspective among others, in which reason typically plays an instrumental role: it is not a value in itself, but is only a tool that is justified for its pragmatic utility within a given communication system.

1. *Convention.*

The lengthy development of European thought, from fourth and fifth century early modernity to Nietzsche, represents the historical theater of conventionalist epistemology, which is characterized by the radical critique, and subsequent refusal, of the "natural order" concept as a general principle of explanation. As early as with Montaigne, the anthropological concept of the early modern age provides evidence that there is no universal human model, but that there are simply a plurality of possible "cultures", each of which is characterized by its own laws. This inspired the positive concept of difference, which consists of recognizing (and desiring) a diversity of ways of life.

This diversity is a good thing. Every cultural enrichment is based on diversity. The diversity of the world's ways of life lies in the fact that every culture, every people (whatever meaning one wishes to give to this concept), has its own rules, and contains a system of meanings whose essential points cannot be changed at will without that change having repercussions upon all the other parts. This gives rise to a radical criticism of universalism, as well as its archetypal source, which can certainly be identified as monotheistic religion. The concept of a single God implies that of a single, absolute truth. Men must submit themselves to this truth because it is the truth-in-itself; those who do not submit themselves are in error, and those who do are entitled to forcibly remove the others from error, by any means necessary, and in good conscience. Due to its intrinsically universalist nature, monotheism tends to produce an epistemological reductionism (all knowledge is ultimately traced back to the unit) and a political egalitarianism (men are equal in the eyes of God because they have a "reason", free of contingencies, that allows them to discern the "truth", and therefore to save themselves).

Conversely, it must be said that the rejection of the "universals" constitutes the defense, and at the same time the guarantee, carried out in an anti-egalitarian manner, of the individual (of each individual) in his specificity, based on the profound conceptual association between the recognition of the fundamental diversity of beings and the normative indication for inequality,[3] which is necessarily derived from this recognition on the level of concrete assessments.

The "order" that we perceive around us is nothing more than what we place there ourselves, most often without even realizing it (see "*Sinn-hineinlegen*", which describes the process of attributing meaning and value to things in Nietzsche).[4] But we are generally prisoners of an "optical illusion" created by the organizing and classifying structures of our mind: we tend to interpret the logical connections that are established for ease of reasoning between facts, series of facts, circumstances, etc., as "data valid at all times". In reality, how-ever, there is no more "logic" beyond man than there are "natural preordained boundaries."

Man is an animal that gives meaning to things: Once he has "inserted meaning" into things, he tends to believe that that meaning has always been there. Similarly, man has a tendency to interpret entirely neutral series of facts in terms of teleology and purpose.[5] We assume necessity where one could just as well assume chance, without realizing that chance and necessity are ultimately one and the same (see Malcolm Lowry: everything that happens takes place *somehow, anyhow*; the fact that things inevitably are as they are, and not otherwise, obviously cannot give rise to idea that their existence meets a predetermined intention). Taken as a whole, the world is an "orderly chaos", a world of relationships in which order, when achievable, is not for man.

2. *Value.*

The epistemological position of conventionalism gives rise to a fundamental problem: upon which criteria can one construct a system of values once the "universals" and the absolute value, seen as the only criterion of truth, have been rejected? And also: what need is there for such a system? The conventionalist position mustn't be con-fused with a generalized, inhibiting and privative relativism, or rather a hyper-subjectivism that can be expressed by formulas such as «to each his own truth», «everything is akin to anything», «anything goes», etc. Conversely, while we attempt to lay the common groundwork for a certain action or attitude, at the same time we deem it necessary to identify a certain number of criteria that will give real value to one idea rather than another, thereby discriminating between contradictory propositions. This rejection of skeptical hyper-subjectivism is associated with two observations.

First observation: as previously mentioned, man is inseparable from his culture, and from the context (the spatial element) and tradition (the temporal element) to which this culture gives shape. Before anything else, man is born as the heir to a tradition of some sort. He doesn't live on another planet, nor on a deserted island: he is born with a specific heritage, which he can either accept or reject, but which he cannot consider to be different from that which it really is. In particular, this heritage implies a certain number of values, and therefore judgments of value: this gives rise to the need to identify the constituent values of one's own culture, but not without critically "filtering" one's own heritage. In this sense it is useful to adopt a genetic approach, or rather to trace the genealogy of the values themselves (consider the classic questions posed by Nietzsche: Who introduced this value? Under what circumstances? Who is the beneficiary? What are the concrete results of its application?). This is the reason for the interest that we might have in our past, even our distant past: the more we look at the long term, the more we can distinguish, within our own historical heritage, that which has been artificially added from that which has pertained to us from the beginning. Everyone's starting point to this approach lies in obtaining knowledge of one's own identity and belonging. Everyone must choose to accept a heritage in order to be able to reformulate it.

Second observation: a subjective normative element imposes itself and "functions" as an absolute at all times, and in every society. In other words, a society only exists to the extent that certain rules temporarily render themselves absolute. There is no historical example of a society without rules, with the obvious exception of societies in decline. What matters here is not so much the content of the rule (which is variable), as the very existence of the rule (which is constant). The fact that the historical content of a rule changes does not make it reasonable to conclude that its existence is optional.

All this is naturally more evident in static societies, in which, over the course of the centuries, the miraculous efficacy of the rules themselves was derived from the fact that they were perceived as absolute. However, a rule that has been "set" as a convention will no longer be able to «function» as an absolute. In this sense, Nietzsche's expression of «God is dead» is somewhat revealing: God «dies» from the moment in which one begins to wonder about his *raison d'être*, and therefore about his «possible death». (A God that is called into question already no longer exists – although the possibility of new gods still remains).

3. *Anthropology.*

This gives rise to a concept of man whose main characteristics, in reference to the Arnold Gehlen school of though, are worth reconstructing. From this perspective, despite being subject to a whole series of constraints due to his biological condition, man is not a living being like all the others. He is set apart by his greater malleability (which is highlighted by a state of neoteny or "constant youth" – a youth that corresponds to a being's availability to undergo a metamorphoses, or rather a sort of "apprenticeship"). In humans, biological determinism is purely negative. That is to say that it is only expressed in the form of potential. Our psychophysical makeup doesn't "tell" us anything about what we will do; it only "tells" us what we won't do. Within the limits and conditions of our "nature", our freedom remains complete.

Herein lies the difference between instinct and that which, in humans, is referred to as impulse: Impulse does not imply planning in relation to the object. Man is not free to be or not to be the theater of a certain number of impulses, but is free to choose the object in relation to which these impulses are exerted. If we inherit a pile of bricks, we can build what we want with those bricks. The only thing we can't do is transform the bricks into slate or marble. The same thing happens with genetic heritage. Starting with a certain heritage, man can always improve. His statute is always incomplete, and from this situation of incompleteness, he progresses. He is not created once and for all, but ceaselessly continues to create himself. This is the source of his superiority, but also his greatest weakness. The same is true for the collective experiences: with each generation, the heritage is called into question. The alternatives of losing oneself or surpassing oneself can always be posed. Man constructs himself. He changes himself by exerting a constraint upon himself, by taking himself as his own object, by establishing webs of habits within his own behavior,[6] and by fixing objectives and principles linked to his image of himself.

We now return to that which was stated earlier: the only "true" ideas and ways of life are those which are embodied, or rather incorporated within a particular way of life – and the more embodiment there is, or rather the more the idea is rooted in the existing, the more "truth" there is. This is not, however, a sanctification of the existing, because one way of life can always be opposed by another, which is rooted in another system of values and will manifest itself according to another design.

The game of the various ways of life does not depend on acts of force, but on availability, or rather, in the Nietzschean lexicon, on the power lent to transformation. That which is good provides us with a *poïesis* that transforms us by constructing us according to the rules that we have set and with which we identify; that which is bad destroys us in relation to these same rules. In the end, even if the work of man (in the most generic sense of the term) were to become futile, man would still have the need construct himself, to give himself a form, by means of a will to constrain himself.[7]

4. *On the Tragic.*

Constructing yourself, giving yourself form, can also mean: transitioning from the state of an undifferentiated atom, equal to all other atoms, to that of an individual. All are single entities, but not all are individuals. We know the Roman distinction between *animus* and *anima*: an individual is a physical entity that has obtained a soul. It would certainly be unjust for all men, indiscriminately, to have a soul; it is just that some of them, at the end of their self-creation, reach the point of obtaining a soul. The idea of "honor" therefore reflects loyalty

146

to the rule that one has imposed upon oneself, and to the image that one has created of oneself. Montherlant argued that promises made to a dog must also be kept, because that which binds us is not the content of the promise or the recipient, but the fact that the promise was made. Similarly, loyalty to a conviction, or to an "idea", is justified by the mere fact of having subscribed to it – when nothing forced us to subscribe to it in the beginning. Such conduct contains its own justification: loyalty to a rule is justified by the fact that it is a rule – perhaps even a chosen, accepted and desired rule. Hence the importance of style. There is an obvious relationship between style and form. Giving form to the world, and giving oneself form, both mean establishing a style. One cannot, therefore, separate the letter from the spirit, the form from the foundation, just as one cannot separate the container from the content.

In Nietzsche, for example, the characterization of this style, which describes aristocratic morality, is clear: the ability to act against one's own interests. It is precisely the opposite of utilitarian morality, according to which man, being essentially driven by a calculation of instrumental rationality, pursues his "best interests." This does not, on the other hand, imply relapsing into negative asceticism or angelism: a society is not made up of heroes. Sombart defined a "hero" as someone who constantly tries to "give" to life, or rather to invent new ways with which to enrich our existence, as opposed to the "merchant", who continually seeks what can be "obtained" from life, and ways to enrich his own existence. Therefore, from this perspective of moral analysis, which ranges from Nietzsche to Sombart, there would appear to be differentiated ethics, that are, at the same time, irreplaceable. This poses the problem of knowing which duties one is entitled to demand from every living individual – and simultaneously provides the measure of the rights that each living individual might claim.

This principle obviously works both ways: while it is true that the person upon whom the most duties are imposed (or who chooses to impose them upon himself) should have even more rights, it is also true that it is unfair to impose many duties upon those who only have few rights. A right that is not harmonized with a duty quickly becomes a privilege (in the sense commonly attributed to this term). It is therefore perceived as an injustice, and this could legitimize an action aimed at overthrowing the rules that permit it.

From a conventionalist perspective, the 'tragic' arises from the clear perception of a double contradiction: on the one hand between the brevity of human existence and the infinitude of the world, and on the other hand between the fact that we are contained in the world on the material plane and the fact that the world, although immense, is at the same time contained in us on the psychic plane, as a well as on the "spiritual" plane (if I might momentarily return to using that cumbersome word). The ancients understood very well that intensity is a form of "revenge" over brevity; that is to say that they had noted that the intensity of an experience varies in a proportionally opposite manner to its duration (one does not constantly live on the peaks). And if individual character somehow affects fate, it is ultimately fate that determines character.[8] The tragic therefore lies in the notion of *fatum*, or "fate".

The sentiment of *fatum* generates two different and seemingly incompatible attitudes: the admission that each of us may have a destiny, without this causing us, in our inescapable character, to see even the slightest reason to cease trying to change it, if we determine that it does not observe the rules we have set for ourselves (this is the constant theme of Greek tragedy). And once everything has been done according to the rules that we have set for ourselves, not merely accepting the course of things that has actually taken place, but also desiring it. This is precisely that which, according to Nietzsche, can be defined as "saying yes" to fate: an attitude that was already known under the ontological morality of the ancients, and was referred to as *amor fati*.

Epilogue

Form, Decision, Myth.
On the Form of a European Civilization

Although the philosophical concept of form – classically set in opposition to "shapeless" material data, on which it exercises its ordering function as an *eidos* – may suggest a unitary thematic complex, it is evident that it is arranged differently according to the areas to which it refers. This determines, as is well known, the start and the progressive development of completely specific "regional" cognitive approaches, often not even in reciprocal communication, which further accentuate the fragmentation of the very concept in the individual, different sectors in which this is applied. Here one of the results of the rationalization process that characterizes mature modernity is easily recognizable, an outcome described in depth in Weber's sociology (and by the Weber's school), in what have become classical developments. As for the legal form, I believe that an adequate analysis of it can start from what Carl Schmitt observes in the conclusion of chapter two of his *Political Theology*, significantly entitled *The Problem of Sovereignty as the Problem of the Legal Form and of the Decision*,[1] from which it emerges that the idea of legal form emanates from its own rules, which essentially differentiate it from the formalism of technique, aesthetic form (relative to sectors in which forms appear as significant units in relation to the way in which the individual manages to express his *paysage intérieur*, the dynamic flow of his interiority)[2] and from general philosophical form itself.

The fundamental characteristic of legal form lies precisely in the link that binds it to the element of decision. Thus Schmitt in *Political Theology*:

> The confusion spreading in philosophy around the concept of form is repeated with especially disastrous results in sociology

and jurisprudence. Legal form, technical form, aesthetic form, and finally the concept of form in transcendental philosophy denote essentially different things. [...] In the contrast between the subject and the content of a decision and in the proper meaning of the subject lies the problem of the juridical form. It does not have the a priori emptiness of the transcendental form because it arises precisely form the juridically concrete. The juridical form is also not the form of technical precision because the latter has a goal-oriented interest that is essentially material and impersonal. Finally, it is also not the form of aesthetic production, because the latter knows no decision.[3]

Starting from this formulation of the problem, we will try here to make a conclusively in-depth assessment of the theoretical status of juridical form by following its development in Schmitt's reasoning (§ 1); by subsequently addressing some aspects that could be defined as degenerative, present in the interpretation of Weber and of neo-Kantian formalism (§ 2); and by trying to identify some possibilities of applying the philosophical instance of a fundamental "decision for the form" - possibilities not lacking today, in relation to the idea of the "form of a people" – that the text of *Political Theology* suggested, albeit only implicitly (§§ 3 and 4).

1. *Giving form to decision. Specificity of legal form.*

The text of *Political Theology* immediately gets to the crux of the matter in the field of the general theory of law, by clarifying how the problem of legal form essentially lies in the dialectic between regulatory content [*normativer Inhalt*] of a norm or decision and act of will of a deciding subject, and in the necessary superiority of the latter over the former, with the result of constituting in it an autonomous, tendentially arbitrary moment that interrupts the rationalistic linearity of the dialectic between the two concepts.

The act of deciding, considered in its purity as an abstract *Entschiedensein*,[4] is thus characterized by an unavoidable arbitrariness, which interrupts the linear circuit of juridical reasoning, manifesting itself (albeit at different levels of intensity) in every concrete determination of law. and in every single phase of judicial activity. Every concrete juridical decision contains «a moment of indifference from the perspective of content, because the juridical deduction is not traceable in the last detail to its premises».[5]

The problem acquires importance in the field of general theory of law in relation to the centrality thesis, which, on the basis of this interpretive approach, must be attributed to the moment of *law implementation* [*Rechtsverwirklichung*] , understood as the moment in which the decision factor interferes more blatantly in the determined normative content. This is linked to what Schmitt claimed in the important 1921 premise to his book on dictatorship:

> The legal value of the decision as such, irrespective of its material content in justice or equity, has already been made the basis of an investigation into legal practice, in my book *Gesetz und Urteil* of 1912. [...] The continuation of this idea finally resulted in the opposition between the norm of law [*Rechtsnorm*] and the norm of its implementation [*Rechtsverwirklichungsnorm*] ... That treatise showed clearly that it was necessary to examine the critical concept of law implementation [*Rechtsverwirklichung*] , hence dictatorship, and to demonstrate through a description of its historical development in modern State theory that it is impossible to deal with dictatorship *ad hoc*, like before, just through casual struggles over isolated articles of the constitution, and basically to ignore the rest.[6]

Hence, starting from the problem of the implementation of the law, these texts already stress the centrality of the relationship between decision and norm, better clarifying what in chapter two of *Political Theology* will be defined as the *problem of legal form*, by forcing the theoretical distinction/opposition, recognized as being of fundamental importance, between *norm of law and norm of legal implementation*. In this sense, the problem must start from a precise theoretical thesis, which Schmitt draws from the context of general public law. The following:

> If dictatorship designates the exception to a norm, it does not mean any arbitrary negation of a random norm. The immanent dialectic of this concept is essentially that what is negated is the norm, whose authority should be guaranteed by dictatorship throughout its historical-political existence. There might be a difference between the rule of law in its making and the method of its exercise. In terms

of philosophy of law, this is the essence of dictatorship: the general possibility of a separation between the norms of justice and the implementation of law [*Rechtsverwirklichung*].[7]

These theses are directly reflected in *Political Theology*, and precisely in the passages which say the following:

> The legal form is governed by the legal idea and by the necessity of applying a legal thought to a factual situation, which means that it is governed by the self-evolving law [*Rechtsverwirklichung*] in the widest sense. Because the legal idea cannot realize itself, it needs a particular organization and form [«*einer besonderen Gestaltung und Formung*»] before it can translated into reality. Thatholds true for the formation of a general legal norm into a positive law as well as for the application of a positive general legal norm by the judiciary or administration. *A discussion of the peculiarity of the legal form must begin with this.*[8]

The important fact, which deserves attention, is in any case the *personalistic element* that emerges from this type of doctrinal reconstruction: an element that the dominant legal theory in Europe between the nineteenth and twentieth centuries, in its early positivist and subsequently normativist outcomes, constantly intended to remove. A sort of *pathos of objectivity* runs through the entire doctrine of European public law between the nineteenth and twentieth centuries, based on the belief that the impersonality of command is a guarantee of freedom within the formal framework of the rule of law. The most diverse theories of sovereignty, Krabbe's, Preuss's, Kelsen's, all aspire – as Schmitt points out in the most polemical pages of *Political Theology* – to such objectivity, for the sake of overcoming intrusions of personality and command, seen as necessarily recessive and as such combated.

> "The law gives authority" said Locke, and he consciously used the word *law* antithetically to *commissio*, which means the personal command of the monarch. But he did not recognize that the law does not designate to whom it gives authority. *It cannot be just anybody who can execute and realize every desired legal prescription.* The legal prescription, as the norm of decision, only designates *how* decisions should be made, not *who* should

decide. In the absence of a pivotal authority, anybody can refer to the correctness of a content [*inhaltliche Richtigkeit*]. But the pivotal authority is not derived from the norm of decision. Accordingly, the question is that of *competence*, a question that cannot be raised by and much less answered form the content of the legal quality of a maxim.[9]

According to Kelsen, Schmitt continues, the concept of personal right to command is rather – as is well known – the peculiar error that characterizes the doctrine of state sovereignty: the imposing mass of texts such as the *Hauptprobleme* (1911)[10] and *Das Problem der Souveränität* (1920),[11] both of which Schmitt discusses in his *Politische Theologie*, aim at eliminating the very concept of state sovereignty by considering it a negation of the idea of law, since in it «the subjectivism of command» intends to replace the objectively valid norm. For Preuss and Krabbe «all conceptions of personality were aftereffects of absolute monarchy».[12] But all these objections, Schmitt argues,

> fail to recognize that the conception of personality and its connection with formal authority arose from a specific juridical interest, namely, an especially clear awareness of what the essence of the legal decision entails. [...] That it is the instance of competence that renders a decision makes the decision relative, but in certain circumstances absolute and independent of the correctness of its content. [...] The decision becomes instantly independent of argumentative substantiation and receives an autonomous value.[13]

With the consequence that

> looked at normatively, *the decision emanates from nothingness.* The legal force of a decision is different from the result of substantiation [because] a point of ascription cannot be derived from a norm. [...] *The peculiarity of the legal form must be recognized in its pure juridical nature.*[14]

In a word, there is an abysmal distance between the concept of juridical form based on a productive dialectic with the moment of decision and the "formalist" concept of form, which appears both in Max Weber and in all doctrine directly or indirectly influenced by Neokantianism. So at this point our analysis must proceed in this direction.

2. *The formalist concept of form. Weber's technicism and the analytical hegemony.*

Form does not refer to formalism. Reflection on the philosophical problem of form, considered in all its complexity in the light of the dialectic between norm and decision, as mentioned above, leads to theoretical results that are absolutely different, and incompatible with those that characterize both the technical and sociological approach to the problem that is proper to Weber's rationalism, and the various theoretical developments of neo-Kantian criticism. At the point in *Political Theology* from which we started, Schmitt briefly addresses only the first of these two aspects, evidently considering the complexity of the second such as to impede even a simple broaching of the discussion.[15]

> It is possible to distinguish three concepts of form in Max Weber's sociology of law. In one instance, the conceptual specification of the legal content whose legal form, the normative regulation, is as he says, but only as the "causal component of consensual acting" [*kausale Komponente des Einverständnishandelns*]. Then, when he speaks of differentiations in the categories of legal thought, he equates the word *formal* with the words rationalized [*rationalisiert*], professionally trained [*fachmäßig*], and, finally, calculable [«*berechenbar*»]. He thus says that a formally developed law is a complex of conscious maxims of decisions, [*ein Komplex bewußter Entscheidungsmaximen*] and what belongs to it sociologically is the participation of trained lawyers, representatives of the judiciary with civil service status, and others. Professional training, which means rational training [*sic!*] , becomes necessary with the increased need for specialized knowledge. From this is derived the modern rationalization of law toward the specifically juridical and the development of "formal qualities".[16]

The three different uses of the concept of form that Schmitt notes in Weber's thought are therefore related (*a*) to a function of mere conceptualization of a particular juridical content: hence form as a simple "conceptual specification" [*"begriffliche Präzisierung"*] of sociologically significant material data. Schmitt must obviously be referring specifically, for this use, to the treatment Weber gives in the second and fifth sections of his *Rechtssoziologie*, devoted, respectively, to the formal character of objective law and to the distinction between formal and material rationalization[17]; (*b*) to a function of rationalization/specialization of the juridical reality detectable in the classification and relative subdivision of objective law in the individual disciplinary fields (with clear reference to section one of the *Rechtssoziologie*); (*c*) to a typically sociological-empirical function of predictability and calculability of social action deriving, as a direct consequence, from the rationalization referred to in the previous point.

Thus form, as Schmitt explains in the passage that immediately follows, can mean

> first, the transcendental "condition" of juridical cognition [*die transzendentale "Bedingung"der juristischen Erkenntnis*]; second, a regularity, an evenness, derived from repeated practice and professional reasoning [*eine gleichmäßige, aus wiederholter Übung und fachmäßigen Durchdenken entstehende Regelmäßigkeit*]. Because of its evenness and calculability, regularity passes over to the third form, the "rationalistic", that is, technical refinement [*eine auf Berechenbarkeit gerichtete technische Vervollkommung*], which, emerging from either the needs of specialized knowledge or the interests of a juridically educated bureaucracy, is oriented toward calculability and gover-ned by the ideal of frictionless functioning.[18]

Hence Weber's theory oscillates between a purely technical-classificatory meaning of form, i.e., relative to the "conceptual clarification" of a given normative content, and a sociological-juridical meaning aimed at the sociological reconstruction of the professional class of jurists who have the task of forming certain regularities of social action, qualified by the presence of the elements of rationality with respect to the purpose of specialization[19] and calculability/predictability. The dualism made up of a simple conceptual technique of clarification of contents, and of a sociology of law conflated on the empirical registration of social facts assumed in their immediate historicity, clearly could not satisfy the need Schmitt felt to arrive at a more sophisticated "sociology of juristic concepts", since it did not have for the latter's decisive importance what is defined in the text as the «sociological peculiarity of the circle of people who professionally deal with the creation of law» [«*die soziologische Eigenart des Personkreises, der sich berufsmäßig mit der Rechtsgestaltung befaßt*»].

On the basis of Schmitt's critique of Weber in this context, Weber's concept of juridical form, by exhausting itself in an attempt to trace the differentiation of legal concepts to the different backgrounds of legal experts (bureaucratic holders of the jurisdiction or honorary magistrates), is not yet a sociology of legal concepts.[20] The peculiarity of the latter consists instead in the fact that

> this sociology of concepts transcends juridical conceptualization oriented to immediate practical interest. It aims to discover the basic, radically systematic structure and to compare this conceptual structure with the conceptually represented social structure of a certain epoch.[21]

Only a sociology of juridical concepts of this type can lead to an adequate understanding of the problem of juridical form, aiming at identifying the substantial identity between the system of juridical concepts and the conceptually elaborated social structure of a given epoch, and thereby also overcoming the radical dichotomy of *Sein* and *Sollen*, fact and norm, empirical sociology of law and normativistic theory, which first Weber and later Kelsen drew from southern occidental neo-Kantianism. While it is true that Weber's sociological approach leads to seeing the law as «a complex of effective determined motives of a real human action»,[22] it is also true – as Weber himself clearly implies – that a purely juridical consideration of law can only come about by analyzing *Sollen*, and therefore taking the path opened up by normativism. However, Schmitt's interest is oriented towards overcoming the empirical sphere of Weber's juridical sociology, in the sense of recovering a clearer juridical-formal conceptuality. Except that for him, in this sense, the formalization of law leads to a decision and not to a norm. The autonomization of the sociology of law therefore is, for Schmitt, nothing more than the reverse side of the neo-Kantian claim to establish, through a "pure" doctrine, the autonomous sphere of ought-to-be as its mirror opposite: a sphere therefore necessarily complementary.

This is not the place to address the question of the defects of the *Sein/Sollen* dichotomy, which represents the fundamental hypothesis on which first the Kantian and later Neo-Kantian epistemological structure was based, by showing how ontological dualism actually fails, since being precedes and establishes the ought-to-be. Rather to confirm the thesis from which we started, namely that formalism is not the obligatory outcome of the problem of juridical form, much less general philosophical form.

In other words, the philosophical problem of form cannot be dealt with or treated satisfactorily in the framework of the transcendental analytics inspired by post-Kantian neocriticism, as indicated above all by the interpretation of schematism and the consequent re-evaluation of the productive role of the imagination proper to transcendental aesthetics (and of the first version of the analytics in the *Critique of Pure Reason*) contained in Heidegger's classic book on Kantian metaphysics.[23]

Hence it is that we must start from Heidegger with the foundation of a formalist's critique of form, aimed at substantially redimensioning what would become the domain of analytical reason in the West's overall epistemological statute.

> The pure power of imagination carries out the forming of the look of the horizon. But then it does not just 'form' [*bildet*] the intuitable perceivability of the horizon in that it 'creates' [this horizon] as a free turning-toward. Although it is formative in this first sense, it is so in yet a second sense as well, namely, in the sense that in general it provides for something like an 'image' [*Bild*] . [...] The formation of a schema [*Schemabildung*] is the making-sensible of concepts. [...] In such intuitability, what is conceptually intended becomes perceivable for the first time, The schema brings the concept into an image. The Transcendental Schematism is consequently the ground for the inner possibility of ontological knowledge. [...] If the transcendental power of imagination may be shown as the root of transcendence, then the problematic of the Transcendental Deduction and the Schematism first achieves its transparency.[24]

Here Heidegger's interpretation of Kant seems to dismantle, with its hermeneutic power, the constructivistic and systematic ambitions of the project of the intellect's analytical domination over the sentience of the world of life: that resistant sentient material that formalism should entirely subdue. In other words, Heidegger's interpretation highlights how Kant also visualizes the "unknown root" of the transcendental imagination, but that

> in opposition to this unequivocal characterization of the transcendental power of imagination as ta third basic faculty along-side pure sensibility and pure understanding, a characterization which grew form the inner problematic of the *Critique of Pure Reason* itself, the clarification which Kant explicitly gave at the beginning and at the end of his work now speaks,

up to concluding that

Kant shrank back from this unknown root.[25]

The reasons for this "shrinking back" of Kant's, which cause the entire cognitive system described in the *Critique of Pure Reason* to undergo a torsion in an analytical-conceptual sense, will have repercussions on the overall concept of form in the entire philosophical approach of nineteenth and twentieth century neocriticism, determining the hegemony of *Sollen* as an unrelated form, dominated by the logic of pure concept, which from the Marburg School (Cohen, Natorp) to the southern occidental one (the "visionary of logical schemes" Lask[26] much more than Windelband and Rickert) will be transmitted to the early Kelsen's *Hauptprobleme*, in which we expressly read that «The contrast between being and duty is a logical-formal contrast [...] and there is no path that leads from one to the other: the two worlds remain separate from each other by an insuperable abyss»,[27] even coming to see in it «the metalogical principle of a dualistic vision of the world».[28]

The result is that logic has taken over being: a stringent analytic has opposed the function of the productive imagination, with the consequence that, in Kantian terms, the constitutive relationship between aesthetics and transcendental dialectic has been severed by the hegemony of a heavily constricting analytics, which soon went into crisis, but not for this did it stop recurring. In other words, the reason of the late West has built its analytics in the epistemological paradigm of functionalism by moving away from the world of life and manifesting itself in the positive form of law as a simple function of domination.

Formalism thus appears as the logical form of domination: as in the Marburg School, in Kelsen too the transcendental is productive – productive of patterns of reason, of regulating tendencies, formal typologies of language, and science. As with what had already occurred in Kant, at the moment analytics act as a screen between aesthetics and transcendental dialectics, where the former is gradually forced to transform itself from an irreducible experience to a simple content of analytics, so too Kelsen's epistemological framework forms the interpretive (and organizational) scheme of law by first making use of the dual function of the logical purity of theory and its transcendental foundation in the *Grundnorm*. But this is not enough, and later on analytics evolve into a nomodynamics. Instead of wanting to record the data of experience by communicating with the world of life, its form becomes a horizon, a pattern of understanding. The system of positive norms is the very form of command, surpassing the apparent rules of the model of political representation in which the democratic mask of the West is still expressed as a mere fiction. The criticisms directed by much of the early Kelsen's doctrine, and pointing against the emptiness of his formalism, are pure and simple commonplaces, especially if understood in the light of his so-called "voluntaristic breakthrough", which marks the last phase of his thought.[29] Kelsen's thought is always one of normative production of domination, exercised without pretenses, where the analytical system serves to effectively retain reality in its logical form. The very sense of reality is produced here by law.

3. *Deciding on a form. Decision for a people's form.*

At this point we might try to formulate a theoretical hypothesis that allows us to test, by measuring it on a concrete problem of the experience of our time, the validity of the considerations made so far in general terms. It is a question of evaluating to what extent the theoretical connection that links form and decision can be further clarified by the parallel interpretation of two particularly representative texts of the philosophical and theoretical-juridical reflection of the late Weimar (and immediately post-Weimar) period, which appeared after a few years from each other: two texts that recognize in the concepts of form and decision something as the driving force for constructing a community of individuals linked by the represensentation of a lived connection of belonging that makes them a collective identity, a "we". I refer to Schmitt's 1928[30] doctrine of constitution and to Heidegger's 1934 summer semester university course on logic and language.[31]

In his *Verfassungslehre* two thematic strands in particular can be recognized, which immediately prove to be fundamental for constructing a new democratic constitutional order: I refer to the doctrine of constitution-making power and to the theory of the people (*Volkslehre*), two conceptual spheres closely related to each other. Schmitt's discourse on these points is developed essentially in chapter I, § 8 ("The Constitution-Making Power") and in chapter III, § 17 ("The Theory of Democracy") and § 18 ("The People and the Democratic Constitution"). In the same text, the famous definition of constituent power is immediately encountered: «The constitution-making power is the political will, whose power or authority is capable of making the concrete, comprehensive decision over the type and form of its own political existence» (*CT*: 125). A constitution is not based indeed «on a norm, whose justness would be the foundation of its validity. It is based on a political decision» (*ibid.*).

Hence two corollaries. The first, relating to what could be defined as the *"inexhaustibility"* of the constituent power: «The constitution-making power is not expended and eliminated because it was exercised once. [...] This political will remains alongside and above the constitution» (*CT*: 125-6). The second, relating to the theoretical foundation of the idea of the people in the myth of identity and belonging, i.e. to "we-consciousness", which leads to the definition of the relationship between the people and the nation in their strictly conceptual dimension:

> Nation [...] denotes, specifically, the people as a unity capable of political action, with the consciousness of its political distinctiveness and with the will to political existence, while the people not existing as a nation is somehow only something that belongs together ethnically or culturally, but it is not necessarily a bonding of men existing *politically*. [...] What ismeant by the the word 'identity' is the *existential quality of the political unity of the people*

in contrast to any normative, schematic, or fictional types of equality. On the whole and in every detail of its political existence, democracy presupposes a people whose members are similar to one another and who have the will to political existence.[32]

A topic immediately resumed in § 18 of the same text:

The people 'anterior to' and 'above' the constitution. – Under democracy, the people are the subject of the constitution-making power. The democratic understanding sees every constitution, even its *Rechtsstaat* component, as resting on the concrete political decision of the people capable of political action. Every democratic constitution presupposes such a people capable of action. [...] Political democracy, therefore, cannot rest on the inability to distinguish among persons, but rather only on the quality of belonging to a *particular people* [...] This quality of belonging to a people can be defined by very different elements (ideas of common race, belief, common destiny, and tradition). The equality that is part of the essence of democracy thus orients itself internally and not externally: within a democratic State system, all members of the State are equal.[33]

The concept of popular sovereignty presupposes a people which – opposing the artificial order of positive law – projects itself into the past as the result of a process of growth in the levels of awareness of its own historical identity. As H. Lübbe observes, «the people, who in a democracy act as the subject of the constituent power, do not derive their identity a posteriori, that is, starting from the constitution it has given itself. This identity is rather a preconstitutional and historical fact, an absolutely contingent yet not arbitrary fact, unavailable to all those who find themselves belonging to a given people».[34] Hence there is in any case a sort of "unavailable link" connected to an origin, understood «as a common ethnic descent or in the broadest sense of a common cultural heritage»,[35] giving rise to a "we-consciousness" that leads to identifying the national principle in the ethnic element, presenting it as a "believed" or "represented" community (in the sense described in Weber's sociology of communities), in the theorization of a nation of people (*Volksnation*). Where it should be specified that on the basis of this idea of "a people's Nation" (*Volksnation*) the *demos* of the citizens of the State – in order to stabilize itself as a legal association of free and equal political partners – is deeply rooted in the *ethnos* of its community members (*Volksgenossen*). To this end, it is evident that the simple cohesive force of the republican community formation, Habermas conceives of it in his liberal-procedural theory of "constitutional patriotism", is insufficient to achieve such a stabilization. Civic loyalty should instead be anchored, as Böckenförde, among others, notes, in the awareness of a historically determined belonging to a people. [36]

The fundamental, critical point of the "ethno-nationalist" version of the construction of a people[37] is however the following: the people is not a naturalistic datum, which should be taken as such in its definitiveness, but something that must be built. Here Heidegger's interpretation of the construction process of the "we" is grafted on, proposing form and decision on a new level.

It is in fact a profound need for form, or rather a tension to "give shape", the constitutive quest that he introduces in his 1934 course:

> It is not simple to pose the form of the determination for ourselves in an adequate sense. [...] Even where a genuine community entirely determines the self-being, this is not in every respect that which is essential for the community. Even the "we" determines itself by decision [...] The "we" is no pushing together of persons into a mere sum, the "we" is a decision-like one. The "we" is a we that is after the manner of decision. Now, however, it is precisely not placed in our will whether we belong to the a determined people or not; that cannot be decided through our passing of a resolution. For, that is always already decided, without our willing, based on our descent, about which we ourselves have not decided. Citizenship, one can perhaps will, but belongingness to a determined people never. [...] The question thus arises: What is that, a people?[38]

Here the Germans as a people are involved in asking themselves, as the essence of "ourselves". But where does the we as a collectivity come from, if we exclude that it consists of a simple numerical series, in a simple algebraic sum of isolated I's? The we-ourselves is located in the answer that each on his own account, as a questioner, should grapple with and make his own. As we have just seen, the course provides a specific indication: «A decision about who we ourselves are has already been made, that is, we are the people». This means that the people are such by virtue of the decision [*Entscheidung*]: it does not receive its own determination from on high, nor does it even possess a potential value that it would be a matter of implementing through the will. How should we interpret this last statement, if, as is pointed out, the German people are *a* people who are questioning themselves and not *the* people?

Heidegger immediately clarifies that the question about "What-is-that, a people?" does not frame the matter in its effectiveness. The "what" definitively fixes the object and crystallizes it in metaphysical terms, and therefore in an inadequate way. In this sense, there were three possibilities for answering the question posed in those terms:

a) People as body [*Körper*]. – Population constitutes the body of the people. […] Often, we use the word 'people' in the sense of 'race'. But 'race' means not only that which is racial [*rassisch*] as the blood-line in the sense of heredity, of hereditary blood connection and of the drive to live, but means, at the same time, often that which is racy [*rassig*]. This is not, however, confined to corporal to corporeal qualities, but we say, for example, also "snazzy [*rassiges*] car". Racial in the first sense does not by a long shot need to be snazzy, it can rather be very drab. 'People' was now, therefore, at first understood as population, residents, connection of lineages – people as *body* of the people. [...]

b) People as soul [*Seele*]. – In the folk songs, folk festivals and folk customs, the emotional life of the people shows itself, the allegorical form of the fundamental bearing of its *Dasein*. The people is here no longer an arbitrary population and residents, but a certain vicinity of human beings, adapted to grown settlements. It is not established in an arbitrary, unrelated region, but with the settlement, the people first of all constitutes itself with its customs [*Gebräuchen*]. 'People' is taken here in their physical conduct *seelisches Gehaben*] – as *soul* […]

c) People as spirit [*Geist*]. – The separation of a people can, in turn, come about out of standards and points of view, which can be taken from the global culture. And the decision power of a people shall bring it back to its own law. In all of this, where it is about classification, autonomous order, decision, the people is as historical, after the manner of knowing, as according to willing, spiritual: people as *spirit*.[39]

None of these traditional answers lives up to the question. For Heidegger, the determination of human beings as essence equipped with reason, as an animal «with mental power»,[40] fixing itself in the three body-soul-spirit divisions [*Körper-Seele-Geist*], is limited to understanding humanity as the appearance of something that can be described, reducing it to a positivity without movement and without plasticity. «We wanted to turn our back precisely on those representations according to which the human being is taken in the composition of body, soul and spirit» (*ibid.*). For this it becomes necessary to transform the What-question into a Who-question.

> It will depend on replying to the question concerning the essence of the people in the same style in which we asked in general – thus in the course of the question to which the answer "We are the people" has been given: in the course of the Who-question [*Werfrage*]. [...] We heard already that the question "What is this people, which we ourselves are?" *is a question of decision*.[41]

But this *Werfrage* places us before the further question:

> "Are we, then, this people, which we ourselves are?" [...] Do we not have the unique privilege that we can stray from our essence and become untrue to it, that we can lose ourselves and turn into the unessence of our essence and persevere for long in it? [...] The question "Are we the people, which ourselves are?" is perhaps in the highest measure pressing and unavoidable. Then, however, our self-being is in a strange way: We are then in being [*seiend*] not those who we are.. [...] This 'Are' and 'Being' stand under a decision. [...] "Who is this people?" is a question that first gains clarity as question of decision, if we know about decision as such.[42]

Here, with this crucial question on the essence of decision, § 15 of the Heidegger's course on logic opens with the title "Reply to the second interposed question: What does decision mean?". Where it is immediately clarified that this is surely not a reflexive decision, which exhausts itself the moment it is made, but a decision "for being-involved or against the same". It is not a matter of deciding whether we are actually present, but deciding whether, in the face of a project of constructing the meaning of a new community, we want to collaborate or if we want to oppose. It is therefore a matter of arriving at a "resoluteness" ["*Entschlossenheit*"] in relation to a real possibility, which implies assuming responsibility on the part of subjects who recognize themselves in it by taking charge of it.

> The decision, as we have meant it hitherto, was the execution of an affirmative or negative choice of the today and of the hitherto. This deciding, this decisiveness is a closing of one's mind vis-à-vis the happening, instead of an opening up of this happening. Now, we could perhaps say: Decisiveness and resoluteness [*Entschieden-heit und Entschlossenheit*] are the same.[43]

The deciding inception, as Heidegger concludes, introduces the historical dimension of happening as "event".[44] The political community, it has been said, is not something that can be defined in ultimately sociological, or biological terms. A "people's form" must instead be designed by resorting to symbolic resources – myths, images, signs of belonging – drawn from the "life-world", which presuppose – one might add – something very similar to what Blumenberg had intended with the idea of an *Arbeit am Mythos*, that is, the conscious deconstruction/re-elaboration of a common spiritual *traditum*.

4. *Building a political myth.*

The Who-question [*Werfrage*] therefore poses the problem of the constitutive decision of a people – in the twofold genitive, subjective (decision taken by a people) and objective (decision on the essence of a people) meaning – through the construction of an effective political myth. The German people, Heidegger argues in a controversial point of his *Beiträge der Philosophie*, in relying on a completely limiting and merely biological conception of the problem of race, did not prove to be up to the task, which would have been to bring to philosophical comprehension the crucial matter of its identity. It helps to give Heidegger words in full:

> What does mean to be ourselves? All 'bustle' [*Betrieb*], all stirring about, places human beings in motion, and the question

remains as to whether they thereby already 'are'. Indeed, it cannot be denied that they are beings of such a kind, but precisely for that reason the question becomes more pointed: 'are' humans already, if they merely 'are' in this way, merely happen to be extant, and 'is' a people itself if it is concerned merely with the increase and decrease of its stock? Obviously, 'more' belongs to the 'being' of a people; this 'being' is in itself characterized by a specific relationality of essential determinations, the 'unity' of which remains even more obscure. *Whence is supposed to come, for example, the endeavor to bring 'form' to the present body of the people through regulations and 'organization'?* That a human being 'consists' of body-soul-spirit does not say much.[45]

And again:

> Whether personality is understood as the unity of 'spirit-soul-body', or whether this hodge-podge is reversed and, merely assertorically, the body is placed first, nothing changes with regard to the confused thinking which rules here and which evades every question. [...] Would one perhaps attempt to provide a biological foundation for the saying of 'I' [*Ich-Sagen biologisch begründen*]? If not, then the reversal just mentioned is mere trifling, which this way of thinking is, even without the reversal, because the concealed metaphysics of 'body' and 'sensibility', 'soul' and 'spirit', remains here presupposed and unquestioned. [...] If it has been so decided, then all experiences and accomplishments are carried out merely as an expression of a 'self-certain life' and are therefore held to be *organizable*.[46]

It is this last adjective, "organizable", that Heidegger stresses, meaning that only in this way is a mechanical and limiting construction of the "we" form that constitutes the community allowed. This would be dominated as such by the powerful *Machenschaft* of technology, giving rise to a technological colonization of the world of life and to the exclusion of the fundamental task of a search for new symbolic resources, i.e. real devices of meaning, which only an effective political myth is able to provide.

Then the question of a little earlier returns: where should the effort to give "shape" through institutions and regulations to the reality of a given people come from? One could answer: essentially from an operative political myth, a myth founded on two main axes: the first deriving from the reworking of the symbolic material produced by a deep-rooted tradition of civilization, which must be regenerated in a new form; the second deriving from the activity of a charismatic power that becomes a vector of transmission of the *traditum* thus reworked, projecting into the future the realization of the historical destiny of the people to which it belongs.[47]

> There is no spiritual life without leadership [*Führung*] – at least in the context of the formation and standardization of a common cultural will. An apparently consociative [*genossenschaftlich*] function like that which is expressed in the formation and survival of a general juridical persuasion reveals itself, in the light of a deeper investigation, as a permanent *directing* and *being directed*. [...] It is always a question of processes that aim to make a certain spiritual content common or to strengthen the experience lived in it of commonality [*Erlebnis der Gemeinsamkeit*] , with the dual effect of intensifying the life of both the community and the individual.[48]

The point at which the juridical form intervenes in this process is that in which the problem of enhancement arises, in the context of constitutional theory and in the broader planning of the political order, the phase of constructing a "possible" political myth, overcoming the relationship of tension between the individual *Erlebnis* of the subject and the collective *Sinnordnung*, objectified in the community. It is here that the "elaboration of the myth" takes place in the first place in the reactivation of the symbols of belonging from the European past, producing a real effect of integration.[49] This is also what Habermas himself recognizes, in a way that may seem unexpected to some, when in his previously quoted essay he observes:

> If we start from the concept of "we-consciousness", founded on an imagined blood relation or on a cultural identity, of people who share a belief in a common origin, identify one another as "members" of the same community, and thereby set themselves apart from their environment [...] and if the national community appears from the perspective of a generalized constructivism as a "believed" or "imagined commonality" (Max Weber), the invention of the ethnic nation [*Volksnation*] can be given a surprisingly affirma-

tive twist. As a specific manifestation of an universal form of social integration, the quasi-natural aspect even for the scientist who assumes that it is constructed. For once we recognize that the nation is merely a variant of a social universal, the resurgence of the national no longer needs to be explained. When the presumption of normality shifts in favor of ethnonationalism it no longer makes any sense to describe the conflicts that today once again command our attention as symptoms of regression and alienation in need of explanation. [50]

In other words, the problem of giving shape to the we-consciousness is an unavoidable problem in the overall framework of a theory of society that as a whole intends to escape the risk of anomie, and it is the same problem that Europe faces today. in its difficult search for an identity that can restore it to its specific nature as a civilization, as well as a power and bloc of homogeneous interests, with respect to which its is worth what careful observers have effectively summarized, with a prediction that is actually quite self-evident:

> If Europe ceases to aspire to suicide, it will be able to try to play a compensatory role in the evolution of the world system by coming to face, at the head of a coalition of cultures and nations, the United States and China; if instead it continues to run towards a political, cultural, social and biological holocaust […] it will disappear from the scenarios and will turn into a wretched, enslaved Sino-American annexation. [51]

In all this, the topic of political myth, which reaffirms itself starting from the dialectic of form and decision that has been discussed up to now, plays a fundamental role. The specific topic in question is the myth of Europe as a civilization. This topic refers to that need for form that till now only prudent observers have been aware of: the fact that it does not manifest itself simply in the dialectic of the geopolitical clash – which even a prospect of realistic analysis continues to indicate as primary and decisive – but which rather implies the task of building an authentic mentality, starting from common symbolic resources that have their roots in the past, in relation to a people, the European people, which as such does not yet exist.

Notes

Introduction

(1) So for Ayer the difficulties that arise in understanding the relationship, expressed in a causal form, between the two entities are all fictitious problems, arising from the metaphysical conception, devoid of meaning, mind and matter, or mind and material things, as substances (Ayer 1936: espec. chapters VII and VIII). Also, for G. Ryle we owe to Descartes the false approach that leads to the well-known image of the "ghost in the machine" (Ryle 1949).

(2) This is the problem that the chapters of the first part deal with.

(3) I refer, on this concept, to the works of Emanuele Severino (See in particular Severino 1980 and 1981).

(4) See in this sense Ilting 1972 and Henrich 1960.

(5) In these studies I have been able, as is obvious, only to graze the surface of this point, around which, I believe, there lies a question of extraordinary importance, that of the constructive *Ansätze* in view of a (still in some measure) possible cognitive ethic.

(6) See Preti 1957, espec. pp. 107 ff., 132 ff. - Note that on the epistemological level (the paradox is only apparent) a Kelsen is more decisionist than a Schmitt, who – in his constant reference to concrete order (*konkretes Ordnungsdenken*) – always leaves open the possibility of an ontological-material development.

(7) Hans Albert speaks picturesquely in this regard of a «Münchhausen trilemma», meaning by this the triple order of logical difficulties in which any procedure of founding a method in epistemology falls: see Albert 1969 (esp. part I: *The Problem of a Foundation*).

(8) It is interesting to note the semantic difference that exists, in German, between *Entscheidung* (an adiaphorous term) and *Dezision*

(and its derivatives: thus the noun *Dezisionismus* and the adverb *dezisionistisch*), which is evaluative – in a positive or negative sense. In our instance it is sufficient to recall that the *Entscheidungsprozesse* may (or may not) be interpreted as *dezisionistisch*. On this topic see especially Lübbe 1971.

(9) Albert 1969: 73 ff.

(10) See chapter VI: *Naphta, or a* katéchon *for Europe.*

(11) Ethics «must be outside of the world» (Wittgenstein, *Tractatus logico-philosophicus*, 6.41). But the *Tractatus* itself ends up inevitably speaking in the language of ethics.

(12) «... die geschichtliche Macht, die das Erscheinen des Antichrist und das Ende des gegenwärtigen Äon *aufzuhalten* vermag, eine Kraft *qui tenet*, gemäß den Worten des Apostels Paulus im 2. Thessalonicherbrief» [«... the historical power to *restrain* the appearence of the Antichrist and the end of the present eon; it was a power that *withholds*, as the Apostle Paul said in his Second Letter to the Thessalonians»] (Schmitt 1950b: 29; engl. tr.: 60).

(13) This is the core of the embedded 'Viennese' problem that implicitly links Wittgenstein and Musil. In Musil's novel, it is above all the experience of Moosbrugger that can be considered as an exploration of that silent world that lies *beyond decision.*

(14) The quotations are drawn from the *Tractatus*, 6.51. In this respect, the studies that constitute the volume's framework here are the third: *The Baroque creature* and fourth: *Ekstatische Sozietät*. But on this point see also Agamben 1982: 104-115 (eighth day). – I find in two contexts very different and far from each other (Schelling and Lukács) elements of a significant philosophical analysis for the purpose of better illustrating what I mean by "possibility of a positive relationship" between mystical experience (see especially Plato, *Letter VII*, 41 c-d) and what can be called *ethical form* (the "good life"): «To be able to enclose itself in a form, it must certainly be outside any form, but its positive aspect does not consist in that, in its being outside of any form, in its being incomprehensible, but in being able to make itself comprehensible, that is in being free to enclose itself or not enclose itself in a form» (F. Schelling, *Erlanger Vorträge*, Schröter V, 13). – «True

life is beyond forms, but ordinary life is on this side of forms, and goodness is the grace to shatter these forms. Of course most men live without life and do not notice it. Their life is only social, only infra-human; they can be content with their duties and fulfill them. Indeed, for them the fulfillment of obligations is the only possibility to elevate life. Because every ethic is formal: duty is postulated, form – and the more perfect a form is, the more it lives a life of its own, the further it falls from any immediacy. Form is a bridge that distances us; a bridge where we come and go and always arrive within ourselves, without ever encountering each other» (G. Lukács, *Von der Armut am Geist* [1912], in Id. 2011).

Chapter I

(1) For Blumenberg «the Copernican world becomes the metaphor for the critical operation that removes the legitimacy of the principle of teleology, the *causa finalis*, in the series of Aristotelian *causae*; and there is no doubt that only the Copernican metaphor caused the pathos of deteleologization to explode, that a new self-consciousness rests solely on it, linked to the cosmic eccentricity of man» (Blumenberg 1960: 138).

(2) On this point, Löwith had already noted that «it is the weakness of modern Christianity that it is so very modern and so little Christian that it fully accepts the language, the methods and the results of our worldly improvements in the illusion that all these inventions are but neutral means which can easily be christened by moral, if not religious, ends. In reality they are the result of extreme worldliness and self-confidence» (Löwith 1949: 114).

(3) «Die Erkenntnis bedarf keiner Rechtsfertigung, sie rechtfertigt sich selbst, sie verdankt sich nicht Gott, hat nichts mehr von Erleuchtung und gnädigem Teilhabenlassen, sondern ruht in ihrer eigenen Evidenz, der sich Gott und Mensch nicht entziehen können» [«Knowledge needs no justification, it justifies itself with no need to resort to a God. It does not even need enlightenment or grace, but rests on its evidence, which neither God nor man can eliminate»] (Blumenberg 1974: 395).

(4) «Eine Kategorie des geschichtlichen Unrechts» (Blumenberg 1974: 9-74).

(5) Schmitt 1970 (*Nachwort*: 124-5).

(6) See in this regard Koselleck 1959 (especially Chapter III: *Crisis and Philosophy of History*).

(7) See Crocker 1970.

(8) «Every Enlightenment ends up sooner or later finding itself in situations of conflict» (Koselleck 1959: 5).

(9) It is obviously not possible here to even begin to deal with the multiple aspects of these important questions. I will only refer to what Walter Benjamin observed: «The unity of the material and the transcendental object, which constitutes the paradox of the theological *symbol*, is distorted into a relationship between appearance and essence […]. Simultaneously with its profane concept of the symbol, classicism develops its speculative counterpart, that of the *allegorical* [...]» (Benjamin 1998: 160-1). The juridical-humanistic presuppositions of the concept of representation appear clearly here: only a *person* can represent in his own sense: as Carl Schmitt points out, «metaphors as 'projection', 'reflection', 'mirroring', 'emanation', 'transference' denote the search for the 'immanent' objective base. The idea of representation, on the contrary, is so dominated by the thought of personal authority, which both the representative and the re-presented must maintain a personal dignity. This is not an 'inherent in things' concept. Only a person can represent in an eminent sense, and a person endowed with authority – what marks the difference with respect to simple "private" substitution – or an idea that, as soon as it is represented, also personifies» (Schmitt 1923: 44-5).

(10) «They who compare a city and its citizens with a man and his members, almost all say, that he who hath the supreme power in the city is in relation to the whole city, such as the head is to the whole man. But it appears [...] that he who is endued with such a power, whether it be a man or a court, hath a relation to the city, not as that of the head, but of the soul to the body. For it is the soul by which a man hath a will, that is, can either will or nill; so by him who hath the supreme power, and no otherwise, the city hath a will, and can either will or nill. A court of counsellors is rather to be compared with the head, or one counsellor, whose only counsel [...] the chief ruler makes use of in matters of greatest moment: for the office of the head is to counsel, as the soul's is to command» (Hobbes, *De Cive* VI, xix: 89).

(11) Schmitt 1923: 45.

(12) «[Hobbes] could not interpret the nature of man from the vantage point of the maximum of differentiation through the experiences of transcendence so that passion, and especially the fundamental passion, *superbia*, could be discerned as the permanently present danger of the fall from true nature; but he had, on the contrary, to interpret the life of passion as the nature of man so that the phenomena of spiritual life appeared as extremes of *superbia*» (Voegelin 1952: 180).

(13) As Voegelin remarks, «the psychological work of Hobbes was paralleled in his own time by the psychology of Pascal, though Pascal preserved the Christian tradition and described the man who was guided by his passions alone as the man who had fallen a prey to one or the other type of *libido*. And also contemporaneously, with La Rochefoucauld, began the psychology of the man of the 'world' who was motivated by his *amour-propre* (the Augustinian *amor sui*). [...] A specifically 'modern' psychology developed as the empirical psychology of 'modern' man, that is, of the man who was intellectually and spiritually disoriented and hence motivated primarily by his passions» (Voegelin 1952: 185).

(14) Further, as Roman Schnur says, «a mechanism can never be totalizing. It is something external, that is to say, usable to obtain external obedience from the citizens, without ever affecting their interiority, their conscience» (Schnur 1963: 74-75). Truly «ein Mechanismus ist keiner Totalität fähig», but the problem arises when the State – and, through it, the machinery of power – has abandoned all mechanistic metaphors (linked to primitive and obsolete schemes of intervention) and instead fully adopts the *functionalist* model.

(15) Schmitt later dealt with Hobbes' very same aporias in the face of Nazi totalitarianism. His position was very similar to the well-known position of Benito Cereno in Melville's tale. Thus G. Schwab: «From the viewpoint of the citizen the essential characteristic of Schmitt's authoritarian State is the acknowledgement of a private sphere which is similar to Hobbes'. In the *Leviathan* (chapter XXXVII) Hobbes distinguished between 'faith' and 'confession' and maintained that 'faith' may be a private matter, but private judgement ceases as soon as public confession is at stake. Only then the sovereign may decide about the content of *veritas*. Schmitt hinted

in 1938 that despite Germany's strength vis-à-vis the outside world, the interference by the Nazis in the private sphere was having the effect of driving some people [...] to seek refuge in their innermost region. At this point, according to Schmitt, "the counterforce of silence and stillness growth"» (Schwab 1970: 146).

(16) Strauss 1953: 7-8.

(17) See Strauss 1953, Chapter II: *Natural right and the distinction between facts and values.*

(18) *Ibid.*: 27.

(19) Perhaps we can spy an analogy within the modes of nihilism, between this "adhering to destiny" and Nietzsche's *Ja-sagen.*

(20) «The names of *just, injust, justice, injustice,* are equivocal, and signify diversly. For justice and injustice [...] signify the same thing with *no injury* and *injury,* and denominate the action *just* or *injust,* but not the man so. For they denominate him *guilty* or *not guilty.* But when justice or injustice are attributed to men, they signify *proneness,* and affection and inclination of nature, that is to say passions of the mind, apt to produce just and injust actions» (Hobbes, *Elements,* I, III, *De Corpore politico*: 97).

(21) Viano 1962: 392.

(22) In fact, this topic appears to have been completely absent in ancient-classical political philosophy: «This is why the ancients did not bother to examine how morality can act on emotions, they did not bother to formulate a theory of duties that would allow ethics to adhere to all the situations of the human condition. But this fundamental conceptual error has its correspondent in a grave error of content of ancient morality: the privilege of the private good over the public good. Methodological inversion – consisting in the consideration of ends regardless of the ins-truments – and inversion of content – consisting in the privilege of the private good over the public good – therefore go hand in hand» (Viano: 362). Here too, Viano adopts an evaluative viewpoint that is the exact opposite of Strauss's.

(23) *Ibid.*: 391.

(24) *Ibid.*: 392.

(25) Strauss 1953: 42. - Weber's quotations are taken from Weber 1920: 204, and from Weber 1922b: 469-470 and 150-151.

(26) We have already mentioned above that Strauss defined «noble nihilism» as the nihilism to which Weber's theses necessarily lead. This in fact stems not «from a primary indifference to everything noble but from the alleged or real insight into the baseless character of everything thought to be noble» (Strauss 1953: 47). Weber recognized – it is true – that «whatever preferences I may have or choose, I must act rationally: I must be honest with myself, I must be consistent in my adherence to my fundamental objectives, and I must rationally choose the means required by my ends». But why? Strauss asks. «What difference can this still make after we have been reduced to a condition in which the maxims of the heartless voluptuary as well as those of the sentimental philistine have to be regarded as no less defensible than those of the idealist, of the gentleman, or the saint?» *(ibid.*: 48). Here Strauss actually touches on the crucial point, the authentic internal weakness in Weber's admirable intellectual construction, namely the desire to control *in extremis* the outcomes of nihilism: an operation about which Nietzsche would have *laughed*.

(27) See Sortais 1920; Pintard 1943; Skinner 1966.

(28) Voltaire 1752 (édition 1878): 138.

(29) *L'Utopie de Thomas Morus, Chancelier d'Angleterre*, Amsterdam: Jean Blaeu 1643. See also Sorbière's translation of *De Cive* (1649): *Elemens philosophiques du Citoyen. Traicté politique, où des Fondemens de la Société civile sont descouverts*, par Thomas Hobbes, *ibidem*.

(30) Sorbière 1657: part II, especially second *discours*: *Si la malice des hommes, qui vient de la Nature corrompue, n'est point augmentée en l'Estat du Gouvernement moins absolu, par les defauts de la société* (: 80-6), and third *discours*: *Où les raisons d'une fausse prudence luy sont proposées à réfuter* (: 113-130).

(31) «Points de départ différents, mais itinéraires entrecroisés: Sorbière va se retrouver bientôt au même carrefour que Hobbes [...]. Ainsi, aux yeux de l'Anglais, parce que l'homme naturel est mauvais, l'autorité et la crainte sont le ciment nécessaire des sociétés: pour son disciple, l'homme naturellement bon s'est corrompu dans l'état de société,

et il faut l'autorité et la crainte pour l'empêcher de nuire. De toute façon la contrainte est indispensable: une anticipation sur les idées de Jean-Jacques ramène à celles de Hobbes l'érudit qu'un souvenir de Montaigne en avait écarté» (Pintard 1943: 554).

(32) «L'histoire de nos guerres civiles est toute recente, et elle est si desadvantageuse à nostre Nation, qu'il seroit à desiderer qu'elle fut supprimée» (Sorbière, *Réflexions politiques sur la sagesse du roy et la fidelité de ses ministres, faites en sept. 1664 à Nantes*, c. 472 v.). – Sorbière draws, like Hobbes, his convictions from the horrors of the English civil war. He sees in the people, especially if in this they are instilled potentially revolutionary religious faiths, the most serious danger for order: «L'on a veu à Londres, que petit pelotons de fanatiques, qui ont couru les rues pour faire souslever le peuple: mais qui n'ont pas esté suivis, et qui se sont tout incontinent dissipez» (Sorbière 1664: 48).

(33) «Ils cherchent chacun ce qu'il leur faut, et font part du superflu à ceux qui n'ont peu aller querir le nécessaire ou qui n'ont pas esté assés heureux por le trouver. La faim, la soif, les injures de l'air, sont tot ce qu'ils craignent. Ils y remedient, et puis se tiennent coys, ou se divertissent sans faire mal à personne» (Sorbière 1657: *Deuxième discours sceptique*: 82-3).

(34) «Je doute si tout nostre malheur et nostre sottise ne vient pas de ce que nous ne vivons pas, dans nos societez civiles de l'Europe, ny tout à fait sous l'Estat de l'Empire, ny rendus à celuy de la Nature. Nous sommes en un certain milieu où se forment, comme en la moyenne region de l'air, la tempeste et les orages. Nos esprits sont partagés entre ces deux Estats; et tantost la sujection aux Puissances souveraines nous abbat le courage, tantost les pensées de liberté nous le relevent» (Sorbière 1657: 83*).

(35) «Relascher un peu de cette vertu rigoreuse dont les Stoïciens nous donnent des idées qu'il est impossible d'imiter» (Sorbière 1657: *Troisième discours sceptique*).

(36) See *Discours de Sorbière à l'ouverture de l'Académie des Physiciens qui s'assemblent chez M. de Montemor* (1663), quoted by Pintard 1943: 558.

(37) Especially by Chinard 1948. But see, in the past, the edition of Pascal's *Pensées* edited by Condorcet, and Sainte-Beuve in *Port-Royal.*

(38) See, approximately, the *Pensées* from 291 to 338 in the Brunschvicg edition. As Del Noce observes, «Sainte-Beuve wrote that Pascal, if

he had not been a Christian, would have been Machiavelli. Let us note the depth of the phrase – not Plato, not St. Augustine, not Aristotle, not St. Thomas – and let us try to penetrate to its core. There is a truly impressive coincidence between Pascal's political ideas and those who followed in Machiavelli's footsteps, the *libertins érudits*: except that, of course, those ideas were reformulated by Pascal as Augustinian pessimism taken to the extreme. Nothing left of ancient Christian natural law. It is in force the principle of legitimacy [...]». It is, in the abbreviated formula, of «a conservatism founded however not on the rationality of the present order, but on the idea that every order, because historical, is neither rational nor sacred [...]». Any social order is *folly*, although – Pascal maintains – «true Christians obey follies» (*Pensées*, fr. 338 Brunschvicg). Del Noce concludes: «The comparison with libertine thought is evident, because what characterized it was the coincidence between the identification of the critical spirit with the search for radical desecration (the will to escape 'naivety') and the most radical denial of the revolutionary spirit [...]. Only that, while libertine thought led to the defense of the Prince in the Machiavellian sense as an ideal type, Pascal wants to reaffirm the indifference of politics for the spiritual life. Of course, politics has its own logic, which must be accepted. But the real good does not lie there; it is a reality from which we must free ourselves internally, in the quest to reach the supernatural level of charity» (Del Noce 1964: 211-3).

(39) Auerbach 1959: 41.

(40) Spink 1960: 82-3.

(41) On the basis of Heidegger's and Löwith's indications, the validity of the theoretical line, at the heart of nihilist thought, between Hobbes and Nietzsche makes here a dramatic return. I believe that a political anthropology – a theme that Arnold Gehlen insisted on – today needs above all to benefit from a disenchanted analysis of historical phenomena linked to the will to power, long exorcised by idealistic and flatly rationalistic interpretations.

(42) Löwith 1949: 192. «If the universe is neither eternal and divine, as it was for the ancients, nor transient but created, as it is for the Christians, there remains only one aspect: the sheer contingency of its mere "existence"» (ibid., 201). See, in addition to the afore-quoted Voegelin, the very personal discussion of Taubes 1947.

(43) Pintard 1943: 570.

(44) Löwith 1949: 269.

(45) *Ibidem.*

(46) Del Noce 1964: 179.

(47) On the problematic qualification of seventeenth-century French free thought as an already "social" thought, see Spink 1960. Naturally, we need to understand the meaning Spink attributes to the term.

(48) See in this sense Del Noce 1965.

(49) Jonas 1963: 290-1. «Freedom from abuse and freedom from non-use, equivalents in their indiscrimination, are only alternative expressions of the same acosmism» (*ibidem*). – In a similar sense one might think of Kierkegaard's comment on the idea of Don Giovanni: that it «belongs to Christianity» (Kierkegaard 1843: 97). While it is true that any position indirectly poses what it excludes, hence the paradoxical but historically stimulating conclusion that sensuality as a principle, a force, a system was proposed for the first time by Christianity. In this sense, Christianity, which ascetically drove sensuality out of the world, is also what led it there, since sensuality became the obligatory correlate of the spirit only through Christianity.

(50) See on this point Goldmann 1955 and Taveneaux 1965.

(51) In the same sense of Schmitt 1947 and 1950.

(52) Benjamin 1998: 66.

Chapter II

(1) Benjamin 1928: 65.

(2) Schmitt 1922: 11 ff. («*Definition der Souveränität*»). – So even Benjamin commences the part dedicated to *Trauerspiel und Tragödie* of his work on German Baroque drama by speaking of «necessary tendency towards the extreme which, in philosophical investigations constitutes the norm in the formation of concepts» [«*die notwendige Richtung aufs Extreme, als welche in philosopphischen Untersuchungen die Norm der Be-*

griffsbildung gibt»] (Benjamin 1998: 57). See also Schnur: «The disagreement between the contenders leads to the extreme situation: while for the conformists there is always normality, conformity to the rule, and for non-conformists all that is interesting is unusual, determined by the exceptional instance» (Schnur 1963: 44).

(3) «The fact that every dictatorship contains the exception with respect to a norm does not mean that it is a casual denial of any rule. The inner dialectic of the concept lies in this, that the negation concerns precisely the norm that is to be enforced and the method adopted to enforce it. In terms of the philosophy of law, here is the essence of dictatorship, that is, in the general possibility of a separation between the norms of law and the norms for enforcing the law [*Rechtsverwirklichung*]» (Schmitt 1921: XVI).

(4) «The sovereign, the principal exponent of history, almost serves as its incarnation. […] This extreme doctrine of princely power had its origins in the Counter-Reformation, and was more intelligent and more profound than its modern version. Whereas the modern concept of sovereignty amounts to a supreme executive power on the part of the prince, the Baroque concept emerges from a discussion of the state of emergency, and makes it the most important function of the prince to avert this. The ruler is designated from the outset as the holder of dictatorial power if war, revolt, or other catastrophes should lead to a state of emergency. […]. The theological-juridical mode of thought, which is so characteristic of the century, is an expression of the retarding effect of the overstrained transcendental impulse, which underlies all the provocatively worldly accents of the Baroque. For as an antithesis to the historical ideal of restoration it is haunted by the idea of catastrophe» (Benjamin 1998: 62, 65-6).

(5) See Schnur 1963, Chapter III: «*Die Suspension. Der Zerfall des Außenhalts und seine Folgen*» [«*Suspension. The dissolution of external support and its consequences*»].

(6) Schnur 1963: Chapters V - VI.

(7) Benjamin 1998: 66. Benjamin himself speaks on more than one occasion of «analogies» existing between his own and Schmitt's own thought (see, for example, Benjamin 1997: 886-7).

(8) «Even order is only a phase of respite in the struggle between parties, on the other hand the abyssal nature of politics may be penetrated only for a short time: it can never be completely eliminated and therefore must be reckoned with» (Schnur 1963: 40). But see also chapters V and VI for the connection – the truth only implicit in Schnur – between the concepts of *Abgrund* and 'nihilism': we can say that this connection is motivated by the need to recognize both the exclusive character of the worldly historical experience and the fact that the latter is constantly placed on the edge of an abyss that can nullify it. Hence the irony and the 'non-total' seriousness into which flows the Mannerist disenchantment of which Arnold Gehlen speaks (see Schnur 1963: 41).

(9) See the second part of Castelli 1953, entitled *L'Umanesimo e il demoniaco*.

(10) Schnur 1963: 23-4.

(11) These are the subtitles of the chapter in question, which treat in the author's unmistakable style a subject halfway between aesthetics and political theory. Of note, in this context, is Gómez Moriana 1968.

(12) The part of Benjamin's *Ursprung* that had been published in «Neue Deutsche Beiträge», directed by Hugo von Hofmannsthal (second series, n. 3, August 1927: 89-110) had been subject to the understandable roasting of Panofsky, who in those years, along with Saxl, had authored *Dürers Melancholia*, and was an intellectual type quite distant from Benjamin.

(13) Schnur 1958 and 1959.

(14) See Schnur 1963, Chapter IV: «*Der manieristischer Ordnungsversuch. Ordnung als einzige tragende Idee*». About the limits inherent in a *waltende Gewalt*, we must remember the words of Rudolph II on the point of forsaking the kingdom, in the drama of Grillparzer *Bruderzwist in Habsburg*, Act IV: «Let Matthias reign. He will learn that […] action is difficult as a reality that must be in harmony with every reality». (See Grillparzer 1848).

(15) Benjamin 1998: 71.

(16) On the «apparent Chaos» («*scheinbares Chaos*») and on the spiritual catastrophe of the late sixteenth century in the Mannerist painter El Greco, see Dvořák 1928.

(17) On this sceptical criticism, Horkheimer 1938

(18) See Metz 1963, Graf von Krockow 1958.

(19) «For their actions are not determined by thought, but by changing physical impulses» [«Denn nicht Gedanken, sondern schwankende physische Impulse bestimmen sie»] (Benjamin 1998: 71).

(20) Buchheim 1962. Consider what Gerhard Oestreich exactly affirms: «It is absolutely impossible to speak of total control of the public and personal sphere by the absolute State» (Oestreich 1968: 335).

(21) The desolate flatness of this claim is the true *Feind* for thought. «The desert grows; woe to him who hides a desert in himself!»: Enrico Castelli in one of his essays cited this Nietzschean phrase, establishing an unexpected Pascal-Nietzsche parallel: the "automaton", the "machine" that man builds against the great fear can lead to destruction of the "inner sphere". But the negative thought that opposes it runs the risk of backsliding into moralistic consequences. (On this point see Castelli 1962).

(22) Schnur 1963: 75.

(23) Schmitt 1938, especially par. 7 on the «Leviathan's shadow».

(24) Neumann 1957: 235.

(25) See instead what is observed above, at note 3.

(26) Dangers demonstrated effectively by Koselleck 1959.

(27) See Hocke 1961, especially the chapter entitled *Mannerism and Baroque.* — On the cultural unity of the European traditional Order as "Romània" between the late Middle Age and the first European Mannerism, see Hofmannsthal 1958b. On this concept, Schnur 1963 and Lazzerini 2012. «The cosmopolitan horizon of the old Habspurg Empire was Hofmannsthal's birthright. Venice and Madrid belonged to it no less than "das Wien des Canaletto, Wien von siebzehnhundertsechzig" ["the Vienna of Canaletto, Vienna of seventeen hundred and sixty"]» (Curtius 1973: 137)

(28) The entire discourse reconnects itself to the problem of the 16th-century reception of Machiavellian 'anticonformity' and its criticism.

(29) Hocke 1961: 176.

(30) Where Aquinas' judgement should be recalled: «Sine gratia faciente non potest esse vera pax, sed solum apparens» (*Summa theol.*, IIa, IIae, qu. 23, cit. 2).

(31) The fact remains that beyond any overindulged objectivism and any *sans sujet* process, the phase of individual subjective decision returns to emerge irrepressible.

Chapter III

(1) Goethe 1831, verses 12104-5: «All things transient are but a parable».

(2) As critics have keenly pointed out, the highest and most mature fruit of scholastic philosophy in the Baroque era was the construction of an ontology independent of both theology and Aristotelian physics: «The scholastic philosophy of the Baroque age dissolved the unification of science of being and science of God, that was the way in which the Middle Ages had absorbed Aristotle's *Metaphysics*. The science of being is constituted to independent ontology. The science of God is abandoned to supernatural theology. Natural theology is either abandoned or is subjected to to such and so many conditions of general ontology as to make its speculative results and its apologetic intents truly difficult» (Di Vona 1968: 35). We might add that, while it is true that in the modern world, following the radical critique of the metaphysical foundations of traditional philosophy, meaning is drawn from the universe, or it survives there only as myth or metaphor, it is Baroque thought that, in the most obvious way, enacts a "metaphorical treatment" of the central arguments of ontology.

(3) See Brémond 1923.

(4) While the symbolic indicates «the intimate unity of idea and phenomenon, the allegorical gives way time after time to this meaningful unity through the indication of some other thing. Symbol is

the coinciding of the sensible and the non-sensible, allegory is the significant reference of the sensible to the non-sensible» (Gadamer 1958: 30). But on the subject we should again consider Benjamin 1998, part III: «*Allegory and Trauerspiel*».

(5) See particularly Brémond 1923, esp. vol. II: *L'invasion mystique (1580-1660)*: 585-605.

(6) For all Klein 1970, especially with regard to Mannerism in sixteenth-century Italian art. But Klein's theses on Neoplatonism can also be extended to some fundamental aspects of the Baroque, as I try to show.

(7) Bouillier 1926. Schopenhauer had translated Gracián's *Oraculo manual*, which Nietzsche had read and appreciated, noting in it remarkable affinities with his own feeling: see Gracián 1861.

(8) Michelstaedter 1910.

(9) «But men get tired on this path, they feel ineffectual in solitude: the voice of pain is too strong. They no longer know how to bear it with their whole person. They look behind them, they look around them, and they ask for a blindfold, they ask to exist for someone, for something [...]. They need for their *filopsychía* to attribute value to things in the very act of seeking them, and at the same time they need to declare that their lives are not in them but that they are free in their persuasion and outside of those needs» (Michelstaedter 1910: 93-4). «As a child in the dark shouts to make himself the sign of its own person, who in its infinite fear feels ineffectual; so men who in the solitude of their empty souls feel ineffectual affirm themselves inadequately by pretending to be something they are not, to have 'knowledge' already in their grasp. They no longer hear the voice of things that say 'You are', and in the darkness they do not have the courage to stand their ground, but each seeks the hand of their companion and says: 'I am, you are, we are'; and together they repeat: 'We are, we are, because we know, because we can repeat to ourselves the words of knowledge, of free and absolute knowledge'. Thus they confound one another» (*ivi*: 99).

(10) «Around a solitary greatness / Birds do not fly, nor do those wanderers / Build their nests beside it. You hear nothing / But silence, see nothing but air» (*Nietzsche*, 1948). – But it is true that those who unmask the ontological void on which the ethics of common coexistence is

based *do not really want* to survive. The unmasking of the reality of evil in Baroque authors who – like Gracián – herald the Nietzsche of the *Posthumous Fragments*, makes it impossible to understand, among other things, what a scholar like J.A. Maravall argues about the alleged anthropocentrism of these authors (see Maravall 1976: 215).

(11) «I would almost conclude that one knows the wax by means of the vision of one's eyes, and not by that of the sole inspection of the spirit, if by chance you did not look from a window at men passing in the street, the sight of the which I do not deny that I see men, just as I say that I see wax. And yet, what do I see from this window, if not hats and cloaks, which could cover ghosts or fake men, moved only by means of springs? But I judge that they are real men» (Descartes, *Med.*: 32).

(12) Gargani 1977: 112-3.

(13) Klossowski 1963: 22 ff. - In this same sense see aphorism 262 of Gracián's *Oráculo manual*: "Saber olvidar".

(14) Perniola 1980: 68, with specific reference to the concept of *cercle vicieux* in Klossowski 1969.

(15) There are numerous steps in this sense in Gracián's *Oráculo manual*. As Perniola notes, it is about «turning humanity into a simulation, ready to play any game, to play any part, to be happy and to win, no matter what happens» (Perniola 1980: 65).

(16) On this point see Agamben 1978.

Chapter IV

(1) The philosophical literature on Musil certainly boasts valuable contributions. Suffice it to mention some of the essays of the fundamental *Robert Musil: Leben - Werk - Wirkung* (= Dinklage 1960): *e.g.* Loebenstein 1960; von Allesch 1960; Strelka 1960. However, below we make brief mention of the most valid works to help the reader understand the slant of our investigation: Uhlig 1953; Boehlich 1954; Braun 1954; Berghahn 1961; Rendi 1961; Leppmann 1962; Magris 1963; Mittner 1971.

(2) As for Foucault, «utopias console: while they have no real place, they nevertheless unfold in a marvelous, smooth space; they open up cities with

wide avenues, well-tended gardens, easy towns, even if their access is chimerical» (Foucault 1989: 7). Musil knows all this and the very concept of the Millennial Kingdom fully reflects, as we shall see, the problematic nature of this awareness of his.

(3) The discursive context of philosophical-political reflection presents already rich in metaphorical values. It can be said that the recurring situation in this reflection is to speak of metaphors by metaphors, remaining closed in the magic circle of equivocation. But an obligatory reference must generally be made on the subject of metaphors, to the studies of Ricoeur 1975, as well as to Blumenberg 1960.

(4) On the central topics these notes touch on, see Cacciari 1975. Cacciari finds in twentieth century European negative thought and in particular in the «serious Viennese apocalypse» a strong element of «effectuality» (p. 8). It involves considering the concept of *negatives Denken* as an *effectually* rational reality aimed at the post-dialectical refoundation of late-Enlightenment ideology dominant in the Austro-German culture of the early twentieth century.

(5) The first concept seems to refer metaphorically to the elements of 'typicality' and 'repetition'; the second to the impossibility of an action based on old values that are reproposed: both, as we see, deeply 'political' concepts.

(6) As for the theoretical basis of this problem, it suffices to refer, in the context of Neokantianism, to the classic Cassirer 1922, or to Georg Simmel's reflections in Simmel 1910 (see especially chapter 3).

(7) Hugo von Hofmannstahl, *Letter from Lord Chandos*: «Mein Fall ist, in Kürze, dieser: es ist mir völlig die Fähigkeit abhanden gekommen, über irgend etwas zusammenhängend zu denken oder zu sprechen» (Hofmannsthal 1958a: 7) (However, see lastly, on *Chandos*, Pétillon 1975: 884-908). – Lord Chandos has a necessary presupposition, in terms of theoretical sensitivity, in Melville's Benito Cereno, a character full of philosophical and political resonances. The solid language of essences – of reassuring metaphysical correspondences, definitively objectifying every practical-bodily activity – is a world that did not yet know the tragic figure of Benito Cereno, whose «inability to act» is a direct projection of the inability to describe experienced by the seventeenth-century Lord Chandos. This was a world in which the uncorrupted

spatiality – at once geographical and symbolic – of the territories dominated by the Eurocentric and possessive ego made it possible to believe in the myth of the full definition of the objects belonging to this world, right down to their essences. Afterwards, history is in this sense marked by a profound epistemological change: the dissolution of the unity of relationships, the disintegration of the individual's geometrical sphere – which is gradually discovered to be no longer legitimized «in its essences» – makes it possible on a practical level only an act «as if» the legitimating value was founded on an essential basis: only convention can support bourgeois subjectivity in its stubborn desire to repropose itself. The European relativistic culture of the early twentieth century, through endless ideological transformations, is the last witness of this process. In it the 'silence' of the world – the silence of essences – thus wavers between complete renunciation of metaphysics and a desperate search for elements of an exact metalanguage that is capable of «talking about silence».

(8) Of this situation Hofmannsthal's Lord Chandos is emblematic: in Chandos the dissolution of the subject as the ordering principle of reality is carried out in such a way that the world reveals itself as a swarm of essences intractable to any arrangement. But if the problem is to chase – while recognizing the impossibility of grasping exactly – the endless warp of life in its every particular detail, which is recognized as «essential and irreplaceable», then we are visibly on the same ground on which the sensitivity of young Musil frets.

(9) Wittgenstein 1922, 6.41. (The year of the *Tractatus logico-philoso-phicus* is 1918). So, again, Wittgenstein: «If there is a value that has value, it must be outside of every future and so-being. Indeed every future and so-being and accidental» (6.41). «Nor, therefore, can there be propositions of ethics," since "propositions cannot express anything higher» (6.42). But on the 'silence of ethics' it is Heidegger who expresses himself incisively: «What does conscience say in his calling the recalled? Exactly: nothing. The call does not state anything, does not give any information about worldly events, has nothing to say... Consciousness speaks uniquely and constantly in the world of silence» (Heidegger, 1927, § 56).

(10) See Wittgenstein 1922, 6.432, 5.632, 5.633.

(11) «Here at the very center of Europe, where the world's old axes crossed...» (*MwQ*: 28-29).

(12) *MwQ II*: 1179.

(13) *MwQ I*: 234.

(14) *Ibidem*.

(15) See further on chapter V: *Moosbrugger and the law*.

(16) The link with one of Nietzsche's last works, the *Götzendämmerung* (= Nietzsche 1889), is quite evident in the chapters on Moosbrugger.

(17) Thus chapter 54 of the first part of *MwQ*. The renounce to the author-Moosbrugger identification is not only the first step on the path that eventually leads to the mystical solution, but also the premise that enables Musil's personal problem to objectify and become a novel, an analysis of his society and his time.

(18) Here society is conceived in such a way as to suppose, at its base, a bodily possession that was fantastically assigned to everyone, without limits, according to his needs, or even his desires.

(19) Sharing things, rights, interests, sensations (see on these concepts the illuminating pages of Cargnello 1966: 23-105). On the same topics, see Castrucci 2015: 119-131.

(20) Hofmannsthal 1958c.

(21) Thus the metaphor of the «inventory of the spirit». As also chapter 37 of the first part: «Count Leinsdorf had aimed at bringing about a powerful demonstration arising spontaneously out of the midst of the people themselves [...], but since his education had been in politics and philosophy to the exclusion of science and technology, he had no way of telling whether there was anything to their proposals or not » (*MwQ I*, 148-149).

(22) Here Musil's 'Nietzschean' side deviates more sharply from his 'ascetic' side and affirms itself with greater violence. Here, with Gottfried Benn, «mir klebt die süsse Leiblichkeit, wie ein Belag am Gaumensaum».

(23) See also, in a metaphorical key, the whole discussion between Ulrich and Clarisse in chapter 82 of the first part: «*Clarisse calls for an*

Ulrich Year», a discussion that introduces to *'Seinesgleichen geschieht'* (chapter 83).

(24) «The world is independent of my will" (Wittgenstein 1922: 6.373). "Even if all we wish to do, yet it would be only, so to speak, a grace of fate, since there is no logical connection between will and world to guarantee such a connection...» (6.374).

(25) *MwQ II*: 1189; *MwQ I*: 23.

(26) *MwQ II*: 1192-4.

(27) «... feeling more comes at the cost of understanding less, and that means through a loss of reality» (*MwQ I*: 983).

(28) The *anderer Zustand* is destined to vanish like snow in the sun in the gap of dimension – and of temporal perception – that separates it from the bodily, possessive world of society; without any possibility of interpreting its image in terms of the naturalistic type pure metaphor of an *Ordnung*, to be projected as such in the historical field. For Musil, however, the ecstatic society could not have been 'guaranteed' by any positive value. As Rendi states: «the new world is reduced to two deck chairs behind a gate» (Rendi 1961: 195)

(29) This is perhaps one of the last meanings of the «*Seinesgleichen geschieht*». For Mittner 1960 they are «the same kind of things» which still retain an "approximate, provisional, fortuitous" character, since they could be «a little or even completely different», as well as «the same or almost same things could happen to the other characters of the novel or even to men of another age». (The realm in which «the same things» happen now excludes any unrepeatability of individual destiny). – Rendi 1961: 53, note 16) observes instead that *Seinesgleichen* [= "people equal to him"] carries in Musil the French meaning of "*tout le monde*", *the world of associated life and external reality"* (italics mine).

(30) *MwQ I*: 1106.

(31) *MwQ I*: 91-92.

(32) Leinsdorf clashes, among other things, with the symptoms of the *Vergesellschaftung* precisely in an attempt to give impulse to Parallel Action: «There was a great impulse forward and Count Leinsdorf began

to feel it. He put on his pince-nez and read all the incoming mail with great seriousness from beginning to end. It was no longer the proposals and desires of unknown, passionate individuals, such as inundated him at the outset, before things had been set on a regular course, and even though these applications or inquiries still came from the heart of the people, they were now signed by the chairmen of alpine clubs, leagues for free thought, female associations, workingmen's organizations, social groups, citizens clubs, *and other such nondescript clusterings that run ahead of the transition from individualism to collectivism* like little heaps of street sweepings before a stiff breeze» (*MwQ I*: 242, italics mine).

(33) *MwQ I*: 91.

(34) Chapter 39 of the second part of the novel is especially meaningful on this point: «*After the meeting*».

(35) Rendi 1961: 147-151.

(36) *MwQ I*: 421, italics mine.

(37) Respectively, Berlin 1918 and 1925.

(38) *MwQ I*: 291.

(39) Thus chapter 14 of part one: «*Friends of youth*».

(40) "At that time music was, for Walter and Clarisse, the source of their keenest hope and anxiety" (*MwQ I*, 46).

(41) *Ibidem*.

(42) *Ibidem*.

(43) The destiny of individualities seems to exhaust itself in a busy swarm whose meaning is elsewhere: "Perhaps we are on the path of the termite State, or some other un-Christian division of labor" (*MwQ I*: 234).

(44) Not without reason, Claudio Magris notes in this regard (Magris 1963: 308) that «there is no history in *The Man without Qualities* [...], there is no sense of the concrete path of man, of historical becoming, of the immanent dynamics of a society. There are very acute pages on the social structure of Austria, which are definitive for reconstructing the physiognomy of the age, but [...] *we look in vain in them for the meaning of the concrete space of human action, which is always the historical one*» (italics mine).

(45) See particularly chapter 46: *Moonbeams by sunlight*: 1182 ff.

(46) *Ibidem*. See also *MeWI* , chapter 62: «*The constellation of brother and sister; or, The unseparated and not united*». It is, however, significant to juxtapose some points of Musil's reflection on love-cohesion with a speculative context of German philosophy that is culturally very distant, but illuminating with respect to our discourse. I refer in particular to a youthful writing of Hegel's: the so-called «*Fragment on love*», In which the young Hegel expresses himself thus: «... the unification of love is complete, but it can be completely so because the separated sol is so opposite, that the One is the lover and the Other is the beloved, so that every separated element is the organ of a living thing. But beyond that, lovers are still in conjunction with much *mortuum*: to each belong many things, that is to say it is in relation with opposites that even for the rapporteur himself are still opposites, objects, and so they are still capable of a multiple opposition in the multiple acquisition and possession of property and rights» (Hegel 1907: 381-382). The observation that the body – that corporeity – eludes a total unification, induces us to consider how lovers can behave before that extension of individual corporeality that is *property*. Because of property, therefore, each of the lovers is still in conjunction with a *mortuum* (*ein Totes*): the material object remains a *mortuum* until it is included and put into a system of relationships that determine its validity. Mere possession becomes property in a legal relationship. But love is not such a unification that it can invest with its form the goods that the lovers own . – As for Musil's inspiration for Ulrich's and Agathe's 'sacred dialogues' on love, Rendi (1960: 190) recalls that they were largely drawn from an anthology of mystical testimonies: *Ekstatische Konfessionen*, ed. by Martin Buber (= Buber 1909).

(47) But the complex analysis of this relationship obviously goes beyond the space of these notes. However, it suffices to observe that here again the question arises in parallel of the interpretive question of those places in the *Tractatus* which correspond, in particular, to propositions 6.4 and later. On this point we can find very incisive indications in Cacciari 1975 (esp. chapters 2 and 3). Nevertheless, I think that Cacciari, in tracing the basic features of his Wittgensteinian Musil, ends up neglecting the presence in the novel of other characters closely intertwined with those surveyed, and of a very different sign. They show how – especially in some places of the *Millennial Kingdom* and the *Tagebücher* – the story

does not lend itself to being interpreted in the univocal sense of the "Wittgenstein razor", with the re-emergence at times of an undeniable tension toward the "profound" beyond the "mystical". See also, on this, Rendi 1961: 58 ff.

(48) See the entire second part of the novel: «*Into the Millennium - (The Criminals)*».

(49) Mittner 1960: 332.

(50) Thus Hösle 1959: 128, rightly states that Ulrich «is ultimately too loyal to forcibly bend the antitheses of his time, in which he sees no synthesis».

(51) For Deleuze, in Proust «the world implied by absence is always a principle of the world in general, a beginning of the universe, an absolute radical beginning» (Deleuze 1964: 45).

(52) On the metaphorical meanings of the light image, see Blumenberg 1957: 432 ff.

(53) Musil 1978: 207.

(54) Thus Musil, according to whom «in every person there is a hunger, and behaves like a greedly animal; yet it is not a hunger, but something ripening sweetly like grapes in the autumn sun, free from greed and satiety. *Indeed, in every one of his emotions, the one is like the other*» (*MwQ II*: 1331, italics mine), as well as the last words of the novel in the alternate draft version 1940-42: «... but they were nihilists and activists, sometimes one and sometimes the other, whichever happened to come up» (*MwQ II*: 1334).

(55) Ironically, Musil: «The utopia of exactness already triumphs: if nowhere else 'in the work day» (quoted from Rendi 1961: 95).

(56) The entire chapter 52 of the novel, which is the last in the alternate draft version 1940-42 , must be kept in mind for the clarity of our discussion: «*Breaths of a summer day*». Musil himself underlines – in a diary entry dated November 8, 1939 – the importance of this 'predatory' aspect: «The fact that the dialogues on love have taken up so much space has the crucial defect that the second pillar of life, that of evil, of the appetitive element and so on, appears on the scene too little and too late!» (quoted by Rendi 1961: 60).

(57) «The conflict between the technical-mechanical world and the ideal romantic world is absolute precisely because they are born from the same root, precisely because their contrast expresses an absolute will to deny the spirit that against life creates its two worlds to cast them against each other, justifying them together in a common theoretical foundation» (Banfi 1961: 237-8).

(58) Banfi 1961: 238-239.

(59) Which is rather the only form of thought able to follow the 'living' rhythm of reality. But on its inconsistencies, to begin with on the 'philosophical' level of this representation, see again Banfi, 1961: 240 ff.

(60) Rendi 1961: 145.

(61) Also in this sense Hösle 1959: 122. For Musil the spirit is not (as it is for the Nietzschean epigone Meingast-Klages) a suspicious «antagonist of the soul».

(62) Musil 1955: 705.

(63) Wittgenstein 1922, 6.51.

(64) See instead Rendi 1961, chapter 9: «*L'altro stato*».

(65) Musil 1955: 638.

(66) Wittgenstein 1922, 6.52.

(67) «But it was a strangely insubstantial reality, not very tangible, for which they felt an expectation; and a half-truth, as familiar as it is unattainable, that aspired to be believed: a reality and a truth not good for everyone, only for lovers» (*MwQ II*: 1198). On the other hand, in his *Tagebücher* Musil explicitly observed that «it is not a matter of making the 'other state' the pillar of associated life. It's too fleeting. I myself can barely remember it. However, it leaves traces in all ideologies, and [...] it is based on the life of these phenomena, which are petrifying» (Musil 1955: 284, quoted in Rendi 1961: 176).

(68) «Let us suppose a community in which all love each other with a pure, total and disinterested love. Will not such a community be ordained? Of course, better than any other. And yet its order will not be external to ordained things: it will be identical to them, that is to the will of individuals relating to each other» (Mathieu 1972: 82). This con-

sideration of the 'ordering' characteristics of the *modus amoris* is suffi-cient to show the *direction* in which we must look, to seek an order no longer external to the ordered thing. All this is particularly relevant to what Musil seems to think of the *Ekstatische Sozietät*.

(69) Thus Cargnello 1966: 33 ff.

(70) See *MwQ II*, alternate draft version 1940-42, chapter 51: *Loving is not simple*.

(71) *MwQ II* (alternate draft version 1940-42): 1324-5 Musil has suggestive images on this score: «This idea seemed to have something special that attracted him. Ulrich would have expounded on it at length and with numerous examples, but while he was still thinking these over, something unanticipated, which quickened his intended line of thought with expectation like a pleasant fragrance coming across fields, appeared to direct his reflections almost inadvertently toward what in painting is called still life or, according to the contrary but just as fitting procedure of a foreign language, *nature morte*» (*MwQ II*, alternate draft version 1940-42: 1323-4).

(72) A.M. Ripellino has very effective pages on this «fantastic picto-rial Baroque painter» – who lived perhaps not by chance between Vienna and Prague – in which there are no longer exactly - it is true – 'still lifes' but something very different: a single image to render nature and man (Ripellino 1973: especially 100-109). Moreover, a very acute obser-vation on the affinities that can be found between the Baroque and the image of silence in Ulrich and Agathe is already found in Rendi 1961: 201.

(73) *MwQ II*, alternate draft version 1940-42: 1331.

(74) On the difference between *scire* and *uti*, having nature as their aim, see Blumenberg 1960: 30 ff. - Blumenberg observes, briefly but acutely, the variations in the relationship between these two concepts in the history of thought. The Talmudic *caveat* against gnosis (*Chagigah*, II, 1): «He who investigates many things, it would be better for him never to have been born: what is above, what is under, what was before and what will come after» – about which Blumenberg notes that for the strict-ness of this verdict there is no Christian parallel – is opposed to the notion of the «violence that man must do to the truth in order to master it»: the machine, or the moment in which «what is plausible is converted into true-

seeming». Here «all truth is acquisition, no longer a gift, and knowledge takes on the character of work».

(75) «The limits of my language signify the limits of my world» (Wittgenstein 1922, 5.6).

(76) This in stark contrast to the irrationalistic philosophical tendencies of the period, mostly falsifying, polemical toward science, the need felt to eliminate the 'negative limit' from the cognitive process. But in Musil the soul is 'scientific,' living always next to the other, without ever hinting at a deterioration.

(77) In Musil there is – as in Rilke – a «mystique of things much more than of God» (Mittner 1960: 179). On the concept of "laic mysticism" of the post-historic scientist see De Martino 2008: 467 ss.

(78) Mittner 1960: 191. Thus there is a decisive juxtaposition between the concept of mystique in Musil and in Wittgenstein, when the silence of the garden is filled with doubts about the ultimate communicability of that «essential part of human life».

(79) Mittner 1971: 1476.

(80) Musil 1955: 478.

(81) Heidegger 1953: 226.

(82) A topic Mittner still insists on. (See Mittner 1960: 327 ff.). The purely consolatory character of utopia, to which reference was made at the outset, is definitively revealed at this point, able to mean only, if at all, for the subject, the useless will to remain in an unproductive illusion.

Chapter V

(1) Mittner 1971: 1461

(2) *MwQ*: 43.

(3) *MwQ*: 126.

(4) *Ibidem*.

(5) *MwQ*: 77.

(6) *MwQ*: 69.

(7) *MwQ*: 259-60.

(8) *MwQ*: 70.

(9) *Ibidem*.

(10) *MwQ*: 123.

(11) Thus for example Gardies 1962. See lastly, for his method of analysis, the interesting essay by an Austrian jurist on a traditionally 'literary topic' in Pernthaler 1974.

(12) *MwQ*: 8-9.

(13) *MwQ*: 70.

(14) *MwQ*: 428.

(15) *MwQ*: 580.

(16) *MwQ*: 255-6.

(17) *MwQ*: 261.

(18) *MwQ*: 262.

(19) *MwQ*: 75-6.

(20) *MwQ*: 152.

Chapter VI

(1) Leaving aside for the moment his *Thesen über den Begriff der Geschichte* (1940), we shall focus our attention on the essay *Zur Kritik der Gewalt* (see the english translation in Benjamin 1996a). The complete works of Benjamin are contained in *Gesammelte Schriften*, hrsg. v. R. Tiedemann - H. Schweppenhäuser (1972). *Zur Kritik der Gewalt* had appeared for the first time in Max Weber's 'Archiv für Sozialwissenschaft und Sozialpolitik', 47, 1920-21.

(2) In the various nuances that this term – in itself polysemic – can have, and that are not of course exhausted in the area, though central in early 20th-century Germany, of neo-Kantian currents, against which a fundamental antiformalist (but not therefore antirationalist) controversy arises.

(3) There is a recurrent mechanism in the formulations of that political theory of the early 20th century, based on the critique of the liberal concept of the rule of law, in the theorization of productivity in the *rationalistic sense (Rationalisierung)* of an *irrational* element introduced into a system whose elements (norms) are in turn taken to be completely rational. In other words, and through an example: the enactment of the law (*Rechtsverwirklichung*) in a given normative-rational system can be ensured in some cases only through a *functional* introduction of an element heterogeneous to the system: a mythical or "charismatic" one: in any case extranormative. And here Weber's critique links up with Carl Schmitt's.

(4) The book *Réflexions sur la violence* appeared in the early 1920's, which also see the *Critique of Violence* in its fifth (1921) and sixth (1923) editions, and they can be counted among the best known and debated political texts of the period. On the *erste Nachkriegsjahre* up to 1923, as well as on Benjamin's "Swiss period" (1918-19), see the memoirs of Scholem (Scholem 1975, 69 ff., 111 ff.).

(5) A rather exceptional style for Benjamin. While the subject of Benjamin's essays is never, as a rule, a straightforwardly specific aspect of reality (as in literature of phenomenological inspiration), in the essay on law and violence, as well as in some other texts of his youthful period, he formulates his philosophical theses outside of a specific hermeneutic instance, seeming almost to neglect his characteristic concern, namely that affirmations about life are always mediated by the analysis and interpretation of a certain 'cultural landscape'.

(6) Which was not the author's intention, if we consider also the size of the essay. Lukács, in his 1920 essay *Legality and Illegality* (in Lukács 1971), presented a very different ideological position in supporting the need for an analysis of the 'motives' that preside over legal or illegal behavior. But between the two essays, Lukács' and Benjamin's, despite the topic which at first seemed interrelated (violence, legality and illegality), they have very little in common.

(7) Benjamin 1996a: 236-243. As Derrida here observes, «Law is not justice. Law is the element of calculation, and it is just that these be law, but justice is incalculable, it demands that one clculates with the incalculable» (Derrida 2002: 244).

(8) Benjamin 1996a: 236.

(9) Benjamin 1996a: 237.

(10) *Ibidem.*

(11) Benjamin 1996a: 239.

(12) Benjamin 1996a: 238.

(13) *Ibidem.*

(14) Benjamin 1996a: 246.

(15) Benjamin 1996a: 243.

(16) Benjamin 1996a: 242 ff.

(17) See on this point Carl Schmitt in his foreword to his book on dictatorship (Schmitt 1921). But it is again Schmitt who in the same period confronts Sorel as a theorist of political myth: see *Die politische Theorie des Mythus* (1923) in Schmitt 1940: 9-18.

(18) Benjamin 1996a: 243.

(19) Benjamin 1996a: 244.

(20) *Ibidem.*

(21) See Benjamin 2005a. But, in speaking of Kraus, see also Elias Canetti's intense pages: Canetti 1979: 29-54.

(22) Benjamin 2005a: 456.

(23) *Ibidem.*

(24) While mythic violence – founder of the law – is a direct projection of mankind's rejection of God as 'governor'. One might add that the conceptual framework 'mythical violence – law' is connected here to the fact that «man has dominated man to his own injury» (*Eccl.*, 8: 9).

(25) *Num.*, 16 (see Benjamin 1996a: 250).

(26) «Just as in all spheres God opposes myth, mythical violence is confronted by the divine. And the latter constitutes it antithesis in all respects. If mythical violence is lawmaking, divine violence is law-destroying; if the former sets boundaries, the latter boundlessly destroys

them; if mythical violence brings at once guilt and retribution, divine power only expiates; if the former threatens, the latter strikes; if the former is bloody, the latter is lethal without spilling blood» (Benjamin 1996a: 249-350).

(27) Benjamin 1996a: 252.

(28) Benjamin 1996a: 247.

(29) Benjamin 1996a: 248.

(30) Benjamin 2005b: 795 ff.

(31) *Ibidem*.

(32) In 'Fate and Character', (see Benjamin 1996b: 201-206).

(33) «History [*Geschichte*] is not the sequence of historical periods but an unique proximity of what is the same, which concerns thinking in the incalculable ways of destiny [*Geschick*] and with variable degrees of immediacy» (Heidegger 2002: 159).

(34) Benjamin 1996b: 203-204, italics mine.

(35) *Ibid.*: 203.

(36) A very brief text – dated by Scholem 1920-21 (see Scholem 1975: 117) – illuminates the meaning of the concept of 'happiness', in the relationship that links messianism and history. This is the so-called *Theologico-Political Fragment*, whose importance is matched only by the hermeticism of the writing and by the extreme concentration of the concepts elaborated therein: «The kingdom of God does not constitute the *telos* of historical *dynamis*; it cannot be set as a goal. From the standpoint of history, it is not a goal, but an end. Therefore the order of the profane cannot be built up on the idea of the kingdom of God, and therefore theocracy does has no political, but only a religious meaning. [...] The order of the profane should be created on the idea of happiness. The relation of this order to the messianic is one of the essential teachings of the philosophy of history. It is the precondition of a mystical conception of history, containing a problem that can be represented figuratively. If one arrow points to the goal towards which the profane *dynamis* acts, and another marks the direction of messianic intensity, the certain quest of free humanity for the happiness runs

counter to the messianic direction; but just as a force can, through acting, increase another that is acting in the opposite direction, so the order of the profane assists, through being profane,the coming of the messianic kingdom. The profane, therefore, although not itself a category of this kingdom, is a decisive category of its quietest approach» (Benjamin 1986 : 312).

(37) Benjamin 1986: 312.

(38) Benjamin 2006: 390.

(39) See Benjamin 2006: thesis 14.

(40) «The forgotten – and with this knowledge we are at a further threshold of Kafka's work – is never purely individual. Each particular object of oblivion merges with the forgotten of prehistory [...]. Oblivion is the vessel from which the inexhaustible intermediate world of Kafka's stories erupts into the light» (*ibid.*: 281).

(41) «In the age of the maximum alienation of people among themselves, of the infinitely mediated relationships that are by now their only ones, motion pictures and the phonograph were invented. In motion pictures mankind does not recognize its own gait, in the grammophone it does not recognize its own voice [...]. The situation of the subject of these experiments is Kafka's. It is the situation that refers to the study» (Benjamin 2005: 287).

(42) *Ibid.*: 280.

(43) *Ibid.*: 288.

Chapter VII

(1) Bourdet 1972.

(2) Th. Mann, *MM*: 382-383. And further: «I was already tolerably well aware that what is called liberalism – individualism, the humanistic conception of citizenship – was the product of the Renaissance. But the fact leaves me entirely cold, realizing. as I do, that your great heroic age is a thing of the past, its ideals defunct, or at least lying at their latest gasp, while the feet of those who will deal them the *coup de grâce* are already before the door. [...] In the past five hundred years,

the principle of freedom has outlived its usefulness. An educational system which still conceives itself as a child of he age of enlightenment, with criticism as its chosen medium of instruction, the liberation and cult of the ego, the solvent of forms of life which are absolutely fixed – such a system may still, for a time, reap an empty rhetorical advantage, but its old-fogey character is, to the initiated, clear beyond any doubt» (*MM*: 399).

(3) *MM*: 395.

(4) *Ibidem*.

(5) *MM*: 396-7.

(6) «Woher weiß man das, daß die wahre Beschaffenheit der Dinge in *diesem* Verhältnis zu unserem Intellekt steht? – Wäre es nicht anders? Daß die ihm am meisten das Gefühl von Macht und Sicherheit gebende Hypothese am meisten von ihm *bevorzugt, geschätzt, und folglich als wahr* bezeichnet wird?» (Nietzsche 1887-88: 386-7).

(7) *MM*: 397.

(8) *Ibidem*.

(9) *Ibidem*.

(10) *MM*: 409.

(11) *MM*: 410.

(12) Hocke 1961: 115.

(13) *MM*: 403.

(14) *MM*: 373.

(15) «It is necessary that the dualism between good and evil, between power and the spirit, here and hereafter, must be for the time abrogated to make way for a single principle, which shall unify ascetism and domination [*Askese und Herrshaft*]» (*MM*: 401-2).

(16) See chapter VI: *Operationes spirituales*: pp. 439 ff.

(17) *MM*: 400.

(18) *MM*: 690.

(19) *MM*: 442.

(20) Dallmayr 1958: 658.

(21) Schmitt 1950a: 38.

(22) Cantimori 1935.

(23) See Sasso 1974, which draws a pretext from the lapsus that Delio Cantimori ran into when he confused Naphta with Fiala (the latter a pseudonym for Karl Löwith) in one of his writings.

(24) In Spengler's analysis of the conflict between man and technique we can find really "true glows of intuitive knowledge" (Brega 2020: 56).

(25) *Logos. Internationale Zeitschrift für die Philosophie der Kultur*, IX, 1921: with essays of K. Joël, L. Curtius, E. Metzger, etc.

(26) Now in Mann 1993.

(27) *Ibid.*: 193.

(28) Cantimori 1962: X-XI.

(29) Jünger 1929: 32.

(30) Löwith 1960: 102.

(31) Mittner 1971: 1447 ff.

(32) Marcuse 1934.

(33) In the same sense of Schmitt 1967.

Chapter VIII

(1) «The precept, it is said, which 'I can wish' were the guide of all men's conduct, is itself the real moral principle. That which I wish is the hinge on which the given direction turns. But what can I truly wish, and what not?» (Schopenhauer, *BM*: 83).

(2) Schopenhauer, *WWR* § 53: 271 and § 66: 368.

(3) Schopenhauer, *BM*: 246.

(4) *BM*: 247.

(5) Schopenhauer sees rationalistic morality as «difficult combinations, rules invented for the purpose, formulae balanced on a needle's point, and stilted maxims, from which it is no longer possible to look down and see life as it really is with all its turmoil. Such niceties are doubtless admirably adapted for the lecture-room, if only with a view to sharpening the wits, but they can never be the cause of the impulse to act justly and to do good, which is found in every man» (*BM*: 133).

(6) *BM*: 28, italics mine.

(7) *BM*: 33.

(8) *BM*: 13.

(9) As is already the case for Spinoza, its purpose «is not to teach a science [...]; it doesn't demand anything from men but obedience, and it only condemns disobedience, not ignorance» (Spinoza, *TTP*: 168). «Postquam novimus, Scripturae intentum non fuisse scientias docere; hinc enim facile judicare possumus, nihil praeter oboedientiam eandem ab hominibus exigere, solamque contumaciam, non autem ignorantiam damnare» (*ibidem*).

(10) *BM*: 44.

(11) *BM*: 63.

(12) And the will «must live on itself, since nothing exists besides it, and it is a hungry will» (*WWR*: 154).

(13) «Due to the subjectivity essential to every consciousness, every-one is his own entire world» (*BM*: 152).

(14) «With his consciousness the world also necessarily ceases to exist for him, in other words its being and non-being become synonymous and indistinguishable. Every knowing individual is therefore in truth, and finds himself as, the whole will-to-live, or as the in-itself of the world itself, and also as the complementary condition of the world as representation, consequently as a microcosm to be valued equally with the macrocosm» (*WWR*: 332).

(15) The general situation of violent hostility between individual atoms «appears more distinctly as soon as any mob is released from all law and order; we then see at once in the most distinct form the *bellum*

omnium contra omnes which Hobbes admirably described in the first chapter of his *De cive*. We see not only how everyone tries to snatch from another what he himself wants, but how one often even destroys another's whole happiness or life, in order to increase by an insignificant amount his own well-being» (*WWR*: 333).

(16) «Now since the will manifests that *self-affirmation* of one's own body in innumerable individuals beside one another, in one individual, by virtue of the egoism peculiar to all, it very easily goes beyond this affirmation to the *denial* of the same will appearing in another individual. The will of the first breaks through the boundary of another's affirmation of will, since the individual either destroys or injures this other body itself, or compels the powers of that other body to serve *his* will, instead of serving the will that appears in that other body» (*WWR*: 334).

(17) *WWR*: 335.

(18) *WWR*: 336. «Kant makes the fundamentally false assertion that, apart from the State, there would be no perfect right to property. According to the deduction we have just made, there is property even in the state of nature with perfect natural, i.e. moral, right, which cannot be encroached on without, wrong, and without wrong can be defended to the uttermost» (*WWR*: 347).

(19) *WWR*: 336.

(20) *WWR*: 337.

(21) «The negative character of justice is also established, little as it may appear, even by the familiar formula "Give to each one his own". Now, there is no need to give a man his own, if he has it. The real meaning is therefore: "Take from none his own"» (*BM*: 183).

(22) *WWR*: 341.

(23) *Ibidem.*

(24) *WWR*: 342.

(25) «The coercive apparatus is the State, whose sole *raison d'être* is to protect its subjects, individually from each other, and collectively from external foes. It is true that a few German would-be philosophers of this venal age wish to distort the State into an institution for the

spread of morality, education, and edifying instruction. But such a view contains, lurking in the background, the jesuitical aim of doing away with personal freedom and individual development, and of making men mere wheels in a huge Chinese governmental and religious machine» (*BM*: 184).

(26) *EM*: 23.

(27) *WWR*: 348.

(28) *Supplements to The World as Will and Representation*, cit., pp. 1518-1519. Schopenhauer observes: «Now here a Kantian would infallibly reply here that, according to this view, the criminal punished would be used "merely as a *means*". This proposition, repeated so indefatigably by all the Kantians, namely that "Man must always be treated only as an end, never as a means", certainly sounds important, and is therefore very suitable for all those who like to have a formula that relieves them of all further thinking. Closely examined, however, it is an extremely vague, indefinite assertion which reaches its aim quite indirectly; it needs for every case of its application a special explanation, definition, and modification, but, taken generally, it is inadequate, says little, and moreover is problematical. The murderer who is condemned to death according to the law must, it is true, be now used as a mere *means,* and with complete right [...]» (*WWR*: 348-9).

(29) *WWR*: 349.

Chapter IX

(1) Heidegger 1954.

(2) See particularly Beaufret 1974 and Severino 1980.

(3) Plato, *Symp.* 208e-209a.

(4) Plato, *Symp.* 205b.

(5) Severino 1980: 137 ff.

(6) «A great demon [...], and indeed every demonic being is between divine and mortal» (Plato, *Symp.,* 202 d-e).

(7) As regards the relationship between *eros* and *logos* see the classic dissertation by Nygren 1936. – On *eros* and *logos* in Plato see Natorp 1920, an essay which corrects the immanent interpretation already given by the author, in *Platos Ideenlehre*, of which it constitutes the *Metakritischer Anhang*. For the interpretation of the *Symposium* see Krüger 1939, Kucharsky 1949 and, on a different level, Kerényi 1966.

(8) Agamben 1978: 3-62.

(9) Valéry 1960: 79 ff.; 148 ff.

(10) Valéry 1956: 121-2, italics mine. «L'homme, te dis-je, fabrique par abstraction; ignorant et oubliant une grande partie des qualités de ce qu'il emploie, s'attachant seulement à des conditions claires et distinctes, qui peuvent, le plus souvent, être simultanément satisfaites non par une seule, mais par plusieurs espèces de matière. Il boit du lait, ou du vin, ou de l'eau, ou de la cervoise, indifféremment dans l'or, dans le verre, dans la corne ou dans l'onyx; et que le vase soit large ou élancé, ou en forme de feuille, ou de fleur, ou bizarrement tordu sur son pied, le buveur ne regarde guère que le boire. Celui même qui a fait cette coupe, n'a jamais pu que grossièrement accorder entre elles sa substance, sa forme et sa fonction. Car la subordination intime de ces trois choses et leur profonde liaison ne pourraient être l'œuvre que de la nature naturante elle-même. L'artisan ne peut faire son ouvrage sans violer ou déranger un ordre, par les forces qu'il applique à la matière pour l'adapter à l'idée qu'il veut imiter, et à l'usage qu'il prévoit. Il est donc conduit inévitablement à produire des objets dont l'ensemble est d'un degré toujours inférieur au degré de leur parties» (1960: 123-4).

(11) Valéry 1960: 82.

(12) Solmi 1976: 66-7.

(13) Valéry 1960: 79.

(14) Valéry 1956: 89-91. «O Phèdre, quand je compose une demeure (qu'elle soit pour les dieux, qu'elle soit pour un homme), et quand je cherche cette forme avec amour, m'étudiant à créer un objet qui réjouisse le regard, qui s'entretienne avec l'esprit, qui s'accorde avec la raison et les nombreuses convenances, ... je te dirai cette chose étrange, *qu'il me semble que mon corps est de la partie*... Laisse-moi dire. Ce corps est un instrument

admirable, dont je m'assure que les vivants, qui l'ont tous à leur service, n'usent pas dans sa plénitude. Ils n'en tirent que du plaisir, de la douleur, et des actes indispensables, comme de vivre. Tantôt ils se confondent avec lui; tantôt ils oublient quelque temps son existence; et tantôt brutes, tantôt purs esprits, ils ignorent quelles liaisons universelles ils contiennent, et de quelle substance prodigieuse ils sont faits [...].

O mon corps, qui me rappelez à tout moment ce tempérament de mes tendances, cet équilibre de vos organes, ces justes proportions de vos parties, qui vous font être et vous rétablir au sein des choses mouvantes; prenez garde à mon ouvrage; enseignez-moi sourdement les exigences de la nature et me communiquez ce grand art dont vous êtes doué, comme vous en êtes fait, de survivre aux saisons, et de vous reprendre des hasards. Donnez-moi de trouver dans votre alliance le sentiment des choses vraies; modérez, renforcez, assurez mes pensées. Tout périssable que vous êtes, vous l'êtes bien moins que mes songes. *Vous durez un peu plus qu'une fantaisie*; vous payez pour mes actes, et vous expiez pour mes erreurs: Instrument vivant de la vie, vous êtes à chacun de nous *l'unique objet qui se compare à l'univers. Vous êtes bien la mesure du monde, dont mon âme ne présente que le dehors.*Elle le connaî t sans profondeur, et si vainement, qu'elle se prend quelquefois à ranger au rang de ses rêves; elle doute du soleil... Infatuée de ses fabrications éphémères, elle se croit capable d'une infinité de réalités différentes; elle imagine qu'il existe d'autres mondes, mais vous la rappelez à vous-même, comme l'ancre, à soi, le navire...» (Valéry 1960: 98-9).

(15) I hereby refer explicitly to Schmitt 1950b. *Nomos* would not be simple *táxis*, but neither *kó smos*. The term *diakó smesis* which appears in the *Symposium*: 209a (but see also *Laws*, 853) constitutes an already more than adequate conceptual representation. (See anyway paragraph 2c).

(16) Valéry 1956: 124, italics mine.

«PHÈDRE: Je conçois maintenant comme tu as pu hésiter entre le construire et le connaî tre.

SOCRATE: Il faut choisir d'être un homme, ou bien un esprit. L'homme ne peut agir que parce qu'il peut ignorer, et se contenter d'une partie de cette connaissance qui est sa bizarrerie particulière, laquelle connaissance est un peu plus grande qu'il ne faut!» (Valéry 1960: 126).

(17) Beaufret 1974, vol. I: 125.

(18) Valéry 1956: 141, italics mine. «SOCRATE: J'eusse bâti, chanté... O perte pensive de mes jours! Quel artiste j'ai fait périr! Quelles choses j'ai dédaignées, mais quelles choses enfantées!... Je me sens contre moi-même le Juge de mes Enfers spirituels. Tandis que la facilité de mes propos fameux me poursuit et m'afflige, voici que je suscite pour Euménides *mes actions que n'ont pas eu lieu, mes oeuvres qui ne sont pas nées, – crimes vagues et énormes que ces absences criantes; et meurtres, dont les victimes sont des choses impérissables!...*» (Valéry 1960: 140).

(19) Particularly in *Wissenschaft und Besinnung,* an essay later included in the *Vorträge und Aufsätze,* cit., but the theme characterizes most of the last Heidegger, including the *Holzwege.*

(20) Heidegger 1954.

(21) «Die Technik ist also nicht bloß ein Mittel. Die Technik ist eine Weise des Entbergens. Achten wir darauf, dann öffnet sich uns ein ganz anderer Bereich für das Wesen der Technik. Es ist der Bereich der Entbergung, d.h. der Wahr-heit» (Heidegger 1954: 16).

(22) Plato, *Letter VII*: 341 c-d.

(23) Heidegger 1954.

(24) See for example: «Dwelling is the fundamental trait of being in accordance with which mortals are» (Heidegger 1954: 98).

(25) Beaufret 1974, vol. II: 171.

(26) Plato, *Rep.*, X (especially 597e: «You call him the imitator in the third generation from nature?»). See also Cassirer 1924.

(27) Brisson 1974.

(28) See Hauriou 1925: 86.

(29) Mortati 1962: 159.

(30) *Ibid.*, 140, italics mine.

(31) Aristotle, *Pol.*, A II, 1253a.

(32) Bergson 1921: 5. See on these topics Minkowski 1956.

(33) Voegelin 1966: 33-56.

(34) Strauss 1953: 136, 131.

(35) Strauss 1953: 131-2, italics mine.

Chapter X

(1) Despite this, every substantialist epistemology seems to suggest that 'true' ideas are such regardless of being embodied, and every materialistic epistemology seems to suggest that ideas that can be said to be ontologically independent, and therefore 'true', generally do not exist. On these topics see Castrucci 2003: part IV, especially p. 914.

(2) «Truth is not […] something that might be found or discovered – but something that must be created and that gives a name to a process […] that has in itself no end» (Nietzsche 1885-87: 384). Spinoza, on the other hand, whose philosophy system was controversially considered by Nietzsche within this context, defined truth starting with the well known definition of substance: «By substance, I understand what is in itself and is conceived through itself, that is, that whose concept does not require the concept of another thing, from which it must be formed» [«Per substantiam intelligo id, quod in se est et per se concipitur: hoc est id, cujus conceptus non indiget conceptu alterius rei, a quo formari debeat»] (Spinoza, *Eth.*: 45). See the entire first part: *God – Definitions*.

(3) Nietzsche would have said: for the hierarchy, since every difference is valued, and constitutes a "position" in the social order and in the pneumatic order.

(4) The Nietzschean *Posthumous Fragments* focus precisely upon this point, particularly that short essay on the «criticism of the logical forms of knowledge», which is contained in section 9 (autumn 1887) of the Colli-Montinari edition. See for example: «The *faith* in reason and its categories, in dialectics, that is, the *valuation* of logic only proves its *utility* for life, evidenced through experience: but *not* its "truth"» [«Das *Vertrauen* zur Vernunft und ihren Kategorien, zur Dialektik, also die *Werthschätzung* der Logik beweist nur die durch Erfahrung bewiesene *Nützlichkeit* derselben für das Leben: *nicht* deren "Wahrheit"»] (Nietzsche 1885-87: 352). This aspect is exactly clarified by Deleuze 1962.

(5) It's the connection between anthropomorphism and teleology that Spinoza definitively critiques in *Eth.*: I, Appendix.

(6) See Gehlen 1940.

(7) This is one of the most vital parts of the Nietzsche's morality, which can be found in *Citadelle* of Saint-Exupéry (= Saint-Exupéry 1959). *Citadelle* is a literary work of considerable philosophical and anthropological importance, which today has been unjustly forgotten: dealing with the apparently opposing viewpoints of Plato and Nietzsche, it contains an analysis and a ruthless critique of modern moral sentiments. From «*Il fut une âge de ma jeunesse où j'eus pitié des mendiants et de leurs ulcères*» to «*La vérité des mes ordonnances, c'est l'homme qui en naîtra*», all of ancient Western Judeo-Christian anthropology is called into question. The rosary of thirteen beads that appears in the exergue is the perfect metaphor for the conventionality of ethics, whose precepts are in no way undermined by this characterization, but – if possible – are rendered even more impelling. «I remember that miscreant who visited my father and said: "You bid your household pray with rosaries of thirteen beads. Why thirteen? May not salvation be had as well with a different number?" Then he advanced subtle reasons why men had better pray with twelve-bead rosaries, and I, who was then a child, was taken by his cunning arguments. Anxiously I gazed at my father, doubting if his answer would outshine that specious brilliance. "Tell me", the man continued, "wherein the rosary of thirteen beads weighs heavier". "The rosary of thirteen beads", my father answered, "has the weight of all the heads I have already cut off in its defense". God en-lightened the miscreant, and he repented» (*Citadelle*, III). A classic case in which a conventionalist ethics and decisionist practices clearly coincide.

(8) As Walter Benjamin noted, «considered in this way, character and fate, far from being theoretically distinct, coincide» (Benjamin 1996b: 305).

Epilogue

(1) Schmitt 1922.

(2) The essay-form came into being from here, understood in the same sense as the philosophical discourse developed in G. Lukács'

classic, *Soul and Form* [1910], in Id. 2011.

(3) Schmitt 1922: 27, 34-35.

(4) This concept refers to the passage from *Grundlinien der Philosophie des Rechts*, in which Hegel observes that in the juridical sphere it is sometimes impossible to rationally determine the decision of a case, but interest in the "fact of deciding" as such prevails: «here the only interest present is that something be actually done, that the matter be settled and decided somehow, no matter how». Indeed «here is one essential element in law and the administration of justice which contains a measure of contingency and which arises from the fact that the law is an universal determination which has to be applied to the individual case. If you wished to declare yourself against this contingency, you would be talking in abstractions» (G.W.F. Hegel, *Outlines of the Philosophy of Right*, § 214 and note, in Id. 2008: 203).

(5) Schmitt 1922: 30.

(6) Schmitt 1921: XLV.

(7) *Ibid.*: XLII.

(8) Schmitt 1922: 28.

(9) Ibid.: 32-33.

(10) Kelsen 1911.

(11) Kelsen 1920, with his peremptory concluding sentence: «Undoubtedly the concept of sovereignty must be radically removed» (*ibid.*: 320).

(12) Schmitt 1922: 30.

(13) *Ibid.*: 30-31.

(14) Ibid.: 31-32, italics mine.

(15) The topic of Kantian form appears in *Political Theology* liquidated with a simple sentence («we need not be detained here by the neo-Kantian conception of form»: 28). But the apparently only theoretical question of the reflections of form elaborated by Kantian criticism on European legal doctrine cannot in reality be avoided, since it is from it that – as we shall see – what can be defined as the primacy of analytics in western rationalist epistemology begins.

(16) Schmitt 1922: 27.

(17) Weber 1922a: II, VII: *Rechtssoziologie*, § 2: *Der Formcharakter des objektiven Rechtes*; § 5: *Formale und materiale Rationalisierung des Rechtes*.

(18) Schmitt 1922: 28.

(19) Where the "sic!" with which Schmitt comments in the text on the comparison, which Weber undeniably made, between rationality and specialization, as if in Weber's view the first were simply reduced to the second.

(20) «To trace a conceptual result back to a sociological carrier is psychology; it involves the determination of a certain kind of motivation of human action. This is a sociological problem, but not a problem of the sociology of a concept» (Schmitt 1922: 44).

(21) *Ibid.*: 45. The reason is that «the metaphysical image that a definite epoch forges of the world has the same structure as what the world immediately understands to be appropriate as a form of its political organization» (*ibid.*: 46).

(22) See Weber 1922a: II, § 1.

(23) See Heidegger 1929.

(24) Heidegger 1929, §§ 19-22 and 27 [engl. tr.: 64-68, 72, 76, 98-99].

(25) *Ibid.*: § 27 and § 31: 95, 112.

(26) The definition is F. Stepun's. See Stepun 1929: 65.

(27) Kelsen 1911: 46.

(28) «Das metalogische Prinzip einer dualistischen Weltanschauung» (Kelsen 1919: 635).

(29) In the *Allgemeine Theorie der Normen* the initial purity of formalism gradually gives way to the realistic harshness of a no longer disguised voluntarism, in light of the principle "kein Imperativ ohne Imperator", according to which pure doctrine is transformed into a simple technology of power.

(30) Schmitt 1928 (en. tr. *Constitutional Theory* = CT).

(31) Heidegger 1934 [en. tr. *Logic as the Question Concerning the Essence of Language (= Logic)*].

(32) *CT* : 127 and 264.

(33) *Ibid.*: 268 and 258.

(34) Lübbe 1999: 38.
(35) Habermas 1998 (en. tr. *The Inclusion of the Other*: 129).

(36) In this perspective, the "pale and bookish" idea of a constitutional patriotism can never replace the awareness of a collective identity of belonging. «This program [of constitutional patriotism] is far-fetched [...]. Recourse to the nation and to the implicit awareness-of-us capable of establishing emotional bonds cannot be evaded [...]. As a countermove, a relative cultural homologizing is necessary, so that the tendentially atomized society is re-assembled and made capable of acting regardless of its internal differentiations. [...] The goal cannot be to overcome and replace collective identity, not even in favor of a universalism of human rights» (Böckenförde 1995). On the subject see Habermas 1998: 131 and ss.).

(37) See on the political concept of ethnonationalism Connor 1994. «Our answer to the frequently asked question: What is a nation? It is a group of people who feel they are related in an ancestral way» (*ibid.*: 202). An answer, however, which, in its evident philosophical indeterminacy, would certainly not have satisfied Heidegger, or even Schmitt.

(38) *Logic* § 13: «'We' are the people by virtue of decision»: 49 ss.

(39) *Ibid.*: 56-59.

(40) *Ibid.*: 59.

(41) *Ibid.*: 60, italics mine.

(42) *Ibid.*: 60-61 (= *Gesamtausgabe*, Bd. 38: 69-70).

(43) *Ibid.*: 66.

(44) The concept of "event" ("*Ereignis*"), developed in the *Beiträge der Philosophie*, characterizes its entry into historicity through decision. According to a note added by Heidegger to the *Brief über den Humanismus*, it can be considered a constitutive concept of Heidegger's late thought

(cf. *Gesamtausgabe*, Bd. 9: 316). As Heidegger himself maintains, «since 1936 'event' is the keyword of my thought».

(45) *Logic*: 40-41, italics mine.

(46) *Ibid.*: 43, italics mine.

(47) The literature on charismatic power in the framework of late Western rationalism has long been unlimited, although not always of high value due to its almost exclusively sociological slant. In addition to S.N. Eisenstadt's classic introduction to Weber 1968, interesting critical insights into the speech given here can be found in Rieff 2007.

(48) Smend 1928: I, 5 and 6 ("Persönliche und funktionelle Integration").

(49) Habermas 1996 (en. tr.: 130).

(50) This is a topic that has long been studied in the constitutional literature of the European tradition, especially in Germany starting from the school of Theodor Litt (including Smend himself in the text cited in the previous note, but also in the short entry *Integrationslehre*: cf. Smend 1956) and later substantially abandoned by the juridical doctrine of the last post-war period, whose positive results – in relation to the theory of the integrative function exercised by symbol – are found instead in some political-anthropological studies, such as M. García Pelayo 1964.

(51) Adinolfi 2002: 224.

Bibliography

Adinolfi, G. (2002) : *Nuovo ordine mondiale. Tra imperialismo e Impero*, SEB, Milano 2002,

Agamben, G. (1978) : *Infanzia e storia. Saggio sulla distruzione dell'esperienza*, Torino: Einaudi [en. tr.: *Infancy and History. The Destruction of Experience*, London & New York: Verso, 1993].

Id. (1982) : *Il linguaggio e la morte. Un seminario sul luogo della negatività*, Turin: Einaudi [en. tr.: *Language and Death. The Place of Negativity*, Minneapolis: University of Minnesota Press, 2006].

Albert, H. (1969) : *Traktat über kritische Vernunft*, Tübingen: Mohr [en. tr.: *Treatise on Critical Reason*, Princeton: Princeton University Press, 1985].

Allesch (von), J. (1960) : 'Robert Musil in der geistigen Bewegung seiner Zeit', in: Dinklage, K. (1960), pp. 133-142.

Aquinas (*Summa*) : *Sancti Thomae de Aquino Summa theologica*, eds. Domenicani italiani, Florence: Salani, 1966.

Aristotle (*Pol.*) : *Politics*, ed. by R.F. Stalley, Oxford: OUP - Oxford Classics, 1995.

Auerbach, E. (1959) : 'On the Political Theory of Pascal', in Id., *Scenes from the Drama of European Literature: Six Essays*, Oldbury: Meridian Books.

Ayer, A.J. (1936) : *Language, Truth and Logic*, London: Victor Gollancz.

Banfi, A. (1961) : 'Ludwig Klages e l'irrazionalismo', in Id., *Filosofi contemporanei*, Firenze: Parenti, pp. 213-254.

Beaufret, J. (1974) : *Dialogue avec Heidegger*, 3 vols., Paris: Minuit.

Benjamin, W. (1986) : 'Theologico-Political Fragment', in Id., *Reflections. Essays, Aphorisms, Autobiographical Writings*, New York: Schocken Books, pp. 312-313.

Id. (1996a) : 'Critique of Violence', in *Selected Writings*, vol. I (1913-1926), Cambridge MA and London: Harvard University Press, pp. 236-252.

Id. (1996b) : 'Fate and Character', in *Selected Writings*, vol. I (1913-1926), Cambridge MA and London: Harvard University Press, pp. 304-311.

Id. (1997) : *Gesammelte Briefe*, Bd. III: Briefe 1925-1930, Frankfurt a.M.: Suhrkamp [en. tr.: *The Correspondence of Walter Benjamin, 1910-1940*, Chicago: University of Chicago Press, 1994].

Id. (1998) : *Der Ursprung des deutschen Trauerspiels* (1928), in Id., *Gesammelte Schriften*, ed. by R. Tiedemann and H. Schweppenhäuser, Bd. I, 1, Frankfurt a.M.: Suhrkamp 1974 [en. tr: *The Origin of German Tragic Drama*, London - New York: Verso, 1998].

Id. (2005a) : 'Karl Kraus', in *Selected Writings*, vol. II, part 2 (1931-1934), Cambridge MA and London: Harvard University Press, pp. 433-458.

Id. (2005b) : 'Franz Kafka. On the Tenth Anniversary of his Death', in *Selected Writings*, vol. II, part 2 (1931-1934), Cambridge MA and London: Harvard University Press, pp. 795-818.

Id. (2006) : 'On the Concept of History', in *Selected Writings*, vol. IV (1938-1940), Cambridge MA and London: Harvard Univ. Press, pp. 289-400.

Berghahn, W. (1961) : 'Robert Musil – Interpretationen und "Parallelaktionen"', *Neue Deutsche Hefte*, 81, pp. 104-113.

Bergson, H. (1907) : *L'évolution créatrice*, Paris: Alcan. [en. tr. *Creative Evolution*, Mineola NY: Dover Publications, 1998].

Blumenberg, H. (1957) : 'Licht als Metapher der Wahrheit', *Studium Generale*, X, pp. 432-447.

Id. (1960) : 'Paradigmen zu einer Metaphorologie', *Archiv für Begriffsgeschichte*, VI, pp. 7-142.

Id. (1974) : *Säkularisierung und Selbstbehauptung*, erweiterte und überarbeitete Neuausgabe von *Die Legitimität der Neuzeit*, Frankfurt a.M.: Suhrkamp [en. tr.: *The Legitimacy of the Modern Age*, Cambridge Mass.: MIT Press, 1985].

Böckenförde, E.-W. (1995) : 'Die Nation', in *Frankfurter Allgemeine Zeitung*, 30 September 1995.

Boehlich, W. (1954) : 'Untergang und Erlösung', *Akzente*, I/1, pp. 35-50.

Bouillier, V. (1926) : 'Baltasar Gracián et Nietzsche', *Revue de littérature comparée*, VI, 3, pp. 381-401.

Bourdet, Y. (1972) : *Figures de Lukács*, Paris: Anthropos.

Braun, W. (1954) : 'Musil's "Erdensekretariat der Genauigkeit und Seele", a Clue to the Philosophy of the Hero of "Der Mann ohne Eigenschaften"', *Monatshefte für deutschen Unterricht*, XLVI, pp. 305-316.

Brega, M.G. (2020) : 'Centralità dell'idea di conflitto in Spengler', *Metabasis.it*, 30, pp. 42-57.

Brémond, H (1923) : *Histoire littéraire du sentiment religieux en France, depuis la fin des guerres de religion jusqu'à nos jours*, vols. IX, Paris: Armand Colin.

Brisson, L. (1975) : 'Du bon usage du dérèglement', in: J.P. Vernant et coll. (eds.), *Divination et rationalité*, Paris: Seuil.

Buber, M. (1909) : *Ekstatische Konfessionen*, Jena: Diederichs Verlag.

Buchheim, H. (1962) : *Totalitäre Herrschaft. Wesen und Merkmale*, München: Kösel Verlag.

Cacciari, M. (1975) : *Krisis, Saggio sulla crisi del pensiero negativo da Nietzsche a Wittgenstein*, Milan: Feltrinelli.

Id. (1981) : 'Diritto e giustizia. Saggio sulle dimensioni teologica e mistica del moderno Politico', *Il Centauro*, 2, pp. 58-81.

Canetti, E. (1979) : 'Karl Kraus: The School of Resistence', in Id., *The Conscience of Words*, New York: Seabury Press, pp. 29-54.

Cantimori, D. (1935) : 'Politica di Carl Schmitt', *Studi germanici*, I, pp. 471-89.

Id. (1962) : 'Nelle ombre del domani'. Introduction to Huizinga, J., *La crisi della civiltà*, Turin: Einaudi.

Cargnello, D. (1966) : *Alterità e alienità*, Milano: Feltrinelli.

Cassirer, E. (1922) : *Das Erkenntnisproblem in der Philosophie und Wissenschaft der neueren Zeit*, Berlin: Bruno Cassirer [en. tr.: *The Problem of Knowledge. Philosophy, Science and History since Hegel*, New Haven CT: Yale University Press, 1950].

Id. (1924) : 'Eidos und Eidolon: das Problem des Schönen und der Kunst in Platos Dialogen', *Vorträge der Bibliotek Warburg*, Braunschweig: Vieweg-Teubner Verlag, pp. 1-27.

Castelli, E. (1953) : *Cristianesimo e Ragion di Stato* (Atti del II Congresso di Studi Umanistici) ed. by E. Castelli, Roma-Milano: Fratelli Bocca Editori.

Id. (1962) : 'Pascal e Nietzsche', *Archivio di Filosofia*, n. 3, pp. 3-25.

Castrucci, E. (2003) : *Convenzione, forma, potenza. Scritti di storia delle idee e di filosofia giuridico-politica*, 2 vols., Milano: Giuffrè.

Id. (2015) *Le radici antropologiche del 'politico'*, Soveria Mannelli: Rubbettino.

Id. (2016) : 'On the Origins of Conventionalist Political Philosophy in the Seventeenth Century', in Id., *On the Idea of Potency. Juridical and Theological Roots of the Western Cultural Tradition*, Edinburgh: EUP, pp. 73-93.

Chinard, G. (1948) : *En lisant Pascal*, Genève: Droz.

Connor, W. (1994) : *Ethnonationalism. The Quest for Understanding*, Princeton University Press, Princeton NJ.

Crocker, L.G. (1970) : *An Age of Crisis. Man and World in Eighteenth Century French Thought*, Baltimore: The Johns Hopkins Press.

Curtius, E.R. (1973) : *Essays on European Literature*, Princeton: Princeton University Press.

Dallmayr (1958) : 'Epimeteo cristiano o Prometeo pagano?', *Rivista internazionale di filosofia del diritto*, XXXV, pp. 657-79.

Deleuze, G. (1962) : *Nietzsche et la philosophie*, Paris: PUF [en. tr.: *Nietzsche and Philosophy*, New York: Columbia University Press, 1983].

Id. (1964) : *Marcel Proust et les signes*, Paris: PUF [en. tr.: *Proust and Signs*, Minneapolis: University of Minnesota Press, 2000].

Del Noce, A. (1964) : *Il problema dell'ateismo*, Bologna: il Mulino.

Id. (1965) : 'Interpretazione filosofica del surrealismo', *Rivista di Estetica*, X, pp. 22-54.

De Martino, M. (2008) : *Mircea Eliade esoterico. Ioan Petru Culianu e i "non detti"*, Rome: Edizioni Settimo Sigillo.

Derrida, J. (2002) : 'Force of Law. The "Mystical Foundation of Authority"', in *Acts of Religion*, New York and London: Routledge, pp. 230-299

Descartes, R. (*Med.*) : *Meditationes de prima philosophia*, in Id., *Oeuvres de Descartes*, ed. by Ch. Adam et P. Tannéry, vol. VII, Paris: Vrin, 1904.

Dinklage, K. (1960) : *Robert Musil: Leben - Werk - Wirkung - im Auftrag des Landes Kärnten und der Stadt Klagenfurt*, ed. by K. Dinklage, Reinbek: Rowohlt.

Di Vona, P. (1968) : *Studi sulla Scolastica della Controriforma. L'esistenza e la sua distinzione metafisica dall'essenza*, Firenze: La Nuova Italia.

Dvorák, M. (1928) : 'Über Greco und den Manierismus', in Id., *Kunstgeschichte als Geistesgeschichte*, München: Piper Verlag.

Foucault, M. (1966) : *Les mots et les choses*, Paris: Gallimard [en. tr.: *The Order of Things*, London: Routledge, 1989].

Gadamer, H.-G. (1950) : 'Symbol und Allegorie', *Arch. di Filosofia*, 75, pp. 23-33.

García Pelayo, M. (1964) : *Mítos y símbolos politicos*, Madrid: Taurus Ediciones.

Gardies, J.-L. (1962) : 'Le droit, l'a priori, l'imaginaire et l'expérience', *Archives de philosophie du droit*, VIII, pp. 171-197.

Gargani A. (1977) : 'Scienza e forme di vita', *Nuova Corrente*, 72-73, pp. 107-141.

Gehlen, A. (1940) : *Der Mensch. Seine Natur und seine Stellung in der Welt*, ed. by K.S. Rehberg, Frankfurt a.M.: Klostermann, 1993 [en. tr.: *Man: His Nature and Place in the World*, New York: Columbia University Press, 1988].

Goethe, J.W. (1831) : *Faust. Der Tragödie Zweiter Teil*, Ditzingen: Reclam, 2008 [en. tr.: *Faust, Part Two*, ed. by D. Luke, Oxford: OUP, 1994].

Goldmann, L. (1955) : *Le dieu caché. Étude sur la vision tragique dans les "Pensées" de Pascal et dans le théâtre de Racine*, Paris: Gallimard.

Gómez-Moriana, A. (1968) : *Derecho de resistencia y tiranicidio. Estudio de una temática en las "Comedias" de Lope de Vega*, Santiago de Compostela: Biblioteca Hispánica de Filosofía del derecho.

Gracián, B. (1861) : *Hand-Orakel und Kunst der Weltklugheit, aus dessen Werken gezogen von Don Vincencio de Lastanosa und aus dem spanischen Original treu und sorgfaltig überstzt von Arthur Schopenhauer*, Leipzig: Brockhaus.

Grillparzer, F. (1848) : *Ein Bruderzwist in Habsburg*, in Id., *Sämtliche Werke*, Bd. VII, München: Hauser, 1965.

Habermas, J. (1998) : *The Inclusion of the Other*, New York: MIT Press, 1998.

Hauriou, M. (1925) : *Théorie de l'institution et de la fondation. Essai de vitalisme social*, Caen: Presses Universitaires de Caen, 1990.

Hegel, G.W.F. (1907) : *Die Liebe*, in *Hegels theologische Jugend-schriften*, ed. by H. Nohl, Tübingen: Mohr, 1907, pp. 379-382.

Id. (2008) : *Grundlinien der Philosophie des Rechts* (1820), in *Werke in 20 Bänden*, Frankfurt a.M.: Suhrkamp, 1986 [en. tr.: *Outlines of the Philosophy of Right*, Oxford: OUP, 2008.

Heidegger, M. (1927) : *Sein und Zeit.*, Tübingen: Niemeyer. English translation: *Being and Time*, Oxford: Blackwell, 1962.

Id. (1929) : *Kant und das Problem der Metaphysik*, in Id., *Gesamtausgabe*, Bd. 3, Frankfurt a. M.: Vittorio Klostermann, 1993 [en. tr. *Kant and the Problem of Metaphysics*, Bloomington: Indiana University Press, 1997].

Id. (1934) : *Logik als die Frage nach dem Wesen der Sprache*, in Id., *Gesamtausgabe*, Bd. 38, Frankfurt a.M.: Vittorio Klostermann, 1998 [en. tr.: *Logic as the Question concerning the Essence of Language*, Albany NY: State University of New York Press, 2009]

Id. (1950) : *Holzwege*, in Id., *Gesamtausgabe*, Bd. 5, Frankfurt a.M.:: Vittorio Klostermann, 1977 [en. tr.: *Off the Beaten Track*, Cambridge: Cambridge University Press, 2002].

Id. (1953) : 'Georg Trakl. Eine Erörterung seines Gedichten', *Merkur*, 61, pp. 226-258.

Id. (1954) : *Vorträge und Aufsätze*, Pfullingen: Neske Verlag.

Henrich, D. (1960) : *Der Begriff der sittilichen Einsicht und Kants Lehre vom Faktum der Vernunft*, in Id. (ed.), *Die Gegenwart der Griechen im neueren Denken*, Tübingen, Mohr.

Hobbes, Th. (*De Cive*) : *Philosophical Rudiments concerning Government and Society*, in Id., *The English Works of Thomas Hobbes of Malmesbury*, ed. by W. Molesworth, vol. II, London: John Bohn, 1841.

Id. (*HN*) : *Human Nature, or the Fundamental Elements of Policy*, in Id., *The English Works of Thomas Hobbes of Malmesbury*, ed. by W. Molesworth, vol. IV, London: John Bohn 1845.

Hocke, G.R. (1961) : *Manierismus in der Literatur*, Reinbek: Rowohlt.

Hofmannsthal (von), H. (1958a) : *Der Brief des Lord Chandos* (1902), in Id., *Gesammelte Werke*, Frankfurt a.M.: Fischer Verlag [en. tr.: *The Lord Chandos Letter and other Writings*, New York: The New York Review of Books, 2004].

Id. (1958b) : *Der Turm*, in Id., *Gesammelte Werke*, Frankfurt a.M.: Fischer Verlag [en. tr.: *The Tower*, Princeton: Princeton University Press, 2009].

Id. (1958c) : *Andreas, oder die Vereinigten*, in Id., *Gesammelte Werke*, Frankfurt a.M.: Fischer Verlag [en. tr.: *Andreas*, London, Pushkin Press, 2001].

Horkheimer, M. (1938), 'Montaigne und die Funktion der Skepsis', *Zeitschrift für Sozialforschung*, VII, pp. 1-54. [en. tr.: 'Montaigne and the Function of Skepticism', in Id., *Between Philosophy and Social Science: Selected Early Writings*, Cambridge MA: MIT Press, 1993].

Hösle, J. (1959) : 'Utopia e realtà ne L'uomo senza qualità', *Rivista di letterature moderne e comparate*, XII/2, pp. 119-132.

Husserl, G. (1925) : *Rechtskraft und Rechtsgeltung. Eine rechts-dogmatische Untersuchung*, Berlin-Wien: Springer.

Ilting, K.-H. (1972) : *Der naturalistische Fehlschluß bei Kant*, in: M. Riedel (ed.), *Rehabilitierung der praktischen Philosophie*, Freiburg i.B.: Rombach Verlag.

Jonas, H. (1963) : *The Gnostic Religion*, Boston: Beacon Press.

Jünger, E. (1929) : *Das abenteuerliche Hertz*, Berlin: Frundsberg Verlag.

Kelsen, H. (1911) : *Hauptptobleme der Staatsrechtslehre, entwickelt aus der Lehre vom Rechtssatze*, Tübingen: Mohr Siebeck.

Id. (1919) : 'Zur Theorie der juristischen Fiktionen', *Annalen der Philoso-phie*, pp. 630 ff.

Id. (1920) : *Das Problem der Souveränität und die Theorie des Völkerrechts. Beitrag zu einer Reinen Rechtslehre*, Tübingen: Mohr Siebeck.

Id. (1979) : *Allgemeine Theorie der Normen*, Wien: Manz Verlag.

Kerényi, K. (1942) : *Der große Daimon des Symposion*, Leipzig: Pantheon Akademische Verlagsanstalt.

Kierkegaard, S. (1843) : *The Immediate Erotic Stages or the Musical Erotic*, in Id., *Either/Or. A Fragment of Life*, London-New York: Penguin Books, 1992.

Klein, R. (1970) : *La forme et l'intelligible*, Paris: Gallimard.

Klossowski, P. (1963) : *Un si funeste désir*, Paris: Gallimard.

Id. (1969) : *Nietzsche et le cercle vicieux*, Paris: Mercure de France.

Koselleck, R. (1959) : *Kritik und Krise. Ein Beitrag zur Pathogenese der bürgerlichen Welt*, Freiburg-München: Alber Verlag.

Krockow (Graf von), Chr. (1958) : *Die Entscheidung. Eine Untersuchung über Ernst Jünger, Carl Schmitt, Martin Heidegger*, Stuttgart: Enke Verlag.

Krüger, Gerhard (1939) : *Eros und Mythus bei Plato*, in Id., *Einsicht und Leidenschaft. Das Wesen des platonischen Denkens*, Frankfurt a.M.: Klostermann.

Kucharsky, P. (1949) : *Les chemins du savoir dans les derniers dialogues de Platon*, Paris: PUF.

Lazzerini, L. (2012) : *Silva portentosa. Enigmi, intertestualità sommerse, significati occulti nella letteratura romanza dalle origini al Cinquecento*, Modena: Mucchi.

Leppmann, W. (1962) : 'Zum Goethebild bei Robert Musil, Hermann Broch und Ernst Jünger', *Monatshefte*, LIV, pp. 145-155.

Loebenstein, J. (1960) : 'Das Problem der Erkenntnis in Musils künstlerichem Werk', in: Dinklage, K. (1960), pp. 77-131.

Löwith, K. (1949) : *Meaning in History. The Theological Implications of the Philosophy of History*, Chicago: University of Chicago Press.

Id. (1960) : 'Der okkasionelle Dezisionismus von Carl Schmitt' (1935), in: Id., *Gesammelte Abhandlungen. Zur Kritik der geschichtlichen Existenz*, Berlin: Kohlhammer, pp. 93-127.

Lübbe, H. (1971) : *Theorie und Entscheidung. Studien zum Primat der praktischen Vernunft*, Freiburg i.B.: Rombach Verlag.

Id.. (1999) : *Abschied vom Superstaat. Vereinigte Staaten von Europa wird es nicht geben*, Siedler, Berlin.

Lukács, G. (2011) : 'Die Seele und die Formen' (1910) - 'Von der Armut am Geist' (1912), in Id., *Die Seele und die Formen*, Werkauswahl in sechs Bänden, Bd. 1, Bielefeld: Aisthesis Verlag [en. tr.: 'On the Poverty of Spirit', in Id., *Soul and Form*, New York: Columbia University Press, 2011].

Id. (1971) : *Geschichte und Klassenbewusstsein. Studien über marxistischen Dialektik* (1923), Berlin: Malik Verlag [en. tr.: *History and Class Consciousness. Studies in Marxist Dialectics*, London: Merlin Press, 1971].

Magris, C. (1963) : 'La sociologia religiosa in Robert Musil', in Id., *Il mito absburgico nella letteratura austriaca moderna*, Turin: Einaudi.

Mann, Th. (*MM*) : *The Magic Mountain*, New York: A. Knopf, 1953.

Id. (1993) : *Gedanken im Kriege*, in Id., *Essays*, vol. 1: *Frühlingssturm 1893-1918*, ed. by H. Kurzke und S. Stachorski, Frankfurt a.M.: Fischer Verlag.

Maravall, J.A. (1976) : 'Antropología y politica en el pensamiento de Gracián', in Id., *Estudios de historia del pensamiento español*, vol. III, Madrid: Marcial Pons.

Marcuse, H. (1934) : 'Der Kampf gegen den Liberalismus in der totalitären Staatsauffassung', *Zeitschrift für Sozialforschung*, III, 2, pp. 161-94.

Mathieu, V. (1972) : *La speranza nella rivoluzione*, Milan: Rizzoli.

Metz, J.B. (1963) : 'Entscheidung', *Handbuch theologischer Grundbegriffe*, Bd. I, München: Kösel Verlag.

Michelstaedter, C. (1910) : *La persuasione e la rettorica*, Milano: Adelphi, 1982 [en. tr.. *Persuasion and Rhetoric*, New Haven CT: Yale University Press, 2004].

Minkowski, E. (1956) : 'L'éphémère, durer, avoir une durée, l'eternel', *Revue de Metaphysique et de Morale*, 3-4, pp. 217-41.

Mittner, L. (1960) : *La letteratura tedesca del Novecento*, Turin: Einaudi.

Id. (1971) : *Storia della letteratura tedesca*, vol. III/2, Turin: Einaudi.

Mortati, C. (1962) : 'Costituzione (Dottrine generali)', *Enciclopedia del diritto*, XI, Milan: Giuffrè, pp. 145 ff.

Musil, R. (1906) : *Die Verwirrungen des Zöglings Törless* in Id., *Gesammelte Werke in Einzelausgaben*, ed. by A. Frisé, Reinbek bei Hamburg: Rowohlt 1978. [en. tr.: *Young Törless*, London: Penguin, 1961].

Id. (1955) : *Tagebücher, Aphorismen, Essays und Reden*, Reinbek bei Hamburg: Rowohlt.

Id. (*MwQ I – II*) : *The Man without Qualities*, by S. Wilkins and B. Pyke, 2 vols., New York: Vintage International, 1996.

Natorp, P. (1920) : 'Logos – Psyche – Eros'. Metakritischer Anhang, in Id., *PlatosIdeenlehre. Eine Einführung in den Idealismus*, Hamburg: Meiner Verlag [en. tr.: *Plato's Theory of Ideas. An Introduction to Idealism*, Sankt Augustin: Academia Verlag, 2004].

Neumann, F. (1957) : *The Democratic and the Authoritarian State*, New York: The Free Press.

Nietzsche, F. (1885-87) : *Nachgelassene Fragmente*, in Id., *Sämtliche Werke. Kritische Studienausgabe*, hrsg. von G. Colli und M. Montinari, Bd. 12, Berlin - New York: de Gruyter 1967.

Id. (1889) : *Götzendämmerung, oder Wie man mit dem Hammer philoso-phiert*, in Id. *Sämtliche Werke. Kritische Studienausgabe*, hrsg. von G. Colli and M. Montinari, Bd. 6, Berlin - New York: de Gruyter 1967.

Nübel, B. (2006) : *Robert Musil - Essaysmus als Selbstreflexion der Moderne*, Berlin - New York: de Gruyter.

Nygren, A. (1936) : *Agape and Eros*, Philadelphia: The Westminster Press.

Oestreich, G. (1968) : 'Strukturprobleme des europäischen Absolu-tismus', *Vierteljahrschrift für Sozial- und Wirtschaftsgeschichte*, Bd. 55, 3, pp. 329-347.

Paci, E. (1955) : 'Silenzio e libertà del linguaggio nel neopositivismo', in *Semantica: Archivio di filosofia*, n. 3, pp. 131-36.

Pascal, B. (1962) : *Oeuvres complètes*, ed. J. Chevallier, Paris: Gallimard.

Perniola, M. (1980) : 'Fenomeno e simulacro', in Id. *La società dei simulacri*, Bologna: Cappelli.

Pernthaler, P. (1974) : 'Das Bild des Recht in drei Werken von F. Kafka. Amerika, Strafkolonie, Prozeß', in *Dimensionen des Rechts. Gedächtnisschrift für René Marcic*, Berlin: Duncker & Humblot.

Pétillon, P.Y. (1975) : 'Chandosbrief, Hofmannsthal: le règne du silence', *Critique*, 31, pp. 884-908.

Pintard, R. (1943) : *Le libertinisme érudit dans la première moitié du XVIIe siècle*, Paris: Boivin.

Plato (*Rep.*) : *Republic,* ed. by R. Waterfield, Oxford: OUP - Oxford Classics, 2008.

Id. (*Symp.*) : *Symposium,* ed. by R. Waterfield, Oxford: OUP - Oxford Classics, 2008.

Reinach, A. (1913) : 'Die aprioristischen Grundlagen des bürgerlichen Rechts', *Jb. f. Phil. und phän. Forschung*, Halle a.d.S.: Niemeyer, pp. 685-847.

Rendi. A. (1961) : *Robert Musil,* Milan: Comunità.

Ricoeur, P. (1975) : *La métaphore vive,* Paris: Seuil.

Rieff, P. (2007) : *Charisma: The Gift of Grace, and how it has been taken away from us,* New York: Pantheon Books.

Ripellino, A.M. (1973) : *Praga magica,* Turin: Einaudi.

Ryle, G. (1949) : *The Concept of Mind,* London - New York: Hutchinson's University Library.

Saint-Exupéry (de), A. (1959) : *Citadelle,* in Id., *Oeuvres,* ed. R. Caillois, Paris: Gallimard.

Sasso, G. (1974) : 'Leo Naphta e Hugo Fiala', *La Cultura,* XII, pp. 100-12.

Schelling, F.W.J. (1821-1825) : *Erlanger Vorträge,* in *Schellings Werke,* ed. by M. Schröter, Bd. V, München: C.H. Beck und R. Oldenbourg.

Schmitt, C. (1921) : *Die Diktatur. Von den Anfängen des modernen Souveränitätsgedankens bis zum proletarischen Klassenkampf,* München-Leipzig: Duncker & Humblot [en. tr.: *Dictatorship. From the Origin of the Modern Concept of Sovereignty to Proletarian Class Struggle,* Cambridge: Polity Press, 2014].

Id. (1922) : *Politische Theologie. Vier Kapitel zur Lehre von der Souveränität,* München - Leipzig: Duncker & Humblot [en. tr.: *Political Theology. Four Chapter on the Concept of Sovereignty,* Chicago: University of Chicago Press, 2006].

Id. (1923) : *Römischer Katholizismus und politische Form,* Hellerau: Jakob Hegner Verlag [en. tr.: *Roman Catholicism and Political Form,* Westport CT: Praeger, 1996].

Id. (1928) : *Verfassungslehre*, Berlin: Duncker & Humblot, 2010 [en. tr.: *Constitutional Theory*, Durham and London: Duke University Press, 2008].

Id. (1938) : *Der Leviathan in der Staatslehre des Thomas Hobbes. Sinn und Fehlschlag eines politischen Symbols*, Hamburg: Hanseatische Verlagsanstalt.

Id. (1940) : *Positionen und Begriffe. Im Kampf mit Weimar - Genf - Versailles (1923-1939)*, Hamburg: Hanseatische Verlagsanstalt.

Id. (1950a) : *Ex Captivitate Salus. Erfahrungen der Zeit 1945-47*, Köln: Greven Verlag [en. tr.: *Ex Captivitate Salus. Experiences 1945-47*, Cambridge: Polity Press, 2017].

Id. (1950b) : *Der Nomos der Erde im Völkerrecht des Jus Publicum Europaeum*, Köln: Greven Verlag [en. tr.: *The Nomos of the Earth in the International Law of the Jus Publicum Europaeum*, ed. by G.L. Ulmen, New York: Telos Press Publishing, 2006].

Id. (1956) : *Hamlet oder Hekuba. Der Einbruch der Zeit in das Spiel*, Düsseldorf - Köln: Diederichs [en. tr.: *Hamlet or Hecuba. The Intrusion of the Time into the Play*, New York: Telos Press, 2006].

Id. (1967) : *Die Tyrannei der Werte*, Stuttgart: Kohlhammer [en. tr.: *The Tyranny of Values*, Washington D.C.: Plutarch Press, 1996].

Id. (1970) : *Politische Theologie II. Die Legende der Erledigung jeder politischen Theologie*, Berlin: Duncker & Humblot. English translation: *Political Theology II. The Myth of the Closure of any Political Theology*, New York: John Wiley and Sons, 2008.

Schnur, R. (1958) : 'Carl Schmitt und die deutsche Staatsrechtslehre', *Wort und Wahrheit*, XIII, pp. 725-7.

Id. (1959) : 'Die französischen Juristen im konfessionellen Bürgerkrieg des 16. Jahrhunderts', *Festschrift für Carl Schmitt zum 70. Geburtstag*, eds. H. Barion - E. Forsthoff - W. Weber, Berlin: Duncker & Humblot, pp. 179-219.

Id. (1963) : *Individualismus und Absolutismus. Zur politischen Theorie vor Thomas Hobbes*, Berlin: Duncker & Humblot.

Id. (1975) : *Staatsräson. Studien zur Geschichte eines politischen Begriffs*, ed. by R. Schnur, Berlin: Duncker & Humblot.

Scholem, G. (1975) : *Walter Benjamin - die Geschichte einer Freundschaft*, Frankfurt a.M. Suhrkamp.

Schopenhauer, A. (*WWR*) : *The World as Will and Representation*, ed. F.J. Payne, 2 vols., New York: Dover Publications.1969.

Id. (*BM*) : *The Basis of Morality*, ed. by A. Brodrick Bullock, London: Schwan & Sonnenschein, 1915.

Id. (*EM*) : *Early Manuscripts (1804-1818)*, in *Manuscript Remains in four volumes*, vol. 1, ed. by A. Hübscher, Oxford: Berg Publishers 1988.

Schwab, G. (1970) : *The Challenge of Exception. An Introduction to the Political Ideas of Carl Schmitt between 1921 and 1936*, Berlin: Duncker & Humblot.

Severino, E. (1980) : *Destino della necessità – Katà tò chreón*, Milan: Adelphi.

Id. (1981) : *La struttura originaria*, Milan: Adelphi.

Id. (1982) : *Essenza del nichilismo*, Milan: Adelphi [en. tr.: *The Essence of Nihilism*, London - New York: Verso, 2016].

Simmel, G. (1910) : *Hauptprobleme der Philosophie*, Berlin-Leipzig: de Gruyter.

Skinner, Q. (1966) : 'Thomas Hobbes and his disciples in France and England', in *Comparative Studies in Society and History*, 8, pp. 153-167.

Smend, R. (1928) : *Verfassung und Verfassungsrecht*, München-Leipzig: Duncker & Humblot.

Id. (1956) : 'Integrationslehre', in *Handwörterbuch der Sozialwissenschaften*, 5, pp. 299-302.

Solmi, S. (1976) : *Il pensiero di Alain*, Pisa: Nistri Lischi.

Sorbière, S. (1657) : *Trois discours sceptiques*, in *Mémoires de M. de Marolles*, part II, Paris: chez A. de Sommaville.

Id. (1664) : *Rélation d'un voyage en Angleterre, où sont touchées plusieures choses, qui regardent l'estat des sciences et de la religion et autres matières curieuses*, Paris: L. Billaine.

Sortais, G. (1920) : *La philosophie moderne. Depuis Bacon jusqu'à Leibniz*, Paris: Paul Lethielleux Éditeur.

Spink, J.S. (1960) : *French Free-Thought from Gassendi to Voltaire*, London: Athlone Press.

Spinoza (*Eth.*) : *Ethica*, in Id., *Opera*, ed. by C. Gebhardt, vol. II, Heidelberg: Carl Winter Verlag, 1925, pp. 41-308.

Id. (*TTP*) : *Tractatus theologico-politicus*, in Id., *Opera*, ed. by C. Gebhard,, vol. III, Heidelberg: Carl Winter Verlag, 1925, pp. 1-267.

Stepun, F. (1929) : *Wie war es möglich? Briefe eines russischen Offiziers*, Hanser, München.

Strauss, L. (1953) : *Natural Right and History*, Chicago: University of Chicago Press.

Strelka, J. (1960) : 'Robert Musil und die Frage des rechten Lebens. Zu den Entwicklungsstufen von Musils Religiosität', in: Dinklage, K. (1960), pp. 175-181.

Taubes, J. (1947) : *Abendländische Eschatologie*, Bern: Rösch Verlag [en. tr.: *Occidental Eschatology*, Stanford: Stanford University Press, 2009].

Taveneaux, R. (1965) : *Jansénisme et politique*, Paris: A. Colin.

Uhlig, H. (1953) : 'Die Periode der Erschütterung', *Frankfurter Hefte*, Jhg. 8, Heft 10, pp. 789-811.

Valéry, P. (1960) : 'Eupalinos, ou l'Architecte', 'L'âme et la danse', in *Oeuvres complètes*, édition établie et annotée par J. Hytier, vol. II, Paris: Gallimard [en. tr.: *Dialogues*, ed. by W. McCausland Stewart, New York: Pantheon Books, 1956].

Viano, C.A. (1962) : 'Analisi della vita emotiva e tecnica politica nella filosofia di Hobbes', *Rivista critica di storia della filosofia*, XVII, n. 4, pp. 355-392.

Voegelin, E. (1952) : *The New Science of Politics. An Introduction*, Chicago-London: Chicago University Press.

Id. (1966) : *Anamnesis. Zur Theorie der Geschichte und Politik*, München: Piper Verlag [en. tr.: *Anamnesis. On the Theory of History and Politics*, The Collected Works of Eric Voegelin, vol. 6, Columbia: University of Missouri Press, 2002].

Voltaire (1752) : *Catalogue de la plupart des écrivains français qui ont paru dans le siècle de Louis XIV*, in Id., *Oeuvres*, tome XIV, Paris: Garnier, 1878.

Weber, M. (1920) : *Gesammelte Aufsätze zur Religionssoziologie*, Tübingen: Mohr [en. tr.: *The Sociology of Religion*, London: Methuen & Co, 1965].

Id. (1922a) : *Wirtschaft und Gesellschaft*, Tübingen: Mohr Siebeck.

Id. (1922b) : *Gesammelte Aufsätze zur Wissenschaftslehre*, Tübingen: Mohr [en. tr.: *Collected Methodological Writings*, ed. by H.H. Bruuns and S. Whimster, Abingdon - New York: Routledge, 2012].

Id. (1968) : *On Charisma and Institution Building*, Chicago-London: The University of Chicago Press.

Wittgenstein, L. (1922) : *Tractatus logico-philosophicus*, New York: Harcourt, Brace & Co.